PLANNING AND ENVIRONMENTAL PROTECTION

Planning and Environmental Protection

A Review of Law and Policy

Edited by
CHRIS MILLER
University of Salford

·HART·
PUBLISHING
OXFORD – PORTLAND OREGON

Hart Publishing
Oxford and Portland, Oregon

Published in North America (US and Canada) by
Hart Publishing c/o
International Specialized Book Services
5804 NE Hassalo Street
Portland, Oregon
97213-3644
USA

Distributed in the Netherlands, Belgium and Luxembourg by
Intersentia, Churchillaan 108
B2900 Schoten
Antwerpen
Belgium

First published 2002. Reprinted 2002

Hart Publishing is a specialist legal publisher based in Oxford, England. To order further copies of this book or to request a list of other publications please write to:

Hart Publishing, Salter's Boatyard, Folly Bridge,
Abingdon Road, Oxford OX1 4LB
Telephone: +44 (0)1865 245533 or Fax: +44 (0)1865 794882
e-mail: mail@hartpub.co.uk
WEBSITE: http//www.hartpub.co.uk

British Library Cataloguing in Publication Data
Data Available
ISBN 1–84113–181–4 (paperback)

Typeset by Hope Services (Abingdon) Ltd.
Printed and bound in Great Britain on acid-free paper by
Biddles Ltd, www.biddles.co.uk

Preface

ACADEMIC INTEREST IN the environmental role of land use planning is hardly novel. What is special about this book that can justify yet another addition to an already overpopulated œuvre?

It is tempting to base the defence on the experience of the contributors. They can boast more than two hundred person-years practising, researching or teaching in a field located at the interface between planning and environmental protection. This familiarity has bred, not contempt, but a continuing curiosity in the changing relationship between these two elements of governance. This curiosity refuses to allow this relationship to be taken for granted. Most of the contributors can remember a time when 'environment' was a specialist term used only by a minority of biologists; they have witnessed the remarkable rise of environmentalism from an assortment of aesthetic concerns to what now offers arguably the most effective critique of capitalism. All of them can not only remember, but were active during, the 1980s when planning, like other forms of state intervention, fell foul of the prevailing political rhetoric in the UK which was motivated by the 'minimal state' idea. They are also aware that town planning emerged from that period largely unscathed and that, despite the abolition of a tier of local government, the remaining local authorities were then to acquire additional responsibilities (environmental assessment, contaminated land, air quality management) with a clear environmental purpose. None of the authors admits to remembering the signing of the Treaty of Rome; but all have seen the emergence of the environmental competence of the European Community from its modest and equivocal beginning, around the time of UK accession, to its current position as a constitutional imperative, with Article 8 of the Treaty (as amended) now obliging Member States to integrate environmental protection requirements into the definition and implementation of *all* Community policies and activities, including the promotion of sustainable development.

The more changes we have observed, the less willing we are to concede that the present arrangements are the last word. In addition, the book is not partisan: it seeks to describe planning's current role and to ponder its future potential, but it does not advocate planning as inherently superior to, say, economic approaches to protecting the environment.

The aims of this book are therefore modest: to attempt to bring a measure of clarity to an area—the role of land use planning in environmental protection—which can so easily succumb, on the one hand, to a welter of empirical detail and, on the other, to theory for theory's own sake. We leave it to others to speculate on the ontology of planning; we are content to ally ourselves with Geoffrey

Vickers in holding that 'planning is what planners do'. And the term 'environment' has experienced such excessive use, both literal and metaphorical, that any consensus on what it should denote is now impossible. Our search for clarity would not be assisted by an (inevitably vain) attempt to offer an exhaustive account, that is, one which leaves no aspect of planning or the environment unconsidered. But we believe we have focussed upon aspects of the environment in which land use is most important.

The book is concerned predominantly with English law (albeit often European in origin) and practice. We have not attempted assiduously to name, where they exist, the Scots, Welsh or Northern Ireland equivalents of every statute, statutory instrument, agency or policy document we have cited. Devolution (of law-making powers) to the Scottish Parliament and to the Welsh and Northern Ireland Assemblies is far too recent for clear departures in attitudes to have emerged. Moreover, we think it unlikely that, where we have drawn conclusions, these would require major revision if applied to the United Kingdom as a whole. It was our aim to state the law as at 1 September 2000. This aim was frustrated by the determination of both the legislature and the judiciary to make interesting additions and amendments which demanded continual revisions through to the proof stage in March 2001.

Acknowledgements

David Gibbs' chapter draws upon research funded by the Economic and Social Research Council (ESRC grant number: R000237997).

The chapter by Simon Marvin and Simon Guy is based on an ESRC research project (L32053149), 'Demand side management and urban infrastructure provision', funded under Phase 3 of the Global Environmental Phase Programme. An earlier version of this chapter appeared as S. Marvin and S. Guy (1997), 'Infrastructure Provision, Development Processes and the Co-production of Environmental Value' *Urban Studies* 34 (12) 2023–36; the permission of Taylor and Francis Ltd (11 New Fetter Lane, London) to allow this paper to be reproduced in part here is acknowledged.

The Editor wishes to express his deep gratitude to United Utilities plc who played host to him and seven of the contributors, over a weekend in November 1998, at one of their holiday cottage complexes in the Peak District. The comfort of the accommodation, coupled with the rugged grandeur of the surrounding Derbyshire hills, instilled the state of mind conducive to embarking upon the task of bringing a measure of coherence to this book.

Contents

Contributors

Chris Miller (Editor) is Senior Lecturer in Environmental Management at Salford University. His interest in planning dates back to a period in the late 1970s when he worked at Manchester University with Chris Wood, with whom he subsequently wrote *Planning and Pollution*. Since then his research interests have become increasingly concerned with environmental law. His *Environmental Rights* was published by Routledge in 1998.

David Gibbs is Professor of Human Geography at the University of Hull. He is an economic geographer with particular interests in local and regional development. Recent research work has focused upon the potential for integrating economic development and environmental agendas at the local and regional scales and the barriers to doing so. He is currently working on a project entitled 'Governance and Regulation in Local Environmental Policy Making' funded by ESRC and is co-ordinator of the ESRC-funded Sustainable Cities Network.

Simon Guy is Reader in Urban Development and Director of the Centre for Urban Technology in the School of Architecture, Planning and Landscape at the University of Newcastle in the United Kingdom. His research interests revolve around the social production of the material environment. He has undertaken sociological research into a wide spectrum of urban design issues including the development of greener commercial office buildings, the role of architecture and property development in urban regeneration and the links between environmental building design and the provision of infrastructure services. Recent publications include: S. Guy and E. Shove, *A Sociology of Energy, Buildings and the Environment: Constructing Knowledge, Designing Practice*, (Routledge, London, 2000) and S. Guy, S. Marvin and T. Moss, *Urban Infrastructure in Transition: Networks, Buildings, Plans* (Earthscan, London, 2000).

John Handley is Groundwork Professor of Land Restoration and Management at the University of Manchester and Director of the Centre for Urban and Regional Ecology (CURE). Originally an applied ecologist at the University of Liverpool, in 1975 he joined the newly formed Merseyside County Council as a principal planning officer responsible for all facets of natural resource management. He returned to academic life in 1994 at the University of Manchester, where he established a new undergraduate programme in Landscape Planning and Management as well as developing research programmes in this field.

William Howarth is Professor of Environmental Law at the University of Kent at Canterbury. He is the author, editor or contributor to several books on environmental law and a specialist in the law relating to the aquatic environment. He is the author of more than one hundred articles in academic journals and has advised several governments on water and fisheries law and policy.

Simon Marvin is the United Utilities Professor of Sustainable Urban and Regional Development and co-director of the Centre for Sustainable Urban and Regional Futures at Salford University. His research interests have focused on the reconfiguring of infrastructure networks across the energy, water, and telecommunication and transport sectors in cities and regions within the UK and comparative research with cities in Germany, Denmark, South America and Southern Africa. He is completing a project on e-commerce and urban sustainability for the Town and Country Planning Association which is part of the Digital Futures Programme co-ordinated by Forum for the Future. Key publications include S. Graham and S. Marvin, *Telecommunications and the City* (Routledge, London, 1996); S. Marvin, S. Graham and S. Guy, *Cities, Regions and Privatised Utilities,* Progress in Planning (Pergamon, Exeter, 1999); S. Guy, S. Marvin and T. Moss, *Urban Infrastructure in Transition: Networks, Buildings, Plans* (Earthscan, London, 2000).

Judith Petts is Professor of Environmental Risk Management at the University of Birmingham. Her interests are in the application of environmental decision tools and particularly how to improve decisions and the public–decision authority interface through effective communication and participation. Her interest in environmental impact assessment has resulted in a jointly authored book *Environmental Impact Assessment for Waste Treatment and Disposal Facilities* (John Wiley, Chichester, 1994) and the editing of the *Handbook of Environmental Impact Assessment* (Blackwell Science). She has published extensively on risk management and public participation, particularly on the use of new deliberative processes.

Christopher Rodgers is Professor of Law at the University of Wales, Aberystwyth, and also Director of its research centre for environmental and rural law issues, the Centre for Law in Rural Areas. He has written widely in the areas of property law and environmental law, and has a particular interest in nature conservation, land management and agri-environment law. He is Editor-in-Chief of the *Environmental Law Review*, and General Editor of the *Environment and Countryside Law* Series.

Gordon Walker is Head of Geography at Staffordshire University. He has researched the interface between planning and risk management for nearly twenty years. His doctoral study on the planning control of major hazard sites was followed by a series of commissioned projects for the Department of

Environment and Health and Safety Executive. Recent work has included questions of risk perception, risk communication and the equity implications of uneven risk distributions. He has recently been appointed to the Advisory Committee on Dangerous Substances, which advises the Health and Safety Commission on the development of policy and legislation in this area.

Christopher Wood is Director of the EIA Centre and Professor of Environmental Planning in the School of Planning and Landscape, University of Manchester. He has had an interest in environmental planning for thirty years. He has been involved in environmental impact assessment (EIA) research and training since 1974 and has a particular interest in the relationship between EIA and land use planning. He is convenor of the RTPI's Environmental Planning and Protection Panel and Editor of the journal *Impact Assessment and Project Appraisal*. He has published extensively on environmental planning generally and on EIA in particular. He is currently working on the second edition of *Environmental Impact Assessment: a Comparative Review* for Longman.

List of Boxes

Table of Cases

1. EUROPEAN COURT OF HUMAN RIGHTS

2. EUROPEAN COURT OF JUSTICE

3. BRITISH COURTS

Table of Legislation

1. INTERNATIONAL CONVENTIONS

2. EUROPEAN COMMUNITIES LEGISLATION

3. UNITED KINGDOM LEGISLATION

Primary legislation

Secondary legislation

1

The Environmental Roles of Town and Country Planning

CHRIS MILLER

INTRODUCTION

BRITAIN'S PLANNING SYSTEM can trace its origins to the 'sanitary reform' period of the middle decades of the nineteenth century. Having provided the infrastructure (sewerage, water supply and waste disposal) which enabled unparalleled improvements in public health, the boroughs (and from 1888, the urban district councils) could extend their role to ensuring minimum standards in housing and to the layout of the suburban estates which were to replace the slums of the old urban centres. As Cherry (1974, 7) has observed, 'when the first town planning powers were provided in 1909, their general provisions followed logically on the approaches of past Public Health legislation'. By the time the Town and Country Planning Act 1947 was passed, any logical connection was far less apparent. A small, highly specialised inspectorate regulated industrial sources of air pollution, and local authority public health departments exercised controls (over sources of smoke, dust, noise and odour) which today would be labelled 'environmental'. Planning had acquired a separate and clear identity; it now had its own Ministry; it had had a professional institution since 1914 whose status (confirmed by the Royal endorsement in 1971) was far superior to that of the equivalent for public health. But the word 'environment' was not in common parlance and it was not to be found in the 1947 Act. The urgency of the immediate task—post-war reconstruction—was such that any discussion of the meaning of planning, or whether it could be said to have its own distinct environmental role, would have been dismissed as idle sophistry.

Nevertheless, the Scott Report (1942)—one of the three most influential policy foundations of the 1947 Act—with its emphasis on conservation of the countryside, would undoubtedly be described as environmental today. Another, the Barlow Report (1940), which recommended the extension of the remit of planning from urban areas to all land in order to facilitate a national plan for the location of industry and population, would probably be claimed by the human geographers. It has recently been argued (Shaw, 1999) that the absence of a 'national spatial planning framework', of which the Barlow Report was an early example, has become a major constraint on the effectiveness of the UK planning system. The Uthwatt Report (1942) was perhaps the least environmental in that it was primarily concerned with an economic problem which, from the experience of planning schemes under earlier legislation from 1909 onwards, was anticipated as an obstacle to further progress. Those whose land value rises as a result of the public control of land enjoy a betterment which, it was argued, should be taxed in order to provide compensation for those who incur losses. Land is an economic good which can be owned and whose ownership can be transferred, originally in return for military service, but now as a financial exchange. Land still forms the subject matter of the vast canons of the law of real property. As a result of one of the latest additions[1] to UK environmental law, the ownership of land polluted by earlier (mostly industrial) uses now carries with it certain obligations regarding the remediation of contamination. (Other recent developments in the relationship between property law and planning are discussed further below.) But the great majority of property transactions (the conveyancing of individual dwellings) have little or no environmental significance. In turn, it is necessary to recognise at the outset that the great majority of decisions taken by planners are 'environmental' simply in that they relate to the use of land.

The recent appearance of the phrase 'environmental planning' serves as a reminder that it is possible to write at length about planning making only scant reference to issues which now form the major concerns of environmentalists. Nevertheless, the overlap between planning and environment, if far short of total, offers a very rewarding area of study. There are few examples of an environmental problem which lack a spatial dimension or have no connection with land use. Sometimes the linkages are all too apparent, as in the siting of nuclear installations, incinerators or even wind turbines. Often the connection needs the trained eye of a practitioner—such as the design of urban forms which minimise reliance upon private motor cars.

In a paper (Miller, 1999a) relating primarily to environmental law, I have sought to identify some semantic structure by distinguishing between a 'weak' usage in which 'environment' refers simply to external surroundings and a 'strong' sense which is driven by an apprehension of ecological collapse brought about by unsustainable economic growth. This apprehension had evolved within the environmental movements of the 1960s; in 1972, Edward Goldsmith and colleagues encapsulated it thus:

> The principal defect of the industrial way of life with its ethos of expansion is that it is not sustainable. Its termination within the lifetime of someone born today is inevitable—unless it continues to be sustained for a while longer by an entrenched minority at the cost of imposing great suffering on the rest of mankind [Goldsmith et al. 1972, 1].

[1] Part IIA, Environmental Protection Act 1990.

The call for sustainability (or more often, sustainable development) has become the key response to this apprehension of climate change, loss of biodiversity, ozone depletion and other environmental threats on a global scale. The later chapters of this book take up the role of planning in the pursuit of sustainability. But it is necessary to remember that the sustainability paradigm, powerful though it is, does not include every aspect of what is understood by the term 'environmental'. If we think in terms of land as soil—as an agricultural resource whose renewability is far from guaranteed—then land too can fall within our strong category. But the word 'land', whether urban or rural, also refers to our immediate surroundings on which all social and economic activities take place; it is therefore environmental in a 'weak' or purely spatial sense. Moreover, the idea of landscape as a source of aesthetic satisfaction, if not timeless, certainly predates late twentieth century environmentalism. Whether we delight in Georgian facades or in rugged upland moors, we have reason to be grateful that *conservation*—both in the town and the country—has been a central aim of planning from the outset. Trees and advertisements continue to require special controls within a more general aim of maintaining visual amenity. Whilst ancient monuments, listed buildings and conservation areas continue to fall within the responsibilities of local planning authorities, this concern with what now tends to be labelled 'heritage', and its desire to retain links with an (often idealised) past, needs to be distinguished from the apprehensions of a bleak future which motivates 'strong' or 'deep green' environmentalism.

The role of land use planning impinges across the environmental spectrum from weak to strong. It follows that, in the exercise of that role, planning authorities will routinely encounter other agencies of the state whose remit is more confined to a particular sector of the environment or to a particular form of environmental harm. Many of those agencies fall within the remit of a single government department in England and Wales. Formed in 1997, the Department of Environment, Transport and the Regions continues the process, begun in 1971 with the creation of the Department of the Environment, of co-ordination and integration within the central executive. The Secretary of State responsible for these departments has also exercised the appellate and other powers conferred upon him by various planning statutes. But the co-ordination of planning and other policies is assisted by the Secretary of State's (non-statutory) power to publish advice in planning circulars and similar documents. The twenty-five planning policy guidance notes (PPGs, see Box 1.1) give some indication of the diversity of planning's concerns. Some, No.6 (the location of shopping centres) for example, are environmental in a purely weak sense. Whilst No. 24 is obviously concerned with an environmental source of nuisance (*viz.* noise) and No.23 explicitly addresses the issue of the relationship between planning and various pollution control agencies. No.25 (on flood risk) might be seen as an anticipation of the need to plan for one of the consequences of climate change, increasingly regarded as the gravest threat to the global environment; whilst No.22 relates to one element in the strategy to reduce that threat.

BOX 1.1: Planning Policy Guidance Notes

PPG01:	General Policy and Principles
PPG02:	Green Belts
PPG03:	Housing
PPG04:	Industrial and Commercial Development and Small Firms
PPG05:	Simplified Planning Zones
PPG06:	Town Centres and Retail Development
PPG07:	The Countryside: environmental quality and economic and social development
PPG08:	Telecommunications
PPG09:	Nature Conservation
PPG10:	Planning and Waste Management
PPG11:	Regional Planning
PPG12:	Development Plans
PPG13:	Transport
PPG14:	Development on Unstable Land
PPG15:	Planning and the Historic Environment
PPG16:	Archaeology and Planning
PPG17:	Sport and Recreation
PPG18:	Enforcing Planning Control
PPG19:	Outdoor Advertisement Control
PPG20:	Coastal Planning
PPG21:	Tourism
PPG22:	Renewable Energy
PPG23:	Planning and Pollution Control
PPG24:	Planning and Noise
PPG25:	Development and flood risk

Following the publication of the White Paper on the environment (HMG, 1990) and the national strategy on sustainable development (HMG, 1994) there has been an increased recognition of the need for an integration of an environmental concern in all planning policies. Thus, PPG1 offers advice on traditional issues like green belt and nature conservation as well as stressing planning's more general role in ensuring that development and growth are sustainable.

THE STRUCTURE OF THIS BOOK

The following chapters of this book make frequent reference to advisory documents published by the central executive, PPGs in particular, which aim to maximise the effectiveness of planning in the pursuit of various environmental objectives. A common theme of these documents is the need for liaison between planning and other agencies. The great majority of contacts consist of little more than the routine consultations and exchanges of information over intended actions. However, it is in the instances of disagreement, even though they constitute a small minority of encounters, that the underlying priorities, in so far as they determine the policies, of the respective agencies become most visible.

Disputes between planners and the bodies responsible for discharges to rivers and coastal waters have tended to attract less public attention than the air pollution counterparts. William Howarth's chapter begins by defining eight "axioms' which, he argues, are descriptive of both the statutory regime of town planning and that of water pollution control, currently in force in England and Wales. From 1973 until 1989, the operation of water treatment plants and the enforcement of water quality standards were exercised by a single public sector body (the regional water authority for the area). Following their privatisation and the creation, first, of the National Rivers Agency and then the Environment Agency, the gamekeeper and poacher roles are now more separate. Inadequate sewerage and failures of water treatment plants still accounted for about a quarter of the 'substantiated water pollution incidents' in England and Wales in 1996 (DETR, 1998a, 3.19). Planners can reduce the risk of such incidents by refusing consent for development which adds further to an already overloaded sewerage system. But in areas of high demand for new housing, such co-operation with what are (following the privatisation of the regional water authorities) private sector bodies may be politically problematic.

The next two chapters consider types of environmental impact for which planning's role—in preventing the juxtaposition of incompatible land uses—has long been recognised. Emissions to the atmosphere from industrial chimneys tend to be viewed with suspicion by those living in the vicinity. Even if the emissions fall short of nuisance, their effects (both real and imaginary) on human health give rise to an apprehension which the regulatory body cannot ignore when justifying authorisation of those emissions. The hostility of local residents is also a factor to be considered by the local planning authority when considering a planning application for a new pollution source. The temptation to assuage local opposition by applying planning powers to control air pollution has in the past given rise to a number of *causes célèbres*. Chapter Three surveys the evolution of this question of overlapping regulatory regimes in the twenty-five years since Chris Wood's (1976) first investigations. Planning's role in regard to major industrial hazards is addressed by Gordon Walker. Technical control over design and operations—to reduce the risk of fire, explosion and major chemical releases—is the statutory responsibility of the Health and Safety Executive. Planning has a recognised role in the siting of hazardous installations and in ensuring that vulnerable land uses (especially schools, hospitals, leisure complexes which are not easily evacuated during an emergency) are not permitted in the vicinity of major hazards. This chapter also explores attempts by local authorities and industry to involve the 'at risk' public more actively in decision-making.

Whilst industrial sources of hazard and pollution may have produced the best known and most controversial cases, the notion of 'overlapping jurisdictions' is also relevant when considering wildlife conservation in rural areas. Ownership of agricultural land, like any other, carries with it rights which are protected by property law, and any intrusion upon those rights in the pursuit of wildlife conservation, such as the designation of a 'site of special scientific interest', has always required the consent of the landowner. But the 'voluntary principle', along with the immunity from planning control which agricultural land has largely enjoyed, is circumscribed when a particular site benefits from the extra level of protection which European Community law now accords. Chris Rodgers' chapter therefore spans a range of ideas from land (principally, rural) as the subject of property law, to landscape as an intrinsic good and to land as the habitat of a threatened species. By introducing the issue of biodiversity, this chapter therefore offers a link between the traditional 'planning versus pollution' role and the 'planning as a vehicle for promoting sustainability' approach which dominates discussion in the latter chapters.

Protection of green field sites in the countryside implies a greater reliance upon derelict and despoiled sites in urban areas. The 1947 Act viewed land as a precious resource, especially in this small and crowded island. The new regime relating to contaminated land brings to that environmental medium a degree of control comparable with that already applicable to air and water. It also has important economic implications, particularly those provisions which seek to make the polluter pay for the costs of remediation. John Handley's chapter is more concerned with planning's role in ensuring that land is also seen as a finite resource in any discussion of sustainability.

Chris Wood describes the UK implementation and practitioners' experience of a statutory system of environmental assessment. British hostility, in the Council of Ministers, to successive drafts of what was to become the 1985 Directive on environmental assessment is well documented (Haigh, 1987, 352). Initially the view was taken that the British planning system was open, transparent and already capable of offering the safeguards which the European Commission was seeking to make mandatory in all Member States, including those whose planning regimes were, in comparison, rudimentary. But the implementation of the Directive in the UK has not been straightforward. It has taken many legal challenges to ensure that the spirit of the original Directive, rather than the letter of the transposing regulations, is observed. These challenges have involved certain principles of European law (supremacy, direct and indirect effect) which are also germane to the subject matter of other chapters (Three and Five in particular); hence a brief summary is included in the discussion of the role of the Courts towards the end of this chapter.

Waste management is invariably accepted as a key element of sustainability; it also has a special status in UK planning in that non-metropolitan county and unitary authorities are statutorily obliged[2] to prepare a local plan which addresses the whole range of waste management issues, such as recycling, trans-

[2] S.38 of the Town and Country Planning Act 1990 (hereafter 'the 1990 Act') as amended.

fer and disposal. The waste plan must be in harmony with the structure plan and must take account of any minerals local plan. Similar obligations are imposed on metropolitan authorities when preparing their unitary development plans. The preparation of such plans provides the public with an opportunity to involve themselves in the policy-making process. Indeed, public participation was the principal motivation in the adoption of the 'new style' development plans in 1968, and it remains central to Part I of the Town and Country Planning Act 1990. No other environmental statute offers any remotely comparable forum for public involvement. Judith Petts' chapter continues the discussion of overlapping jurisdictions but also goes on to consider the need for new approaches for public participation, not only at the site specific stage but at a more strategic level. Such approaches, she suggests, could reduce the conflict which is often seen as inherent in planning (see below).

A similar optimism is present in Marvin and Guy's chapter, which extends the discussion of sustainability into (water, waste, transport and energy) infrastructures. They contrast management of demand with the supply-side orientation prevailing during the period of public ownership of the utilities. Demand management, they argue, holds the promise of developers, planners and providers negotiating more sustainable arrangements tailored to the particular needs of the development. The chapter by David Gibbs argues that the implementation of policies promoting sustainable development, on a scale commensurate with the problems posed, requires planning at the regional level to be given a far more prominent role than it has enjoyed hitherto in England. He recognises that sustainable development discourses have been adopted at the sub-regional level to justify policies for restraint and that some areas (especially in the South East of England) cannot accommodate allocations of new housing proposed within the relevant Regional Planning Guidance Note. He then pursues the question whether the existing planning system is equipped, given its emphasis on land use, to address the broader economic and social issues entailed in sustainable development.

Gibbs' chapter and, to a lesser extent, Marvin and Guy's depend for their sources largely upon recent policy documents and the insights of fellow academics who have considered the same issues. The fact that they do not refer to any legal cases (either in a British or a European jurisdiction) is due to the fact that sustainability *per se* has yet to be cited in a legal challenge. However, the weak end of the environmental spectrum has given rise to a vast volume of planning case law. As long as the refusal of planning consent has enormous financial implications, aggrieved appellants will continue to have every reason to challenge the legality of such decisions. This seemingly inexorable accumulation of case law is arguably as important an influence on the role of planning as ministerial guidance notes. This book must pay special attention to recent additions to that case law which relate to challenges to planning's environmental role, especially in pollution control, nature conservation and environmental assessment. In addition, it must not overlook developments in both private and public law which also shape that role.

PLANNING, CONFLICT AND THE ROLE OF THE COURTS

A study of the relationship between planning and environment is, no less than an academic analysis of any other aspect of governance, dependent primarily upon published sources. Inter-departmental consensus tends to produce few documents for successive generations of scholars to rediscover and reinterpret. It is discord which tends to generate the more substantive records. Planning appeals and judicial reviews are responses to disagreement; and it is to reports of inquiries, ministerial decision letters and reported cases (especially those heard in the higher courts) that analysts are irresistibly drawn. We should therefore be constantly aware of the paradox that public administration would be impossible without general consensus but our understanding of its processes comes largely from studies of dissent. But there are few incentives (and fewer funding opportunities) to research the commonplace. In the absence of more information, we cannot dismiss the possibility either that the conflicts represent occasional anomalies within a deeper consensus or that they are indicative of a widespread dissatisfaction which, but for the costs incurred by objectors, would be far more apparent. Notwithstanding our concern to keep discord in perspective, one authoritative source continues to argue that 'Politics, conflict and dispute are at the centre of land use planning' (Cullingworth and Nadin, 1997, 2).

In so far as appeals are indicative of conflicts of interest, it is useful to have some measure of overall numbers. Box 1.2 gives recent data on the annual numbers of planning and related appeals in England. Appeals[3] against planning refusal (and planning conditions) are clearly the largest single category, although applications 'called in'[4] for determination by the Secretary of State could contain the more strongly environmental cases. It is necessary to bear in mind that approximately eighty-eight per cent of the (half million or so) planning applications submitted annually in England are approved; planning appeals therefore arise in less than a quarter of the remainder. Less than one per cent of these appeals are challenged by statutory review[5] in the High Court; but their importance in shaping planning law and policy belies their numbers (see Box 1.3). It should be noted that these figures exclude the judicial reviews taken by third parties against planning approvals by local planning authorities. Reform of the legal aid system has meant that few private individuals (as distinct from environmental pressure groups) can now risk the enormous costs which an unsuccessful action might entail. However, action has been taken on a number of occasions to challenge the legality of certain planning applications decided without consideration of an environmental assessment. This sub-set of judicial reviews demands attention in this chapter. In Chapter Three below, reference is made to a number of appeals under the Environmental Protection Act 1990 (see

[3] S.78 of the 1990 Act.
[4] S.77 of the 1990 Act.
[5] S.288 of the 1990 Act.

BOX 1.2 Planning and related appeals (England) 1996/97–1999/2000

Case Type	1996/97	1997/98	1998/99	1999/00
Planning Appeals	12,029	13,051	12,877	12,619
Called in Planning Applications	67	90	119	133
Development Plan Inquiries[1] opened	59	48	38	36
Enforcement Notice Appeals[2]	2,230	3,147	2,370	2,746
Listed Building & Conservation Area Consent Appeals	678	780	603	633
Listed Building Enforcement Notice Appeals	144	196	143	161
Lawful Development Certificate Appeals	77	123	183	128
Public Path and Definitive Map Orders	454	307	317	336
Advertisement Appeals	1,925	2,442	2,014	2195
Applications for Costs	1,667	1,511	1,583	1,407
Compulsory Purchase Orders[3]	45	82	103	90
Appeals[3] under Environmental Protection, Environment and Water Resources Acts	203	214	185	60

[1] England *and Wales*.

[2] Includes appeals under s.39 of the Planning (Listed Buildings and Conservation Areas) Act 1990 and s.174 of the 1990 Act.

[3] Number of cases *received* during the year.

Source: *Planning Inspectorate Executive Agency Statistical Reports 1996/97–1999/2000.*

the final row of Box 1.2) and related judicial reviews, which may come to have an influence, comparable with the equivalents under planning law, in terms of their effect upon the regime of environmental protection at the local level.

1. Planning, environmental assessment and the courts

Environmental assessment seeks to ensure that appropriate scientific techniques are applied to the prediction, and hence the amelioration or prevention, of the impact of projects potentially harmful to the environment. But the EC Directive[6] which obliged the UK government to overcome its antipathy and to

[6] Directive 85/337/EEC [1985] OJ L175/40.

BOX 1.3: Outcome of Planning Appeals (England) 1996/97–1999/2000

Planning Appeals determined by:	1996/97	1997/98	1998/99	1999/2000
written representation	9,686 (57)	9,922 (34)	9,420 (15)	9,201 (24)
public inquiry	831 (100)	999 (78)	997 (61)	882 (50)
hearing	1,512 ([a])	2,130 (13)	2,460 (14)	2,536 (8)
Total	**12,029 (157)**	**13,051 (125)**	**12,877 (90)**	**12,619 (82)**
Percentage allowed	35% (32%)	36% (33%)	35% (36%)	36% (32%)
Appeals challenged[b]	72	77	80	68
Outcome: won	36	38	30	3
lost	8	13	11	1
awaited	28	26	39	64

(numbers in parentheses denote appeals determined by the Secretary of State)

[a] 1997/98 was the first year in which hearings were used to determine appeals by the Secretary of State.

[b] in the High Court under s. 288 of the 1990 Act.

Source: *Planning Inspectorate Executive Agency Statistical Reports 1996/97–1999/2000.*

implement a statutory regime of environmental assessment also sought to involve the 'public concerned' in the assessment process. Given this combination of technical and participatory aims, it is not surprising that the planning system was employed as the principal vehicle for implementing the Directive in the UK. While there have been grounds for concern over the technical content of environmental statements (Jones et al. 1998), it has tended to be procedural questions—especially the failure of planning authorities to demand an assessment of any description—which has motivated disputes resolved by litigation. These cases have, until very recently, fallen foul of a wider dispute over the standing of individuals to take legal action in the public interest. Alder (1993) encapsulated the issues in his review of the early cases (including *Twyford Down*[7]; for a discussion of some later cases, see Stallworthy, 1998). Subsequently, a more relaxed attitude to standing and an important ruling in the '*Dutch Dykes*'[8] case by the European Court of Justice have assisted the higher courts to remove a lot of the earlier confusion. A 1997 case involving quarrying in North Yorkshire came to represent something of a turning-point.

The 1947 Act gave many quarries a form of planning consent but without specifying conditions or time limits. In 1991 a registration scheme[9] was introduced in an attempt to forestall the potential problem of 'old mining permissions' (of which there may be some 1,000 in England and Wales) becoming

[7] *Twyford Parish Council and others* v. *Secretary of State for Transport* (1992) 4 JEL 273.

[8] Case C–72/95 *Aanemersberdijf PK Kraajeveld BV* v. *Gedeputeerde Staten van Zuid Holland* [1996] ECR I–5403.

[9] S.22 of the Planning and Compensation Act 1991.

activated with no environmental safeguards. Owners of such permissions were given a six-month period in which to register them with the local mineral planning authority, whereupon conditions might be applied. Wensley Quarries, near Preston under Scar, were registered in 1993 and conditions were determined by North Yorkshire County Council two years later. Quarrying falls within Annex II to the 1985 Directive, which lists those projects which must be subject to an assessment where they are likely to give rise to significant effects. Local residents argued that the county council had acted unlawfully by determining the conditions without requiring the operators to submit an environmental statement. The key issue was whether 'development consent'—the phrase defined in Article 1 of the Directive—lay in the interim development order (conferred by the 1947 Act) or in the determination of conditions under the 1991 Act. At first instance, Hidden J argued for the former.[10] In taking the opposite view, the Court of Appeal had the benefit of the ECJ ruling[11] that 'the wording of the [EA] directive indicates that it has a wide scope and a broad purpose'.[12] In the instant case, a purposive interpretation suggested that it was not the passing of the 1947 development order but the determination of conditions (relating to operational matters, restoration and aftercare) which was the point at which the developer was permitted to proceed. The determination of conditions without consideration of an environmental statement was therefore unlawful. The House of Lords subsequently affirmed this verdict and offered a little further advice on activities requiring multiple or staged permissions:

> the principle in this and similar cases seems to me to be clear: the Directive does not apply to decisions which involve merely the detailed regulation of activities for which the principal consent, raising the substantial environmental issues, has already been given.[13]

In a similar case involving a quarry in County Durham, the Court of Appeal has resolved a longstanding legal question by holding that the Directive[14] is capable of 'direct effect'. This is the principle of European Community law which enables individuals to rely upon provisions of directives, which are precise and unconditional, in their national courts. As an emanation of the (UK) state, Durham County Council was bound by the terms of the Directive and it had therefore to receive and consider an assessment before approving the proposed operations. But this would result, Durham argued, in an obligation being imposed on a private individual (the quarry operator) or, in other words, it would be an example of horizontal direct effect—a directive should impose an obligation on Member States not on individuals—something which the case law[15] of the European Court of Justice has sought to avoid. In resolving this

[10] R. v. *North Yorkshire County Council ex parte Brown* [1997] Env. LR 391.
[11] Above n.8.
[12] R. v. *North Yorkshire County Council ex parte Brown* [1998] JPL 764.
[13] R. v. *North Yorkshire County Council ex parte Brown* [1999] JPL 616.
[14] Above n.6, Art. 4.1 requires the submission of an assessment prior to project approval.
[15] Case C–91/92 *Faccini Dori* v. *Recreb Srl* [1994] ECR I–3325.

dilemma, Sedley LJ argued that Mr Huddleston's (the resident who brought the judicial review) 'interest in the legal protection of the environment'[16] could be protected without imposing criminal liability on the operator.

There are very few reported instances of the successful use of the 'direct effect' of a provision of an environmental directive in any member state; this is almost certainly the first instance in the English Supreme Court. A private individual has used a principle to be found, not in the Treaty of Rome, but in the case law of the European Court[17] to persuade the Court of Appeal to adopt a purposive interpretation of a directive, rather than rely upon a literal reading of the implementing regulations. It is a procedural victory but not necessarily a substantive one: having received and considered the assessment, the County Council will still enjoy wide discretion (constrained only by *Wednesbury*[18] reasonableness) in the conditions it chooses to impose. But coming as it did, in the first months of the new millennium, this case may come to be seen as a milestone[19] in the conflict between public and private interests which, according to Professor MacAuslan (1980), planning seeks to mediate. It represents a clear departure from judicial attitudes in earlier cases. If nothing else, it will remove the 'busybody' stigma from those who seek to invoke their public law rights to challenge planning (and related) decisions. Twyford Down might just conceivably have been saved had Sedley LJ's reasoning preceded, rather than followed, that tragic case.

2. Planning and property rights

By way of complementing the following chapters' references to the overlap between planning and other statutory regimes of environmental protection, it is also necessary at this stage to make some reference to recent cases which illuminate the relationship between planning and the environmental dimensions of English common law. Planning control has always amounted to an intrusion on the rights of property. Although Mrs Thatcher's privatisations did not extend to a general reversal of the 'nationalisation' of landowners' rights to develop their property which, Cullingworth (1997, 23) claims, had taken place in 1947. Even when her deregulation rhetoric was at its height, extensive dismantling of the planning system was not attempted; although the faintness of the praise—'in many ways [town and country planning] has served the country well and the Government has no intention of abolishing it' (HMG, 1985, para. 3.1)—suggests that this had been contemplated.

[16] R. v. *Durham County Council and others ex parte Huddleston* [2000] JPL 409.

[17] Case C–41/74 *Van Duyn* v. *Home Office* [1974] ECR 1337.

[18] *Associated Provincial Picture Houses Ltd* v. *Wednesbury Corporation* [1948] 1 KB 223, [1947] 2 All ER 680.

[19] As might *Berkeley* v. *Secretary of State for the Environment* [2000] 3 All ER 897 (HL) in which their Lordships held that an environmental statement must be submitted even though it is unlikely to influence a decision-maker, who already has all the relevant information but in a different form.

The right to enjoy one's property without interference from noise, odour and fumes from adjoining land is protected by the ancient tort of nuisance, from which modern environmental law is descended. When the activities which give rise to complaints (concerning smoke, fumes, noise, odour etc.) are carried out by a body acting under statutory authority then, in general, that authority will amount to a defence in nuisance. In a case[20] involving noise from traffic entering and leaving a commercial port, Buckley J held that planning consent was analogous to statutory authority in conferring a defence against claims in nuisance. If this decision is interpreted as extinguishing a private right (to sue in nuisance) without remedy or compensation, it is contrary to English law. If however, the planning permission is understood as bringing about a marked change in the nature of the area, then the locality test (of what is a reasonable amount of noise, dust or fumes to be expected in an industrial, residential or commercial area) remains the basis of a defence against nuisance. Given the criticism which this decision attracted, it was not surprising that the Court of Appeal chose to narrow further the latter interpretation when considering a similar case.[21] It concluded that a defence in nuisance might attach to a planning permission which had demanded a consideration of 'strategic issues' as to where the wider public interest (stemming, for example, from a commercial port) was deemed to have outweighed the local residents' detriment. Secondly, the development had to make a specific change to the nature of the locality, which, in this later case, the operation of pig units in a rural area did not. The High Court has also held that, whilst the possibility of actions in nuisance had to be considered by a planning authority, that did not oblige the authority to withhold consent for housing in the vicinity of an existing source of odour (an animal treatment works).[22]

It is interesting to compare the notion of planning permission conferring a defence in nuisance with the House of Lords' ruling in *Hunter*,[23] where it was stated *obiter* that development control could have foreseen and prevented the circumstances which gave rise to the nuisance allegedly associated with poor TV reception. Interference caused by an exceptionally tall building (Canary Wharf in East London) was deemed not to constitute a nuisance. Citing precedents dating from the seventeenth century that the interruption of view and other passive effects of one building upon another were not (in the absence of some easement or covenant) unlawful, their Lordships declined the opportunity to modernise nuisance by recognising that receiving adequate TV signals is, for many people, a necessary precondition of the full enjoyment of their homes. Instead they held that the effects on television reception should form but one of many 'material considerations' to be taken into account (along with the development plan and any representations made by local residents) by the planning authority before

20 *Gillingham BC* v. *Medway (Chatham) Dock Company* [1992] Env. LR 98.
21 *Wheeler and Anr* v. *J.J. Saunders Ltd and others* [1995] 2 All ER 697.
22 R. v. *Exeter CC ex parte J.L. Thomas and Co.* [1990] 1 All ER 413.
23 *Hunter and others* v. *Canary Wharf Ltd* [1997] AC 655, [1997] 2 All ER 426.

giving planning consent for any large building. However, this development took place within the boundary of an enterprise zone (Isle of Dogs) where even a building of this height (250 metres) required the agreement only of the London Docklands Development Corporation. Notwithstanding this point, nuisance cannot be used in an *ad hoc* manner to compensate for the adverse consequences of 'fast track' planning.

The erection or extension of even a single-storey building can impair the view previously enjoyed by neighbours. For those affected it represents the loss of a private good. But whether any given instance involves the public interest to such an extent as to make it a 'material consideration' for planning purposes is 'for the decision-maker to determine'.[24] If loss of sunlight or an intrusion upon a treasured view are to carry an 'environmental' label, then it must be of our weak variety. By analogy, interference with TV signals simply by the presence of a tall building must also fall within that category. However, it is possible to point to an earlier case involving planning and electromagnetic radiation which, despite being only 'weakly environmental' in our sense, did lead to the fundamental principle of planning law that *any* consideration which relates to the use of land is capable of being a 'material consideration'.[25]

Underlying all these judgments (and countless others) is the need to strike a balance between individual rights and the public interest. Nuisance serves to protect the former whilst recognising the latter; planning pursues the latter whilst ensuring that the extinction of any property right (as, for example, in compulsory purchase) is appropriately compensated. Planning is inherently utilitarian: it is recognised that there may be losers as well as gainers as a result of any planning decision or development plan policy. But provided that decision or policy is in pursuit of the overall interests of the area, and it is not unreasonable in the *Wednesbury* sense, then the planning authority is not liable in negligence to any person who consequently incurs loss.[26] If planning and property law have come to enjoy a largely peaceful co-existence, there are signs that the relationship between planning and the rights protected by the Human Rights Act 1998 could become more vexatious.

3. Planning and human rights

The Human Rights regime represents yet another overlapping jurisdiction and one which can be expected to disturb the equilibrium between public and private interests. Planning authorities and the various environmental agencies referred to in this book are 'public bodies' and therefore fall within the remit of

[24] *AL Wood-Robinson* v. *Secretary of State and Wandsworth LBC* [1998] JPL 977.

[25] *Stringer* v. *Minister of Housing and Local Government* [1971] 1 All ER 65 at 77, in which the operators of the radio-telescope at Jodrell Bank (Cheshire) opposed a development which would increase the local background radiation (from electrical machinery in the proposed garage).

[26] *Ryeford Homes* v. *Sevenoaks District Council* [1990] JPL 36.

the 1998 Act. Judges are obliged to 'take account of'[27] the case law of the European Court of Human Rights (ECHR) when hearing any action under the 1998 Act; and it is possible to point to a number of cases, with an environmental dimension, which raise the possibility of conflict with UK planning's utilitarian ethic.

In *Lopez Ostra* v. *Spain*,[28] the ECHR held that the applicant's (Article 8) right to privacy and respect for family life had been violated by a local authority's ineffectual response to her complaints about odorous fumes from a tannery near her home. In determining whether, in cases of this type, a state had breached its duty to protect private and family life, home and correspondence, the Court held that:

> regard must be had to the fair balance that has to be struck between the competing interests of the individual and of the community as a whole, and in any case the State enjoys a certain margin of appreciation.[29]

On the evidence in this case, especially that given by a paediatrician on the effects of hydrogen sulphide emissions on the health of the applicant's daughter, the margin of appreciation had been exceeded. It was similarly deemed to have been exceeded in another case[30] in which the same (Article 8) right was adjudged to have been violated, on this occasion, by an Italian local authority's failure to inform the residents about the evacuation procedures to be followed in the event of an emergency at a plant manufacturing fertiliser.

It was the margin of appreciation which, by a six to three majority of the judges in the ECHR, saved the United Kingdom from considerable embarrassment in the *Buckley*[31] case. Mrs Buckley, a gypsy, argued that her right to family life had been infringed when the local planning authority took enforcement action after she had parked her two caravans on land which she owned but which was not designated for that purpose in the local plan. A ruling in Mrs Buckley's favour would have seriously undermined the basis of the UK planning system. However, it could well be that the more lasting effect on the UK planning system will come from *Bryan* v. *UK*[32] and subsequent cases which are concerned with the procedural, as distinct from the substantive, rights which the planning system confers.

Article 6(1) of the Convention provides that: 'in the determination of his civil rights and obligations . . . everyone is entitled to a fair and a public hearing by an independent and impartial tribunal established by law'. In the *Bryan* case, the ECHR decided that an Inspector determining an appeal against an enforcement notice could not be 'an independent and impartial tribunal' by virtue of the existence of the power of the Secretary of State to determine the appeal himself and

[27] S.2 of the Human Rights Act 1998.
[28] *Lopez Ostra* v. *Spain* (1995) 20 EHRR 277.
[29] *Ibid.* para.51.
[30] *Guerra and others* v. *Italy* (1998) 26 EHRR 357.
[31] *Buckley* v. *UK* (1997) 23 EHRR 101, [1996] JPL 1018.
[32] *Bryan* v. *UK* (1995) 21 EHRR 342, [1996] JPL 386.

because the Inspector was bound to consider policies, especially those contained in the various planning policy guidance notes, published by the Secretary of State. However, the ECHR went on to accept that the right of an aggrieved appellant[33] to refer the decision in an enforcement notice appeal to the High Court was sufficient to ensure that Article 6(1) was not violated by the existing UK procedures.

The limited 'independence' of the Planning Inspectorate and the executive was one of a number of concerns which led the government to commission a study, by Malcolm Grant, of the feasibility of a specialist environmental court for England and Wales. This innovation had been suggested earlier by the planning lawyer, Robert Carnwath (1992), and by Sir Harry (later, Lord) Woolf, who argued (1991, 12) that the growing number and complexity of environmental disputes necessitated the establishment of a specialist tribunal. When he became Master of the Rolls, his report (Woolf, 1996) on reform of the civil justice system made few explicit references to the environment, but he could not have been unaware of the European Commission's concern over the need to improve access (especially by third parties) to national courts for environmental justice.[34] Professor Grant's preferred model envisages a two-tier system with a tribunal, incorporating the existing Planning Inspectorate and possibly the Lands Tribunal, and a court-tier, hearing *inter alia* applications for judicial review, statutory review of planning decisions, and appeals in criminal cases as well as civil litigation with a clear environmental dimension. Grant's report (DETR, 2000a) does not understate the problems (analogous to distinguishing between our weak and strong categories) of selecting the cases to be heard by the new environmental jurisdiction and those which are to be left, as now, to the Queen's Bench Division.

The absence of a 'readily definable body of environmental law' was one of the reasons HM Government was, according to a House of Lords spokesman,[35] not persuaded of the need for an environmental tribunal. It remains to be seen whether this initial disinclination can survive a ruling, eagerly awaited as this book goes to press, in the Inner House of the Court of Session (Scotland's equivalent of the Court of Appeal) in the case of *County Properties Ltd.* v. *The Scottish Ministers*.[36] Although this case is strictly concerned with an appeal over listed building consent, it raises issues which are not confined to this weak end of the spectrum and, if not reversed, it has implications for appeals involving mainstream planning matters. In summary, the argument advanced in *Bryan*[37] (*viz.* that the provision for statutory review of appeal decisions in the High Court overcomes the objection that the Planning Inspectorate is not an inde-

33 '[O]r the local planning authority or any other person having an interest': s.289 of the 1990 Act.

34 EC Commission Report on Access to Environmental Justice [1995] OJ C254/47; see also the European Convention on Access to Information, Public Participation in Decision Making and Access to Justice in Environmental Matters (the 'Aarhus Convention') 1998.

35 House of Lords Debates 9 October 2000.

36 (Outer House) *Scots Law Times*, 25 August 2000 at 27.

37 Above n.32.

pendent tribunal) does not answer the objection that that review is confined to matters of law. And since the review does not allow a reconsideration of the merits (which in this case involves aesthetic judgments) of the original decision, the Article 6 requirement for a truly 'independent' tribunal is not satisfied. However, offering property developers a means of challenging their obligations in the conservation of Georgian facades was, I suspect, not uppermost in the minds of the original authors of the European Convention or of those who drafted the Human Rights Act 1998.

Whatever the precise structure of any environment court which is eventually implemented, it is likely that the appeals, reviews and cases, which have been of most interest to the contributors to this volume would tend to be considered by a multi-disciplinary body including lawyers, planners, surveyors and scientists. One might therefore anticipate the gradual emergence of a more consistent approach. But whilst the appellate role of the Secretary of State might be removed, the role of the central executive in setting out the overall policy aims of planning will remain. If denied the opportunity to determine the most controversial appeals, the executive, mindful that PPGs and planning circulars constitute 'material considerations' which must[38] be taken into account, might be tempted to become far more prescriptive when preparing or revising these advisory documents. Governments are elected to govern in the public interest. Within the 'public interest', green concerns are becoming dominant and these often involves difficult decisions over land use. Passing such decisions to the judiciary will not make them any easier or, indeed, any less political.

SUMMARY

The use of the plural in the title of this introductory chapter is deliberate. It is necessary from the outset to remind the reader that the more prolific the use of the term 'environment', the more its meaning has become fragmented. It may be that the book will identify a coherence in planning's role across the range of environmental sectors but that has to be established, not assumed. The weak/strong environmental spectrum which I have introduced can be criticised in that it reduces all environmental concerns, no matter how complex, to a one-dimensional scale. But it is simply a heuristic device—a belated attempt to impose some structure in the semantic chaos which attends the uncritical and metaphorical use (as in 'social environment') of any concept.

Planning seeks to regulate the use of land in the public interest. The 'public interests' which planning has traditionally sought to regulate—green belt, landscape, and amenity—are environmental in the sense that they are aspects of our immediate surroundings—aspects which are still seen as a source of aesthetic satisfaction. Such concerns are far from trivial and they continue to give rise to

[38] *J A Pye (Oxford) Estates Ltd* v. *West Oxfordshire DC* [1982] JPL 577.

important additions to planning case law. But contemporary environmentalism is motivated and characterised by a deep apprehension that the true external costs of industrialism may outweigh the benefits. Sustainability is a 'public interest' in a rather special sense—one which embraces both intra- and inter-generational equity. We do not claim that the following chapters represent an exhaustive account, that is, one which leaves no aspect of planning or environment unconsidered. But we believe we examine those aspects which enable the reader to form a view of planning's contributions to environmental protection in the immediate future.

2

Town and Country Planning and Water Quality Planning

WILLIAM HOWARTH

OBJECTIVES AND APPROACH

THE PURPOSE OF this chapter is to examine the parallels between town and country planning and water quality planning and to consider whether the general separation between the two regulatory systems is justified or beneficial in securing strategic environmental objectives. From a distance, it may appear that the anticipation of environmentally unacceptable activities and impacts in relation to land use, on the one hand, and water use, on the other, have much in common. Both may be seen as mechanisms by which environmental protection may be directed towards overall objectives and the conformity of particular proposals with those objectives may be secured. However, it is remarkable that, in the United Kingdom, the regulatory systems which apply to land use planning and water use planning have evolved, to a great extent, independently of one another. Whatever justification exists for this is largely historical in character, but the new emphasis upon holistic environmental regulation places in contention any legal or administrative barriers between the control of different activities which impact upon the environment. Hence, the time is ripe to revisit the separation between town and country planning and water quality planning and to reassess whether this regulatory separation is genuinely conducive to better protection of the environment as a whole and the ecosystems which are dependent upon it.

Having embarked upon this, potentially wide-ranging, line of enquiry some qualifications are needed to confine the discussion within manageable limits. The first is to note that, following the general theme of this work, the comparisons and contrasts that are to be drawn are between town and country planning and water *quality* planning. That is to say, that the weighty concern of water *quantity* management, the reconciliation of water demands upon limited supplies and the consequences of over-use of water supplies upon the aquatic environment, will be addressed here only incidentally (but see Chapter Nine). Whilst the role of land use planning in preventing developments which impose unacceptable demands upon vulnerable watercourses and groundwater supplies is a fundamental concern in the protection of the aquatic environment, the respective use of the two planning regimes to prevent water pollution and the deterioration of water quality is taken as the central focus of attention.

Secondly, it must be recognised that the system of town and country planning operative in England and Wales is of bewildering intricacy and the danger of being swamped by detail must be avoided if useful general inferences are to be drawn. For the purpose of emphasising comparisons and contrasts with water quality planning a strongly thematic approach is needed. This involves identifying the centrally important features of the regulatory regimes at the expense of leaving out much of the detail that would properly feature in a fuller account of either system of control. It is to be stressed, therefore, that the coverage that follows seeks to provide a basis for a comparative discussion rather than anything approaching a comprehensive account of the law and policy on land use planning or water quality planning.

Finally, it is necessary to acknowledge that any analysis based mainly on legislative principles may be neglecting institutional and political factors which might support quite different inferences. Local authorities, for example, which undertake the greater part of the responsibility for administering the town and country planning system in practice, have a local democratic mandate. The elected representatives of local people will be unavoidably subject to a corresponding political obligation to be responsive to environmental and other primarily local concerns. By contrast, the Environment Agency, which has the principal responsibility for the administration of water quality planning, has no directly corresponding political mandate and draws its remit from its allocation of responsibilities under national legislation and policy and the considerable body of technical expertise that it possesses in relation to the implementation of its environmental responsibilities. The key point to appreciate is that the practical effect of a body of law is capable of being greatly influenced by the nature of the body that is entrusted with its implementation, and the actual impact of the two regulatory regimes under consideration may be strongly dependent upon different perceptions of environmental priorities as between local authorities and the Environment Agency. Moreover, the legally-based analysis that follows may not give adequate weight to the contrasts that arise because of the different perspectives of those entrusted with administrative and law-enforcement responsibilities.

AXIOMS OF TOWN AND COUNTRY PLANNING LAW

In any comparative legal study, some effort must be made to distil the key features of the areas of law to be compared and, necessarily, this is the case in comparing town and country planning law and water quality planning law. Unavoidably, this involves quite a large measure of subjectivity, since equally well-informed commentators are likely to reach different conclusions about which parts of a subject area are properly identified as 'key principles' and which are to be relegated to 'matters of detail'. Nonetheless, for any progress to be made, some judgement has to be exercised, even if it is not likely to be met with universal endorsement. It is, tentatively, proposed, therefore, that the following may be treated as the axioms of town and country planning law:

(1) the Executive Responsibility Principle;
(2) the Plan Formulation Responsibility;
(3) the Development Definition;
(4) the *De Minimis* Exception;
(5) the Authorisation Principle;
(6) the Consultation Obligation;
(7) the Materiality Principle; and
(8) the Determination Principle.

The suggestion is that these principles are 'axiomatic' in the sense that they identify the basic structure of planning regulation whilst minimising the need to go into matters of detail other than to illustrate the meaning of the principles. In terms of their basic functions, within the town and country planning system, the principles are outlined in the following paragraphs.

1. The executive responsibility principle

Whilst practical responsibilities for formulating development plans and determining applications for development consent are normally allocated to local planning authorities, the appropriate Secretary of State has ultimate control over the town and country planning system by means of a range of legislative, administrative and adjudicative powers. In relation to legislative powers, the Secretary of State is provided with extensive powers to facilitate the implementation of the principle enactment, the Town and Country Planning Act 1990 (the '1990 Act'), by making secondary regulations and orders[1] and for most practical purposes the implementation of the Act requires legislative action on his part (see, for example, the Use Classes Order,[2] the General Permitted Development Order[3] and the General Development Procedure Order,[4] discussed below). At the administrative level, the Secretary of State has wide-ranging powers to issue guidance to local authorities to ensure that they act in accordance with general planning policy. Hence, control over structure plans adopted by local authorities is maintained by a requirement that, in formulating a structure plan, the local authority must have regard to any regional or strategic planning guidance

[1] S.333 of the 1990 Act.
[2] Town and Country Planning (Use Classes) Order 1987 (SI 1987, No.764).
[3] Town and Country Planning (General Permitted Development) Order 1995 (SI 1995, No.418).
[4] Town and Country Planning (General Development Procedure) Order 1995 (SI 1995, No.419).

given to assist in the preparation of the plan,[5] and where relevant policy guidance exists this will be a material consideration in determining any particular planning application. At the adjudicative level, the Secretary of State has various powers to determine planning appeals, such as appeals against a refusal to grant planning permission or the grant of a permission subject to conditions[6] and also has the power to 'call in' particular applications for planning permission for his own determination.[7] Whilst this range of functions may serve to demonstrate the Secretary of State's role in the planning system as a neat contradiction of Montesquieu's theory of the desirability of the separation of the powers of government (see Vile, 1967, 90), it also serves to confine the decision-making power of local authorities in planning matters. The system may be characterised as one of 'bounded discretion' in which a local authority's scope for decision-making is placed within the powers given by statute *and* does not encroach upon those matters which are subject to the overall control of the Secretary of State.

2. The plan formulation responsibility

A duty is imposed upon planning authorities to formulate development plans for a range of different kinds of purpose (under Part II of the 1990 Act). Of central relevance, under the so-called 'new style' of development plans, this involves, for most areas, two tiers of planning, with responsibilities allocated at county level for structure plans and at district level for the local plans. The purpose of the structure plan is to provide a general account of policies applicable to land use within the area, whereas local plans apply policies stated in the structure plan in relation to identified areas of land. Broadly, the function of development plans is twofold: first, to provide a statement of the manner in which national and local policies are to be applied within the relevant area and, secondly, to provide a guide to determinations of whether particular kinds of development will be allowed in particular locations. Hence, at one level plans indicate how strategic objectives for land use, such as the realisation of targets for the provision of housing, are to be realised; at another level they are location-specific in indicating whether a certain kind of development is likely to be authorised in a specific location. The location-specific element is never entirely conclusive of whether a particular development proposal will be authorised, but will generally be useful to prospective developers in identifying areas where specific kinds of development are most likely to be given approval.

[5] S.31(6)(a) of the 1990 Act.
[6] S.78 of the 1990 Act.
[7] S.77 of the 1990 Act.

3. The development definition

Development means 'the carrying out of building, engineering, mining or other operations in, on, over or under land, or the making of any material change in the use of any building or other land'.[8] Because the concept of development is so centrally important in planning law, the case law on the interpretation of these words is considerable, and wildly diverse kinds of land use have been intimately scrutinised to ascertain whether they fall within the scope of the definition. However, for present purposes, the key feature to be recognised is the essential function of the definition in providing a general and *preliminary* identification of the matters that are to be subject to the system of planning regulation. This 'preliminary' identification of regulated kinds of land use is subject to statutory refinement in that, 'for the avoidance of doubt', certain matters are declared to constitute development or are stated not to constitute development[9] and detailed secondary legislation is enacted seeking further to define what degree of change in land use will constitute a 'material' change of use (see the Use Classes Order 1987).[10]

4. The '*de minimis*' exception

To prevent the development control system becoming overloaded with applications for authorisation of minor developments, which are not thought to need explicit consideration by planning authorities, a wide range of developments are given deemed planning permission.[11] That is, even after the definition of 'development' has been refined by secondary legislation, the concept remains too broad to be practicable as a test to determine which land use activities need to be made subject to the full rigour of the planning system and further limitations must be provided for to exempt minor kinds of development from the need for explicit consideration. Whilst this challenge to practicability might have been met by a narrower definition of 'development' being formulated in the first place, the solution that is adopted keeps minor operations within the meaning of 'development' but dispenses with the need for an explicit planning application to be made for such projects by the stipulation that they are 'deemed' to be granted by the Secretary of State without the need for further permission to be given by a local authority. This approach has the advantage that the deemed permission may be withdrawn in certain cases where the Secretary of State or the local planning authority is satisfied that it is expedient that certain

[8] S.55(1) of the 1990 Act.
[9] S.55(2) of the 1990 Act.
[10] Above n.2.
[11] Above n.3.

categories of, otherwise, permitted development in specified areas should be the subject of explicit consideration.[12]

5. The authorisation principle

'Planning permission is required for the carrying out of any development of land'.[13] The key to any system of regulatory control is that, ultimately, failure to comply with regulatory requirements will result in a sanction of some kind, otherwise there would be no compelling reason for adherence to other regulatory requirements. A peculiarity of the town and country planning system is that development of land without planning permission is not, by itself, a criminal offence. However, unauthorised development will allow the local planning authority to instigate the enforcement machinery relating to planning control (see DOE, 1997a, 1997b). This will normally involve the service of an enforcement notice against the person responsible for the unauthorised development which will require the development to cease or to be removed. It is only when the action required under the enforcement notice is not undertaken within the time allowed that a criminal offence is committed.[14] Hence, strictly, the fundamental prohibition upon which the planning system rests is that it is unlawful to contravene an enforcement notice. Nevertheless, the execution of unauthorised development of land is properly characterised as the first step towards commission of the criminal offence.

6. The consultation obligation

Opinions of specified consultees must be sought on applications for particular categories of development and, in determining an application, the local planning authority must take into account representations made by consultees and other representations made. This principle, alongside the obligation upon local planning authorities generally to publicise planning applications, seeks to ensure that determination of applications is made on the basis of the fullest practicable input of relevant opinion and expertise, and implies that authorities are to be responsive to representations which raise significant objections. However, the consultation obligation remains no stronger than that, and providing that an authority adheres to the procedural requirement that such representations are taken into account there will be no grounds for overturning a planning permission that the opinions of a consultee have not been accepted in making the determination (see Box 2.1). Similarly, in relation to development plans, where a local planning authority is preparing a development plan it is

12 Above n.3, Art. 4.
13 S.57(1) of the 1990 Act.
14 S.179 of the 1990 Act.

BOX 2.1: The *Ynys Mon BC* Case

Ynys Mon BC v. *Secretary of State for Wales*[1] concerned an application for planning permission for six houses and was strongly opposed by the National Rivers Authority (the predecessor of the Environment Agency). Following construction of the houses, it would have been the statutory right of the developer to be allowed to make a connection into the local sewerage system.[2] The contention of the Authority was that the local sewerage system was inadequate in that it allowed untreated foul sewage to be discharged into coastal waters. As a consequence, the Authority had formulated a policy to oppose all developments involving further connections to the sewerage system and, consequently, recommended refusal of the application until such time as the relevant sewerage undertaker had brought about adequate improvements to the sewerage system. This was accepted by the local planning authority, which declined the application, but not by the Planning Inspector, who took the view that, although the discharge of raw sewage into the sea was unsatisfactory, the discharge of effluent from an addition six small dwellings was not a sufficient reason to justify the refusal of the development. Accordingly, the Inspector granted the permission.

In an appeal by the Council to quash the Inspector's decision, the Deputy Judge accepted that the duties upon the Authority were of high importance in the public interest and that the conditions at the existing sewage outfalls in the locality were unsatisfactory. Nevertheless, he declined to accept that the total embargo policy adopted by the Authority could conclusively determine in relation to any particular proposed development. To do so would make the Authority's policy conclusive of any decision in the development control context where other relevant considerations needed to be addressed. Whilst the policy objectives of the Authority were important material considerations, it was imperative that they should be weighed together with all other relevant matters. In essence, this is what the Inspector had done by not treating the policy of the Authority as conclusive of the matter for determination and the decision that he had arrived at could not be challenged as unlawful simply because it conflicted with the policy. He was entitled to conclude that, despite the policy, the discharge contributed by the additional houses would not give rise to deleterious consequences in the planning context. It was held that the Inspector had had proper regard to the evidence, and the weight to be attached to this was a matter for his judgment, consequently, the Court declined to overturn the decision.

A key passage from the judgment of Graham Eyre QC, sitting as a Deputy Judge, states that 'a planning decision properly arrived at which, as a result breached this [National Rivers Authority] policy embargo could not be attacked on the grounds that it was unlawful simply by virtue of the existence of the policy'. This shows that a planning application which, if allowed, will contravene Environment Agency policy on pollution control will not necessarily be refused, since the policy is only one material consideration and should not be followed where it is outweighed by other material planning considerations.

[1] [1993] JPL 225.
[2] Under s.98 or s.106 of the Water Industry Act 1991.

bound, before finally determining the contents of the plan, to consider any representations.[15]

7. The materiality principle

In determining a planning application, the planning authority must have regard to provisions of the development plan, so far as material to the application, and to any other material considerations.[16] The test of what is a 'material consideration' in the preparation of plans or in the control of development 'is whether it serves a planning purpose [that is] one which relates to the character and use of the land'.[17] This principle seems to allow, and require, planning authorities to take into account the widest conceivable range of factors in exercising planning functions.

8. The determination principle

'Where, in making any determination under the planning Acts, regard is to be had to the development plan, the determination shall be made in accordance with the plan unless material considerations indicate otherwise'.[18] The effect of this requirement is to emphasise the importance of the relevant development plan in the determination process by creating a presumption that the plan should be followed where there are no material considerations to the contrary. Nonetheless, the possibility is left open that other material considerations might be of sufficient weight to justify a departure from the development plan in some circumstances. In essence, this 'plan-led' presumption seems to take the development plan as a starting point and to give it a weight above that of other factors relevant to the determination. In practice, however, the difficulty will

[15] S.33 of the 1990 Act and Town and Country Planning (Development Plan) Regulations 1991 (SI 1991, No. 2794).
[16] S.70(2) of the 1990 Act.
[17] *Per* Lord Scarman, in *Great Portland Estates plc* v. *Westminster City Council* [1984] 3 All ER 744 at 750.
[18] S.54A of the 1990 Act.

always be that of deciding whether the strength of other material considerations is sufficient to outweigh the presumption in favour of the development plan, or whether not following the plan would cause demonstrable harm to an interest of acknowledged importance (DOE, 1997c, para.39).

AXIOMS (THE SAME ONES) OF WATER QUALITY PLANNING

Having suggested a set of axioms of town and country planning law, the second part of the exercise is to ascertain to what extent the principles that have been outlined have counterparts within the regulatory system applicable to water quality planning. Accordingly, the same set of headings are used in this section to outline the comparisons and contrasts within water quality planning.

1. The executive responsibility principle

Although the practical responsibility for water quality planning in England and Wales rests with the Environment Agency, through the exercise of its powers and duties under the Water Resources Act 1991(the '1991 Act') and the Environment Act 1995 (the '1995 Act'), this is subject to the extensive powers of the Ministers with responsibility for the environment and agriculture (and now the National Assembly for Wales[19]) to enact secondary legislation, to give guidance and directions to the Agency and to exercise certain judicial functions in relation to appeals. The legislative powers of the Ministers enable the enactment of extensive secondary legislation concerning the determination of applications for discharge consents to controlled waters under the 1991 Act.[20] The general guidance (DOE, 1996a) to the Agency indicates the contribution that the Agency should be making towards the achievement of sustainable development and the general objectives it should be pursuing in discharging its functions.[21] In addition to the general guidance, the appropriate Minister may give the Agency directions of a general or specific character with respect to the carrying out any of its functions, and particularly where such directions are necessary for the implementation of European Community or international obligations.[22] In relation to various judicial matters, rights of appeal, against decisions of the Agency, are given to the Secretary of State, for example, where a discharge consent application has been refused or been allowed subject to conditions.[23]

[19] Government of Wales Act 1998 and National Assembly for Wales (Transfer of Functions) Order 1999 (SI 1999, No. 672).

[20] See Control of Pollution (Applications, Appeals and Registers) Regulations 1996 (SI 1996, No. 2971).

[21] S.4 of the 1995 Act.

[22] S.40 of the 1995 Act.

[23] S.91 of the1991 Act and Control of Pollution (Applications, Appeals and Registers) Regulations 1996 (SI 1996, No.2971), though see below on the role of the Planning Inspectorate in relation to the hearing of appeals.

Hence, as under the town and country planning system, the Ministers are empowered to exercise a wide range of legislative, executive and judicial functions in relation to the supervision of the Agency in discharging its water quality function. However, some contrast may be drawn in the level of detail to be found in some respects. Whilst an extensive list of Planning Policy Guidance Notes is in place to guide local planning authorities across the range of matters over which they exercise powers and duties, the guidance provided to the Agency in relation to water quality planning is neither so extensive nor so detailed. In part, the explanation for this may lie in the perception of water quality function of the Agency being comprehensively provided for in legislation, in part it may also lie in technical aspects of water quality planning being left to the discretion of experts within the Agency.

2. The plan preparation responsibility

In so far as water quality management is a strategic activity, formal requirements for the specification and realisation of water quality objectives are legally provided for through the mechanism for establishing statutory water quality objectives. In essence, the Secretary of State is possessed of enabling powers which allow systems of water quality classification to be formally established and for him to specify that particular waters must meet, and be maintained at, at least the quality required by a specified quality classification. Where this is done, the Agency will be legally bound to exercise its legal powers, so far as practicable, for the purpose of achieving and maintaining water quality at the level required by the classification specified for a particular water.[24]

However, two points should be noted concerning the procedure over statutory water quality objectives. The first is that the water quality 'planning' mechanism is formulated as a power, rather than a duty, upon the Secretary of State, and he has so far chosen to exercise this power only where specification of statutory water quality objectives is necessary to meet requirements arising under European Community water directives. A 'national' classification system has been enacted for the ecological quality of waters[25] but no statutory water quality objectives are thought to have been so far specified in relation to ecological quality for any particular waters. By contrast with other areas of environmental law, such as air quality[26] and waste management,[27] there is no duty upon the Secretary of State to formulate a national water quality strategy or plan. The most pertinent policy statement available is the rather terse observation to be found in the guidance on Sustainable Development to the Agency: 'The Government's policy objective for water protection is where possible to prevent

[24] Ss.82 to 84 of the 1991 Act.

[25] Surface Waters (River Ecosystem) (Classification) Regulations 1994 (SI 1994, No.1057).

[26] S.80 of the 1995 Act and see HMG (2000a).

[27] S.44A of the Environmental Protection Act 1990, as amended, and see HMG (2000b).

deterioration in water quality and to seek to secure improvements in accordance with agreed priorities which reflect the requirements of Community legislation' (DOE,1996a, para.6.23).

Secondly, in so far as duties are statutorily imposed upon the Environment Agency they appear to relate only remotely to any possible water quality planning role. Hence, the general environmental duty upon the Agency to have regard to the desirability of conserving flora and fauna when considering any proposals relating to its pollution control functions[28] might be construed as an obligation to ensure a satisfactory ecological quality of receiving waters when determining an application for a discharge consent. However, it is far from explicit to what extent the general environmental duty upon the Agency implies a strategic water quality planning role.

Perhaps because of the lack of explicit statutory guidance in respect of its role in water quality planning, the Agency has imposed upon itself, with Government endorsement, various non-statutory kinds of environmental planning objectives such as the aim 'to achieve major and continuous improvement in the quality of air, land and water' (Environment Agency, 1998a, para.2.4). This is interpreted as a commitment to delivery of environmental improvement at the local level through Local Environment Agency Plans (LEAPs) which are intended to 'set out and assess local environmental issues, and present an integrated action plan for the Agency and other bodies with responsibilities to protect and improve the environment, taking into account the views of local communities, local authorities, industry and environmental groups' (Environment Agency, 1998a, para.2.7). Further implications of LEAPs are stated as follows:

> River-basin management planning is the foundation for safeguarding the water environment. LEAPs provide an opportunity for the Agency to describe existing and propose future targets for water quality. These include targets to ensure waters are fit for their uses and are in good condition to be passed on to the next generation. We believe that the investment plans of water companies being determined in the Periodic Review for 2000–2005 should meet, or at least be tailored to, the targets determine set out in River Quality Objectives (RQOs), as accepted by the Government in 1989. LEAPS provide a key mechanism for reviewing RQOs and to target investment. We will also use the LEAPs process to prevent deterioration in water quality [Environment Agency, 1998a, para.6.17].

In practical effect, LEAPs, formulated at river catchment levels, serve as a useful consultation mechanism which allows greater transparency in informing the public and regulated bodies about how the Agency intends to use its legal powers to achieve water quality and other environmental improvements. However, the contrast with statutory water quality objectives is that failure to meet a statutory water quality objective, where it is reasonably practicable to do so, would be a breach of a legal duty on the part of the Agency, whereas failure to

[28] S.7(1)(b) of the 1995 Act.

meet a commitment set out in a LEAP would have no direct legal consequences. Similarly, the relative informality of LEAPs, by contrast with town and country planning development plans should be noted, in that there appears to be nothing more formal than a self-imposed obligation to take particular actions, such as the determination of discharge consent applications, in accordance with the relevant LEAP.

Further, self-imposed objectives for water quality planning by the Agency are to be found in *An Action Plan for Water Quality*, which incorporates a commitment to develop an Environment Agency National Plan for Water Quality 'to develop a firm planning base for the maintenance and future improvement of water quality' and a commitment to 'vigorously enforce discharge consent control standards' (Environment Agency, 1998b, 13; on enforcement generally, see Environment Agency, 1998c).

The inference from this must be that, by comparison with town and country planning, water quality planning is regarded as a considerably less strategic activity. It is apparent that there is no direct analogy to the duty upon local planning authorities to establish development plans, and in so far as the Secretary of State has a plan-making role in specifying statutory water quality objectives, it is a power that has been exercised only where necessary to ensure European Community water quality objectives are met in national waters. Whilst the Agency has taken various initiatives to plan for water quality management, all of these lack the firm legal foundation that is provided for in relation to town and country planning development plans.

3. The development (discharge) definition

In water quality planning the functional counterpart of the concept of 'development' of land is that of 'discharge' of effluent which, at least traditionally, has been regarded as the principal activity to be regulated. However, whilst, as has been noted, the definition of 'development' is a matter of some legal intricacy, the question of what is to constitute a 'discharge' into controlled waters is unproblematically assumed to be the passage of a liquid from an effluent conduit into the aquatic environment and, therefore, something which is not the subject of any explicit statutory definition. Whilst it is statutorily provided that it will be a defence to the principal water pollution offences[29] to make a discharge under and in accordance with a discharge consent under Chapter II of Part III of the Water Resources Act 1991,[30] there is no further indication of what kinds of discharge need to be the subject of the consenting procedure.[31]

However, the traditional assumption that water quality management objectives are capable of being achieved by the control of 'discharges' alone is less

[29] S.85 of the 1991 Act.
[30] S.88(1)(a) of the 1991 Act.
[31] Sched. 10 of the 1991 Act, as amended.

credible today than in the past. In particular, it is now appreciated that a range of contaminants which have an adverse effect upon water quality, without necessarily resulting in dramatic pollution incidents, result from gradual emissions from diffuse, rather than point, sources. So, for example, where fertiliser or pesticide is applied to agricultural land, and is gradually washed into an adjoining watercourse resulting in a deterioration of water quality, it would be unrealistic to seek to regulate the problem in the same way as for a piped discharge of industrial effluent.

Increasingly, various types of land use are recognised to be in need of regulation for the purpose of protecting water quality, and water quality planning should be characterised as encompassing these kinds of control, alongside the longstanding mechanisms for control of discharges from point sources. A good example of this approach to water quality management is to be found in the power of the Secretary of State to enact regulations to prevent water pollution[32] and those[33] which impose construction standards upon containment facilities for silage, slurry and fuel oil on farms. Similarly, the power to designate water protection zones and to prohibit or restrict activities within such areas[34] allows a range of controls to be imposed upon the storage of substances that are hazardous to the aquatic environment and these powers have recently been exercised in the establishment of the River Dee Water Protection Zone.[35] In addition, the need to control the application of nitrate, as fertiliser applied to agricultural land, has resulted in national provisions allowing for the designation of nitrate sensitive areas[36] and further regulations to implement the Nitrates Directive[37] and to regulate activities in nitrate vulnerable zones identified for the purpose of the Directive.[38]

Two points are usefully made about this range of controls upon land use for the purpose of protecting water quality. The first is that the various regulations that have been enacted involve a clear shift of emphasis from water pollution control to land use control. Hence, in most respects, criminal offences are provided for in relation to infringement of the regulations regardless of whether any actual pollution of water occurs. The more recent wave of regulation seeks to anticipate water quality problems by recognising that particular kinds of land use represent a threat to water quality and, accordingly, the appropriate

[32] S.92 of the 1991 Act.

[33] Control of Pollution (Silage, Slurry and Agricultural Fuel Oil) Regulations 1991 (SI 1991, No. 324) as amended by SI 1996, No. 2044.

[34] S.93 of the 1991 Act.

[35] See Water Protection Zone (River Dee Catchment) Designation Order 1999 (SI 1999, No 915) and Water Protection Zone (River Dee Catchment) (Procedural and Other Provisions) Regulations 1999 (SI 1999 No.916).

[36] Ss.94 and 95 of the 1991 Act and Nitrate Sensitive Areas (Designation) Order 1990 (SI 1990, No.1013) as amended.

[37] Directive 91/676/EEC [1991] OJ L375/1.

[38] Protection of Water Against Agricultural Nitrate Pollution (England and Wales) Regulations 1996 (SI 1996, No.888).

application of regulation is to various kinds of *failure to prevent* water pollution and contamination.

Secondly, the new emphasis upon control of land use, rather than direct discharges into the aquatic environment, takes water quality planning a step closer to development control in town and country planning law. For example, restricting the right of a farmer to construct a slurry tank, other than in accordance with fairly specific conditions, might naturally be thought of as a matter falling under town and country planning law. The fact remains, however, that the restrictions which are imposed arise under water resources legislation rather than town and country planning law. It might be an exaggeration to suggest that the Environment Agency has been given a range of powers to control 'development' of land, but the similarity between some of its preventive powers and those of local authorities in planning matters deserves to be noted.

4. The *de minimis* exception

In so far as water quality planning objectives are sought to be realised through the control of discharges of effluent to controlled waters, there is no formal exception allowed for in relation to the authorisation of minor discharges, since the relevant offence is formulated in terms of 'any' discharge of effluent, with no explicit exception for minor discharges.[39]

By contrast with the definition of 'development' under town and country planning law, the theory of discharge control envisages that every discharge to controlled waters will be the subject of regulation. However, the actual practice is that there are innumerable minor discharges, which are unlikely to be environmentally problematic, and to regulate all of these would impose a considerable burden upon the resources of the Agency and would bring little environmental benefit. For example, it has been estimated that four per cent of properties in England and Wales are not connected to public sewers (DOE, 1994a,16) and many of these properties will be making minor discharges to watercourses. Because of the environmental insignificance of these, the practice of the Agency is not to require such discharges to be subject to discharge consent requirements. Even where a discharge consent is required, the impracticability of subjecting every application to the full system of controls is recognised in that exemption from publicity requirements is provided for in relation to minor discharges. Thus, exemption from advertising requirements is provided for where the Agency considers that the activities which are the subject matter of the application are 'unlikely to have an appreciable effect' on the water in the locality.[40] It is understood that, in practice, the majority of discharges which are the subject of discharge consents fall into this category.

39 S.85(3) of the 1991 Act.
40 Above n.20, reg.4 and see DOE (1984).

More broadly, the contrasting treatment of the concept of 'development' under town and country planning law and 'discharge' under water quality law should be noted. Whilst the range of *de minimis* exceptions to the concept of 'development' are formally, and fairly comprehensively, provided for in the legislation, the treatment of minor discharges in water quality is a matter of relative informality and left largely to the discretion of the Agency.

5. The authorisation principle

The key prohibition that underlies water quality planning it that it is an offence to cause or knowingly permit the discharge effluent into a controlled water[41] but it is a defence to this to show that the discharge was made under and in accordance with a discharge consent.[42] There may be circumstances where the interpretation of 'under and in accordance with' is open to dispute, such as where a consent exists but does not specifically indicate whether a particular substance is authorised to be discharged. However, it has become the practice of the Environment Agency to formulate consents exhaustively so that a consent to discharge substances A, B and C will explicitly indicate that it does not authorise the discharge of further substances that have not been expressly indicated.

The contrast with town and country planning law is that, whilst undertaking an unauthorised development of land is not, by itself, a criminal offence, the making of an unauthorised discharge is, without more, an offence. Powers were provided to the Agency under the Environment Act 1995 to issue enforcement notices where the holder of a consent is contravening, or likely to contravene, the conditions of a consent, and to specify the steps that must be taken to remedy the contravention.[43] However, the power to issue enforcement notices, and to prosecute where they are not complied with, does not detract from the fact that an unauthorised discharge, or a discharge which contravenes the conditions of a discharge consent, will constitute a criminal offence. Similarly, the Agency has powers to impose prohibitions on discharges which are not the subject of a consent[44] and to impose consents upon unconsented discharges,[45] but these powers are, again, in addition to, and do not detract from, the power of the Agency to bring a prosecution for a water pollution offence.

There is a marked contrast between the extreme breadth of the principal water pollution offences, and the strict liability associated with causing water pollution[46] and the relatively infrequent actual use of these powers by comparison with the situations in which, theoretically, prosecution proceedings could

41 S.85(3) of the 1991 Act.
42 S.88(1)(a) of the 1991 Act.
43 S.90B of the 1991 Act, as amended.
44 S.86 of the 1991 Act.
45 Para.6 of Sched. 10 to the 1991 Act.
46 See *Empress Car Co. (Abertillery) Ltd.* v. *National Rivers Authority* [1998] 1 All ER 481.

be brought. To a degree, this disparity between the scope of the law and the extent of its actual use is provided for under the Environment Agency's (1998c) *Enforcement and Prosecution Policy*. The Policy emphasises the belief of the Agency in firm but fair regulation, and interprets this in terms of four principles: proportionality, consistency, transparency and targeting. In accordance with these principles, a range of considerations are outlined as to when the prosecution powers of the Agency are likely to be exercised. Clearly, as with any law enforcement authority, a wide range of factors must influence the decision whether a prosecution should be brought and, in this respect, comparisons may be drawn with the predicament of a local planning authority deliberating on whether to pursue enforcement proceedings for a breach of planning control.

6. The consultation obligation

Consultation is provided for in relation to applications for discharge consents by way of a requirement that the Agency must give notice of a discharge consent to prescribed persons and advertised generally in a prescribed manner and representations made within the period allowed must be considered in determining the application.[47] The detailed requirements relating to these matters are set out in Regulations.[48] Hence, by way of reciprocation to the consultation requirement for town and country planning applications (described above), the Agency is bound to consult every local authority within whose area a discharge is to be made.[49] Generally, the fairly close parallel with planning requirements should be noted, in ensuring that every reasonable opportunity is given for interested bodies and members of the public to comment on a discharge consent application.

7. The materiality principle

Whilst the concept of 'material considerations' has been extensively considered, and broadly construed, in town and country planning law, the matters that are properly regarded as material considerations in relation to a discharge consent application are relatively less well defined. A starting point is the requirement that an applicant for discharge consent must provide 'such information as the Agency may reasonably require'.[50] It is reasonable to suppose that the information which may reasonably be required is that which may be used to identify and formulate any conditions that may be required in an eventual consent. Hence, it is relevant to note that although the Agency may make a consent subject to such

[47] Paras. 1 and 2 of Sched. 10 to the 1991 Act.
[48] Above n.20.
[49] *Ibid*, para. 5(1)(a).
[50] Sched. 10 para.1 to the 1991 Act.

conditions as it 'may think fit', explicit reference is made to a range of particular conditions that may be included. These encompass conditions as to the place at which the discharge may be made and the design and construction of the outlet; the nature, origin, composition, temperature, volume and rate of discharge and the periods in which the discharge may be made; steps to be taken to subject the substances discharged to treatment or any other process for minimising the polluting effects of the discharge; also, various sampling, measuring and recording requirements may be imposed and the making of returns on these matters to the Agency.[51] Since it is explicitly provided that these matters may be the subject of conditions in a consent, the implication is that they must, where relevant, be material considerations in the determination of the consent.

Beyond the particular matters which are identified as the potential subject matter of discharge consent conditions, the identification of which further matters are 'material' is somewhat uncertain (see Box 2.2). The Agency will be bound to exercise its discharge consenting function in accordance with its general powers and duties, and from this it follows that it must have regard to its principal aim of contributing towards the achievement of sustainable development.[52] Also relevant will be its general environmental duty to have regard to the desirability of conserving flora and fauna in exercising its pollution control functions.[53] Along with this, the Agency is under a general duty to have regard to likely costs and benefits when exercising its powers, including costs to persons and costs the environment.[54] Although only remotely related to the practicalities of determining a consent application, conceivably relationships might be drawn, as where, for example, it is claimed that a condition in a consent would be unduly costly for the discharger to meet in comparison to any environmental improvement which would be secured. Also of relevance is the status of the Agency as the competent authority with regard to the implementation of European Community water directives, and the duty upon the Agency to use its powers to ensure statutory water quality objectives are met and maintained where these have been imposed for the purpose of securing conformity with Community directives.

BOX 2.2: Material Considerations in Case Law

A couple of cases have a useful bearing on the issue of materiality in relation to discharge consent. An interesting factual situation arose in R. v. *Ettrick Trout Co. Ltd. and Baxter*[1] where a fish farm director had a discharge consent which limited the volume of the discharge to a specified amount in any 24-hour period. In a prosecution brought against him for having exceeded

[51] Para.4(4) of Sched. 10 to the 1991 Act.
[52] S.4 of the 1995 Act.
[53] S.7(1)(b) of the 1995 Act.
[54] Ss.39 and 56(1) of the 1995 Act.

the volume condition in the consent, he mounted a collateral challenge to the prosecution on the basis that the condition was invalid. He maintained that the condition had not been imposed for the permitted purpose of pollution control but rather for the allegedly illegitimate purpose of limiting the volume of water that he was allowed to abstract from a watercourse to pass through the fish farm. Because the abstracted water flowed through the fish farm and was returned to the watercourse without diminution of quantity, the discharge consent effectively limited the amount of water that could be abstracted. The outcome, however, was that the validity of the discharge consent could not be contested in criminal proceedings since this was an attempt to by-pass both judicial review procedures and the statutory appeal procedure, and to allow the challenge would be an abuse of process. In effect, the possibility that the discharge consent was being used for the ulterior purpose of controlling water abstraction was not resolved. It remains an open question, therefore, whether such water quantity issues should feature as a material consideration in the determination of a discharge consent.

Further challenges to the materiality of considerations applied in the determination of a discharge consent arose in *R.* v. *National Rivers Authority ex parte Moreton*,[2] where judicial review proceedings were brought to contest the granting of a discharge consent by the National Rivers Authority to allow a sewerage undertaker, Welsh Water, to discharge sewage effluent into the sea. The applicant, who was a regular swimmer in the sea in the vicinity of the discharge, sought to challenge the granting of the consent on three grounds. The first was that the Authority wrongly took into account the investment budget of Welsh Water. The second was that the Authority had unlawfully failed to have regard to the requirements of the European Community Bathing Water Directive.[3] The third was that the Authority had misunderstood the requirements of the European Community Urban Waste Water Treatment Directive.[4]

In respect of the first challenge, relating to the investment budget of the sewerage undertaker, it was noted that investment budgets had been published indicating the funds available to the undertaker in relation to environmental improvements. In relation to the initial budget, it was noted that amounts allocated for basic investments would not have been sufficient to deal with existing problems by 2000, the date for compliance with the Bathing Water Directive. A further budget for discretionary schemes had allocated funds to projects which were regarded by the undertaker as more pressing than the particular outfall which was the subject of the complaint. The applicant's contention was that the Authority had wrongly taken these budgets into account and thereby fettered its discretion in determining the application and had failed to consider the application on its merits.

On the second challenge, concerning the implementation of the Bathing Water Directive, it was alleged that the Authority had failed to have regard to the imperative standard under the Directive. Specifically, it had failed to adhere to a duty under national legislation[5] and the National Rivers Authority (Bathing Waters) Directions 1995 to ensure that standards for bathing water were achieved so far as it was practicable to do so.

With regard to the third challenge, it was alleged that the Authority had misunderstood the requirements of the Urban Waste Water Treatment Directive. Although the Directive allowed less stringent treatment for waters identified as 'less sensitive',[6] this was with the proviso that discharges received primary treatment and that such discharges did not adversely affect the receiving environment. It was alleged that the Authority had neglected to mention the proviso and had thereby misdirected itself.

In dismissing the application, it was held that the Authority had not improperly fettered its discretion in considering what conditions to impose upon the discharge consent since its decision had not been predetermined by the statements regarding the undertaker's investment budgets. The Authority had no interest in the resource implications of the engineering solutions needed to meet the mandatory environmental standards and had concerned itself merely with the question whether the standards would be met. In relation to the compliance with the Bathing Water Directive, it was found that there was no evidence that the Authority had failed to implement the imperative standard required by the Directive. In respect of the failure of the Authority to mention the proviso in relation to the Urban Waste Water Treatment Directive, this failure did not mean that it had misunderstood the Directive. By the time the Directive came into force, 2000, the sewage treatment scheme for the discharge would include both primary and secondary treatment as required by the Directive.

The decision is an important one in considering the criteria and procedures that must be applied in the determination of discharge consents by the Environment Agency. Essentially, the applicant failed to establish the key points of fact which would have substantiated the allegations. Nevertheless, implicitly, it affirms that having improper regard to financial considerations or failing to adhere to requirements under Community water quality directives by the Agency may constitute a valid ground for judicial review of a discharge consent determination. Similarly, it may be observed that, in the circumstances at issue, financial considerations were not be regarded as a material consideration and the need to adhere to the requirements of Community water directives was a material consideration.

1 [1994] Env. LR 165.

2 [1996] Env. LR 234.

3 Directive 76/160/EEC [1976] OJ L194/26.

4 Directive 91/271/EEC [1991] OJ L135/40.

5 The Bathing Water (Classification) Regulations 1991(SI 1991 No.1597).

6 Under Article 6 and see R. v. *Secretary of State for the Environment ex p Kingston upon Hull* [1996] Env. LR 248.

On the other hand, it is specifically stated that the Agency's pollution control powers are to be exercisable for the purpose of preventing or minimising, or remedying or mitigating the effects of, pollution of the environment.[55] The implication of this is that determination of a discharge consent application on a ground which fell outside this remit might be unlawful, or that matters not related to the effects of pollution are not be regarded as material considerations. However, it is to be noted that the concern of the Agency is with the 'effects' of pollution, rather than pollution itself. An interpretation of this is that matters such as public health impacts and ecological impacts are material considerations in determining a discharge consent.

8. The determination principle

It is nowhere stated on what basis the determination of an application for a discharge consent is to be made. This is in stark contrast to the obligation under town and country planning law that determinations of planning applications should be in accordance with the relevant development plan, in the absence of material considerations indicating otherwise (see above). The explanation for this disparity is, of course, that water quality plans do not exist in anything like the same form as development plans. Nonetheless, many of the things that have been identified as material considerations in the determination of discharge consent applications might equally be regarded as a basis for determination of applications. Accordingly, an 'upper limit' is set upon determinations by the need to secure conformity with Community water directives and statutory water quality objectives established for the purpose of implementing directives. However, the absence of a more comprehensive mechanism for expressing the range of objectives to be sought in water quality planning and the lack of explicit basis for making consent determinations in relation to local circumstances do demonstrate a lacuna in water quality planning in comparison to the approach adopted in town and country planning law.

Although the 'axiom by axiom' comparative study of town and country planning and water quality planning that has been undertaken has served to draw attention to the similarities between and differences in the two regimes, the question remains whether the relative insulation between the two systems of environmental regulation is justified or beneficial. This issue is usefully approached through case studies of particular areas which involve both systems and draws attention to the difficulties arising because of the separation between them.

[55] S.5(1) of the 1995 Act.

THE ENVIRONMENT AGENCY AND THE TOWN AND COUNTRY PLANNING SYSTEM

The water-related functions of the Environment Agency have been defined as:

(a) the former functions of the National Rivers Authority, that is,
- (i) its functions concerning water resources management;
- (ii) its functions concerning control of pollution of water resources;
- (iii) its functions concerning flood defence and land drainage;
- (iv) its functions concerning land and works powers;
- (v) its functions relating to fisheries;
- (vi) its functions as a navigation authority, harbour authority or conservancy authority;
- (vii) its functions under Schedule 2 to the Water Resources Act 1991;
- (viii) functions assigned to the National Rivers Authority by or under any other enactment, apart from the Environment Act 1995.[56]

The notable omission from this list is any explicit reference to a land use planning function of the Agency in relation to water or other matters. Conceivably, this might come under (viii), but this depends upon how the term 'function' is to be understood. Normally, a function would imply the possession of both powers and duties by the Agency, but in relation to planning its role consists of various powers without any specific duties, so that it is arguable whether it is genuinely a 'function' of the Agency or whether it should be separately categorised.

However classified, the role of the Environment Agency in the town and country planning system is of considerable significance. In relation to the formulation of development plans under the Town and Country Planning Act 1990, local planning authorities are under a duty to consult various bodies.[57] This allows the Agency to comment upon the implications of a draft development plan in respect of any function exercised by it including pollution control. In relation to particular applications for development consent, local planning authorities are under a duty to make planning information available to statutory consultees. Accordingly, a planning authority will be bound to consult the Agency in relation to a proposed development which involves the carrying out of works or operations in the bed or on the banks of a river or stream, and other kinds of development which may have an impact upon the aquatic environment, and the planning authority will be bound to take recommendations into account in making the planning determination.[58] Beyond this role as a statutory consultee, the Agency is entitled to make representations in relation to any planning

[56] S.2(1)(a) of the the Environment Act 1995

[57] Art. 10 of the Town and Country Planning (Development Plan) Regulations 1991 (SI 1991, No.2794).

[58] Art. 10 of the Town and Country Planning (General Development Procedure) Order 1995 (SI 1995, No.419).

application which it considers may have a damaging effect upon the aquatic environment.[59] For the Agency, the critical difficulty is, of course, that its view of the undesirability of a particular development proposal is only one amongst many material considerations that the local planning authority will have to take into account in determining whether to grant the planning permission which is sought (see Box 2.1).

The guidance on what use the Agency should make of its powers in relation to the town and country planning system is to be found in *The Environment Agency and Sustainable Development* (DOE, 1996a, 26). This indicates that the Agency will become involved in land use planning by responding to consultations by local planning authorities in relation to environmental assessment; responding to requests from developers for information; responding to consultations on planning applications; responding and providing input to the preparation of development plans; responding to general enquiries about proposed developments; and providing technical advice to the Government at regional or national level in response to requests for information about the significance of any likely pollution from a proposed development. The advice to local planning authorities should be provided in a manner that is consistent, reasonably and in the public interest, and consistent with Planning Policy Guidance Note 23: *Planning and Pollution Control* (DOE, 1994b). Understandably, however, this guidance is presented at a high level of generality and gives little insight into the way in which the Agency should deploy its limited resources so as to give priority to those matters where it may be most influential and beneficial in relation to development planning and development control.

In practice, the Agency comments upon approximately 100,000 planning applications annually. The concerns of the Agency are that a new development should proceed only where it does not adversely affect river corridors and the natural water environment; pose an unacceptable risk of flooding; create an unacceptable risk of contamination to air, land and ground and surface waters; or require additional water resources beyond that available for industrial and public supply (Environment Agency, 1997).

TOWN AND COUNTRY PLANNING AND SEWAGE TREATMENT WORKS

The most common single cause of pollution incidents in England and Wales is the inadequate treatment of sewage effluent (Environment Agency, 1999) with twenty-four per cent of incidents, identified by source, arising from sewage treatment. The Agency has as its principal aim and objective the discharging of its functions to protect or enhance the environment, taken as a whole, so as to make the contribution towards attaining the objective of sustainable development that is indicated by ministerial guidance.[60] One interpretation of this, in

[59] SI 1995, No.419, Art. 19.

[60] S.4 of the 1995 Act.

the town and country planning context, is that the Agency should be using its powers as a consultee to oppose those development projects which are likely to have adverse environmental impacts. In relation to sewage treatment works, for example, this might involve opposing such developments unless a satisfactory level of protection or enhancement of the aquatic environment is shown.

However, under section 15 of the Water Resources Act 1991 the Agency is subject to a further duty, in exercising any of its powers, under any enactment, to have particular regard to the duties imposed (under Parts II to IV of the Water Industry Act 1991) on any water or sewerage undertaker which appears likely to be affected by the exercise of the power in question. Amongst other things, this will mean that the Agency must have regard to the duty upon sewerage undertakers to 'provide, improve and extend a system of public sewers and so to cleanse and maintain those sewers as to ensure that the [undertaker's] area is effectually drained', and to 'make provision for the emptying of those sewers and such further provision as is necessary from time to time for effectually dealing, by means of sewage disposal works or otherwise, with the contents of those sewers'.[61] The implication of the duty upon the Agency to have regard to the responsibilities of sewerage undertakers is that, when exercising its role as a consultee in the town and country planning process, it must recognise the legal duties upon sewerage undertakers. Hence, the Agency should not raise objections to activities which are necessary to allow undertakers to fulfil their statutory functions.

The critical issue is, in cases of conflict, how the Agency's duty to protect and enhance the aquatic environment so as to contribute towards sustainable development is to be reconciled with the duty to take account of the responsibilities of sewerage undertakes for sewerage provision.

The issue of determining planning applications concerning sewage treatment infrastructure is further complicated by the advice that is given to local planning authorities in this context. The DOE Circular, *Water Industry Investment: Planning Considerations* (DOE, 1991a) was issued because of the need to comply with various European Community water directives (including the Bathing Water Directive[62]) and the ban upon sludge disposal at sea (confirmed in the Urban Waste Water Treatment Directive[63]). The Circular was prompted by the need to comply with a series of schedules for water quality measures prompted by the directives, and refers to the need to implement land-based sewage sludge disposal by the end of 1998 and to achieve compliance with the Bathing Water Directive by 1995 'in all but a few exceptional cases'. Nonetheless, the guidance that it offers to local planning authorities remains instructive. In particular, local planning authorities are requested to work expeditiously with the water industry to find suitable sites for sewage treatment works and give sympathetic consideration to proposals for enhancing sewage treatment; and local plans and

[61] S.94(1) of the Water Industry Act 1991.
[62] Directive 76/160/EEC [1976] OJ L194/26.
[63] Directive 91/271/EEC [1991] OJ L135/40.

unitary development plans should identify suitable locations for sewage treatment works. Notwithstanding this, if the relevant development plan contains no site-specific proposal which relates to the particular development proposed, nor more general policies that are material, the planning application should be determined on its merits in the light of the other material considerations.

The Circular tends to put pressure upon local planning authorities to be sympathetic towards proposals for new sewage treatment facilities and to process them swiftly, whilst the general remit of the Agency in protecting the aquatic environment is diminished by the effect of the Circular and moderated by its duty to have regard to the sewage treatment obligations upon undertakers. Hopefully, any 'improvement' of sewerage treatment infrastructure should be conducive to a reduction in the alarming numbers of incidents attributable to inadequate functioning of treatment works, and should be supported by the Agency, but the constraints which are placed upon it in raising planning concerns relating to such works are remarkable when compared with its role in making representations about other kinds of project that may represent a water pollution hazard.

OVERLAP AND SEPARATION

Whilst recognising the disparities that have been outlined between the town and country planning system and the water quality planning system, these must be balanced against the considerable overlaps which have been identified. Most significant, perhaps, are the reciprocal arrangements which exist for consultation. As has been noted, the Environment Agency is a statutory consultee in relation to certain kinds of town and country planning applications and, reciprocally, local authorities must be consulted in relation to discharge consent applications in their areas.

Beyond the reciprocal consultation obligations, a further mechanism for the linking of town and country planning and water quality planning has been provided by the Environment Agency encouraging planning authorities to incorporate water planning principles in development plans. Most recently this has been advocated in the Agency's manual *Liaison with Local Planning Authorities* (Environment Agency, 1997). A memorandum of understanding entered into by the Agency and the local authority associations outlines the general intention to build a co-operative relationship based upon openness and the exchange of information. The stated aim is to further a shared commitment to the protection and enhancement of the environment and envisages a further protocol on land use planning.

Another key link of a procedural kind has been forged by the decision of the Secretary of State to arrange, as from 1 January 1997, for his power to determine discharge consent and associated appeals to be exercised by the Planning Inspectorate. Consequently, all determinations of this kind will be taken by the

Inspectors on behalf of the Secretary of State, in accordance with procedures which are similar to those governing planning appeals, except in rare cases of major importance or difficulty, where the Secretary of State may exercise this power himself (DOE, 1996b). At a practical level, having the same people determining town and country planning and discharge consent appeals must be likely to encourage a similarity of approach.

Nevertheless, despite the overlaps that have been indicated, the dominant theme is that town and country planning possesses a high degree of separation from water quality planning notwithstanding the many parallels between the two systems that have been referred to. A key policy statement emphasising this separation is PPG 23 (DOE, 1994b), which gives guidance on the relevance of pollution control to the exercise of planning functions and advises on the relationship between local authority's planning responsibilities and the *separate* statutory responsibilities exercised by pollution control authorities under environmental legislation. Key passages from this document read as follows:

> The planning system should not be operated so as to duplicate controls which are the statutory responsibility of other bodies (including local authorities in their non-planning functions). Planning controls, except where they are applied in the context of hazardous substances consents, are not an appropriate means of regulating the detailed characteristics of potentially polluting activities [paragraph 1.3].

> The role of the planning system focuses on whether the development itself is an acceptable use of the land rather than the control of the processes or substances themselves. It also assumes that the pollution control regime will operate effectively. . . . Planning controls can therefore complement the pollution control regime, and thus help to secure the proper operation and rehabilitation of potentially polluting developments [paragraph 1.33].

> In deciding whether to grant planning permission, planning authorities must be satisfied that planning permission can be granted on land-use grounds, and that concerns about potential releases can be left for the pollution control authority to take into account in considering the application for the authorisation or licence. Alternatively, they may conclude that the wider impact of potential releases on the environment and use of land is unacceptable in all the circumstances on planning grounds, despite the grant, or potential grant, of a pollution control authorisation or licence [paragraph 1.36].

Despite these injunctions, there are indications that the practical trend is in the opposite direction, with planning authorities becoming ever more closely involved in consideration of the environmental consequences of granting planning applications. A good example of this is to be found in *R.* v. *Bolton MBC ex parte Kirkman*[64] where the best practicable environmental option for a waste incineration facility was recognised to be a material consideration for a planning authority to consider. Another example is the case of environmental assessment of projects with a water quality dimension (referred to above) where

[64] [1998] Env. LR 719, see also ch. 3 below.

planning authorities are obliged to become intimately engaged in assessing the aquatic impact aspects of development projects and to evaluate the environmental effects of effluent discharges.

Arguably, this assimilative trend is to be welcomed, first, because the determination of planning applications has, otherwise, to be made on the basis of incomplete information, with the planning authority being obliged to assume that the environmental regulator will be able to license a discharge satisfactorily, and enforce licensing controls with sufficient stringency to safeguard against environmental harm. Secondly, there is a fear that granting planning permission for a development will force the hand of the Agency to grant a discharge consent when the development is operational. Thirdly, the separation of controls means that objectors to a development proposal are placed at a considerable procedural disadvantage because they may have insufficient information about the discharge consent conditions that are to be applied to a discharge from a development at the time the planning application is being considered. This is because this information is likely to become available only subsequently, at the time when the environmental licence is determined. Whilst the facility exists for a public hearing to be held in relation to an appeal against the adverse determination of a discharge consent, this is available only where this is requested by the Agency or the intending discharger.[65] Even where a hearing is requested by either of the parties, members of the public will be allowed to participate in the hearing only if they have previously made representations with respect to the grant of the discharge consent.[66]

The case for greater integration has also be firmly expressed by those professionally involved in the town and country planning system:

> The Town and Country Planning Association proposes that integration should go further still by integrating pollution control, waste management and land-use planning, thus recognising that these are interdependent processes. Land-use policies affect the location of pollution activities. Plans for recycling, waste minimisation and pollution control all have a land-use component. This interaction between land use and environmental policies is already recognised in the environmental programmes of many local authorities and it is now time to bring the separate traditions together to create a proper environmental planning process [Blowers, 1993, 15 and see also Purdue, 1999].

However, a potentially problematic aspect of the assimilative trend is whether local planning authorities are genuinely equipped with the expertise that is required to assess the impacts of a development project upon a distinctive sector of the environment such as the aquatic environment. For so long as the Agency is the principal repository of technical expertise for sectors such as the aquatic environment, over which local authorities have relatively limited jurisdiction, the capacity of local authorities alone to make this kind of determination will be open to question.

[65] S.91(2C) of the 1991 Act.
[66] Above n.20, para.12(6)(c).

The crucial question is whether the perceived tension between the democratic mandate of local authorities and the technical mandate of the Agency is genuine or not. Whilst it might seem undemocratic to give the, non-elected, Agency power to overturn decisions reached by the, elected, local authority, the reality may be that decisions of local planning authorities are so confined by law and policy guidance that the scope for political considerations to enter into planning determinations is relatively limited. Given also the common ultimate allocation of executive responsibility to the Secretary of State, under both systems of controls, it might be argued that the real tension is between national and local, democratically determined, environmental imperatives. If this is so, the perceived lack of political and policy accountability of the Agency should not be a serious concern. The central objective is that the national and international imperative of achieving sustainable development should not be undermined by decision-making procedures which fail to give sufficient weight to the opinions of those having the greatest amount of relevant expertise. In addressing this, it is a matter of finding the right balance between technical environmental expertise, appreciation of local concerns and accountability.

CONCLUSION

Whilst differences have been shown to exist between town and country planning and water quality planning, these are not so great as to preclude a more unified approach within the two systems of control which are, ultimately, for the common purpose of securing sustainable development. Moreover, where disparities of approach exist, it is thought that evolution of the water quality planning system towards greater assimilation to the town and country planning approach would be no bad thing. In particular, if the Agency were legally required to formulate explicit water quality plans, at national, regional and local levels, would it then be unreasonable to expect it to make discharge consent determinations in accordance with such plans 'unless material considerations indicate otherwise'? Similarly, with the other axioms considered above, to the extent that approaches differ, water quality planning might be greatly improved by a shift towards the approach more explicitly adopted in town and country planning.

The overall conclusion is that a greater degree of co-determination should be sought in relation to the control of developments which impact upon the aquatic environment. The procedures for granting planning permission for new developments could, in many respects, be consolidated with the environmental licensing procedures so that an application for planning consent would be considered alongside any applications for environmental licences, and particularly discharge consents, which are needed to undertake the activities that are envisaged by the development. Water quality planning should cease to be the 'poor relation' of its more precocious and effective sibling, and family ties should be emphatically reaffirmed.

3

Planning and Air Pollution

CHRIS MILLER

INTRODUCTION

WITH THE NEAR completion of the domestic smoke control programme, very few areas of the United Kingdom can ever again experience conditions remotely comparable with the last great London smog of December 1952. There are also far fewer factory chimneys and the smoke issuing from those that remain is no longer welcomed as a sign of a strong local economy. But even with a declining manufacturing sector, the UK economy still needs incinerators, refineries, cement kilns and power stations. Regulation of emissions from major sources using 'integrated pollution control' (IPC) remains the responsibility of a specialist agency of central government, *viz.* the Environment Agency. Planning consent is still required for new sources and for significant modifications of existing plant, and an environmental impact assessment (including atmospheric effects) will accompany the planning application for the more important proposals. When determining such applications, as well as those for housing or any other development in the vicinity of large industrial installations, the local planning authority is expected to consult the pollution control agency (DOE, 1994b, para. 1.34).

The 'enterprise culture' and the deregulatory phase of Thatcherism left few parts of the UK state untouched. Among the obligations imposed on planning authorities was a presumption 'in favour of development' (DOE, 1985, para. 3), relegating any relevant development plan policy to being but one among other material considerations. In 1991, development plans recovered[1] something of their original status; and although the great majority do make reference to air pollution, these have tended to consist of little more than bland statements of good intent which, by themselves, have insufficient weight to counter the regional (and often national) need which developments like incinerators, for all the public hostility they generate, are designed to meet. These statements—by way of a typical example, Box 3.1 reproduces the pollution control policy contained in the unitary development plan of the City of Salford—tend to reflect an orthodoxy which has developed in a long succession of white papers, circulars and policy guidelines issued by central government. This orthodoxy—on the

[1] S.54A of the 1990 Act, as inserted by the Planning and Compensation Act 1991.

BOX 3.1: Unitary development plan, City of Salford

Pollution Control

Policy (Part I)

EN20—The City Council will encourage and support measures to reduce air and water pollution, land contamination and the problems of noise dust and vibration. Development will not normally be allowed if it is considered likely to:

i) have an unacceptable effect on the quality of the City's rivers, water course, water bodies and ground waters, or
i) cause unacceptable ground contamination, or
ii) cause an unacceptable increase in existing air pollution, noise or vibration levels, particularly around sensitive uses such as housing, schools or hospitals.

Unacceptable air, water, noise, odour or other sorts of pollution will be judged by reference to standards set by relevant regulatory bodies such as Her Majesty's Inspectorate of Pollution and the National Rivers Authority [to become the Environment Agency in 1996], the Health and Safety Executive as well as the Local Authority itself.

Environmentally sensitive development, such as housing, schools or hospitals, will not normally be permitted where existing pollution (air, water, noise, land contamination, dust, vibration and odour) is unacceptable unless it can be demonstrated to the satisfaction of the City Council that the development includes sufficient improvement measures to reduce the nuisance to an acceptable level.

Source: *Unitary Development Plan* (adopted November 1995), City of Salford, p.57

relationship between planning and other statutory controls over pollution—was to receive judicial endorsement in a statutory review of a ministerial approval for a clinical waste incinerator in Gateshead.

This chapter must therefore begin with a consideration of the *Gateshead*[2] and *Bolton*[3] cases and their implications for planning's role over sources of air pollution. This is followed by an examination of what some might term 'quasi incinerators' *viz.* cement and lime kilns partially fuelled by solvent residues and other 'waste' products. This controversial practice has tended to be seen as a technical issue and one which, with its reduced reliance on fossil fuels, has clear sustainability credentials. But it also has land use implications even if they are

[2] *Gateshead MBC* v. *Secretary of State for the Environment* [1995] JPL 432.
[3] *R.* v. *Bolton MBC ex parte Kirkman* [1998] JPL 787.

not 'material' in the legal sense. Odour from industrial processes has always been accepted as a material consideration. When the technology of odour abatement was rudimentary, remote siting was the only way of ensuring that the amenity of an area was not threatened by this more common category of LULU (locally unwanted land use). It is necessary therefore to pay some attention to a number of cases in which, despite the extension of the regime of 'best available techniques not entailing excessive costs' (BATNEEC) to industrial sources of odour, the most effective and enforceable deterrents have consisted of conditions (of the process authorisation) which could equally well have formed conditions of the respective planning consent.

Despite a remarkable decline in total emissions of the classic pollutants (*viz.* smoke and sulphur dioxide), public concern over air quality has not disappeared; but it has become focused upon pollutants (such as nitrogen dioxide) less tangible than smoke. Since 1997, the National Air Quality Strategy has sought to bring 'a comprehensive approach to maintaining and improving the quality of ambient air in the United Kingdom' (DETR, 1997a). Whilst the success of this strategy depends primarily upon the effective enforcement of European Community standards of air quality,[4] the continued need for intervention at the local level is recognised in the major role given to district and unitary councils in England and Wales. These bodies are now required to carry out periodic reviews of air quality in their areas and to compare the data thus collected against objectives set out in regulations[5] which form part of UK implementation of the European Directive. The seven pollutants specified (see Box 3.2) in these regulations are largely associated with exhaust emissions from vehicles. Whilst fixed points of emission cannot be neglected, transport sources must be seen as the principal threat to overall air quality in the UK. (In Box 3.3 below, the decline in total annual emissions of sulphur dioxide can be compared with a more static trend in nitrogen dioxide.)

Land use planning is repeatedly cited in official documents as an important factor in the development of sustainable transport policies. The spatial form of urban areas is seen as the key to reducing trips by private cars and then, according to the conventional wisdom, reduced exhaust emissions and lower consumption of fossil fuel will be but two of a number of 'environmental' benefits. However, evidence of a specific concern with poor air quality—as distinct from a more general apprehension of traffic congestion—being the primary motivation of remedial action by planners is hard to find. The author is unaware of any instance in which air pollution considerations, whether actual or potential, have resulted in the cancellation, or even the re-routing, of any proposed road scheme. But there have been attempts by planners to limit development in the vicinity of major roads and also development which attracts traffic to areas already polluted. This chapter must therefore include among its case studies the

[4] Directive 96/62/EEC [1996] OJ L296/55.

[5] Air Quality (England) Regulations 2000 (SI 2000, No. 928).

BOX 3.2: Air Quality Objectives

Pollutant	Concentration	Measured as	To be met by
Benzene	5 ppb	running annual mean	31.12.2003
1,3–Butadiene	1 ppb	running annual mean	31.12.2003
Carbon Monoxide	10 ppm	running 8 hour mean	31.12.2003
Lead	0.5 µg/m³	annual mean	31.12.2004
	0.25 µg/m³	annual mean	31.12.2008
Nitrogen Dioxide	105 ppb not to be exceeded more than 18 times per year	1 hour mean	31.12.2005
	21 ppb	annual mean	31.12.2005
PM_{10}	50 µg/m³ not to be exceeded more than 35 times per year	24 hour mean	31.12.2004
	40 µg/m³	annual mean	31.12.2004
Sulphur Dioxide	100 ppb not to be exceeded more than 35 times per year	15 minute mean	31.12.2005
	132 ppb not to be exceeded more than 24 times per year	1 hour mean	31.12.2004
	47 ppb not to be exceeded more than 3 times per year	24 hour mean	31.12.2004

(In view of its transboundary character, ozone is seen as more appropriately controlled at the national rather the local level. It is not therefore included within these objectives. However, reduced emissions of nitrogen dioxide will also cause ozone levels to fall.)
Source: Air Quality (England) Regulations 2000 (SI 2000, No. 928)

Secretary of State's decision to uphold an appeal against a refusal of planning consent for a large retail development near the centre of Bath.

In the exercise of his appellate role, whether in respect of planning or pollution control, the Secretary of State (or some person appointed by him) should be exemplary in observing his own advice, any lapse invites challenge by judicial review. But of course, when faced with the particular exigencies of any decision, a cabinet Minister is no less immune than local councillors from political influences which may dictate a course of action which deviates from that indicated by the relevant policy guidelines. Appeals and judicial reviews form the principal data sources in the case studies presented in this chapter. It is in the

BOX 3.3: Trends in Annual Emissions (ktonnes) to UK Atmosphere 1970–95

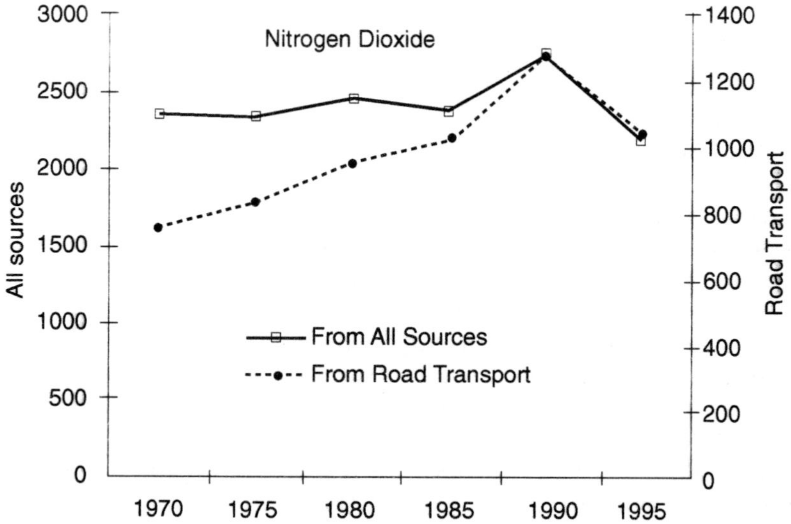

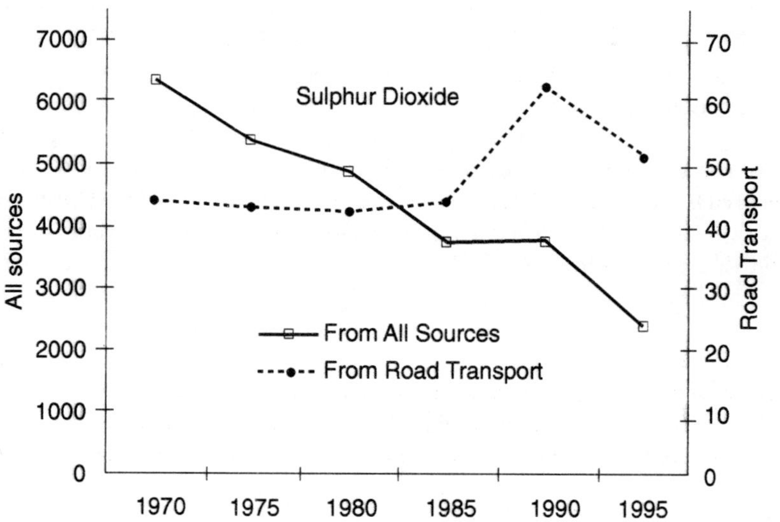

Source: DETR (1998a)

conflicts, rather than in the far more numerous instances of straightforward consents, that the key determinants of policy become exposed to public scrutiny.

WASTE INCINERATION

1. Gateshead

Given the tall chimneys and the pollution abatement equipment which incinerators—whether for toxic, clinical or municipal waste—are now required to install, their contribution to ambient air quality, even in their immediate vicinity, is small compared with that of road traffic. Although incinerators form one category of LULU which will remain a regrettable necessity even in the most service-dominated economies, they are invariably viewed with great suspicion. International obligations to eliminate waste dumping at sea and stricter controls over landfill mean that the determination of planning applications for these vexatious developments is not as rare an occurrence as planners might wish. In determining a planning application for a clinical waste incinerator, Gateshead MBC was not only concerned over its impact on air quality in this semi-rural area but was also mindful of public apprehension about the risk of dioxin emissions. The applicant (Northumbrian Water Group) appealed against refusal of consent. After an inquiry, the planning inspector, assisted by a chemical engineer who sat as an assessor, held that these concerns were sufficient grounds for refusing consent and recommended that the appeal be dismissed. The Secretary of State did not accept this recommendation (nor, by implication, the view that public concern over perceived risk should obviate development). In justifying his decision to grant planning consent, he relied principally upon the existence of the statutory controls over emissions from the incinerator which would be exercised by, at that time, Her Majesty's Inspectorate of Pollution (HMIP). The legality of this justification was challenged by the local planning authority in the High Court. Here the Deputy Judge presiding held that, whilst the threat of harm to the environment and to public health was undeniably a 'material consideration', so too was the existence of a control regime statutorily obliged to address these threats; and it was for the Secretary of State to consider their relative weights and to decide accordingly. This view was subsequently endorsed in the Court of Appeal, where Glidewell LJ went on to make an observation which gets to the nub of this particular genus of environmental problem:

> Public concern is, of course, and must be recognised by the Secretary of State to be, a material consideration for him to take into account. But if in the end that public concern is not justified, it cannot be conclusive. If it were, no industrial development—indeed very little development of any kind—would ever be permitted.[6]

[6] Above n.2.

Although the judge does not elaborate the point, it is clear that it is the central executive, especially the pollution control body, which determines which concerns are 'justified' and which are not. Since that body has few resources to commission independent research, it must perforce rely on the existing scientific orthodoxy. Even if the development is one which requires the developers to submit an environmental statement, this too will be based upon the conventional science and technology in which the affected public has little confidence. Outright refusal of planning consent for development of this type will almost invariably result in appeal and therefore *de facto* centralisation of decision-making, leaving the local planning authority with no controls of its own to point to when seeking to reassure concerned residents. The temptation to approve the development, but with planning conditions which offer the prospect of future intervention if the pollution abatement technology should fail to meet expectations, is therefore considerable; as is the incentive, for an applicant, not to delay development by appealing against such conditions.

The problem of overlapping jurisdictions is hardly new. A draft planning circular in 1972 stressed the need for early consultation with HM Alkali and Clean Air Inspectorate (a precursor of HMIP) during the planning process (DOE, 1972). The draft circular particularly deprecated the practice of applying planning conditions to 'scheduled works' which imposed more stringent controls over air pollution than those demanded by the Inspectorate. Publication of the circular was suspended when the Royal Commission on Environmental Pollution (RCEP) announced its intention to review the air pollution control as a whole. The 1976 Report of the Commission generally endorsed the pragmatic tradition of the Inspectorate and was scathing in its opposition to duplicative planning conditions (RCEP, 1976).

It was a commitment given in the White Paper 'This Common Inheritance' (HMG, 1990) which finally led to the publication in June 1992 of draft advice on planning and pollution control. The desire for a clear division of the respective jurisdictions of the planning and pollution control authorities was very apparent in this draft:

> Planning controls are not an appropriate means of regulating the detailed characteristics of industrial processes. Nor should planning authorities substitute their own judgement on pollution control issues for that of the bodies with the relevant expertise and responsibility for statutory control over those matters [DOE, 1992a, para. 1.25].

In August of that year, the inspector submitted his report of the inquiry into the Gateshead incinerator appeal. His recommendation to refuse consent, the Secretary of State's contrary decision and the subsequent judgments in the High Court and in the Court of Appeal were all in the public domain before the final version (substantially revised and with a reference to Glidewell LJ's ruling: DOE, 1994b, para. 1.3) eventually appeared in July 1994.

The published version of PPG 23 revisited the issue of overlapping jurisdictions:

> Lack of confidence in the effectiveness of controls imposed under pollution control legislation [IPC] is not a legitimate ground for the refusal of planning permission or for the imposition of conditions on a planning permission that merely duplicate such controls [DOE, 1994b, para. 3.23].

In 1998, these issues were raised again when yet another disputed incinerator application led to litigation.

2. Bolton

It is often stated that third parties enjoy no right of appeal against planning consent under existing planning law. This deficit is rectified to some extent by the more general public law right to seek judicial review of any planning decision. Environmental pressure groups are usually deemed to lack the personal interest necessary to establish standing; and individuals who meet this criterion still face the considerable financial obstacles (now increasingly rarely mitigated by legal aid) in bringing an action to court. But Mr Kirkman, assisted by Friends of the Earth, initiated a challenge[7] to Bolton MBC's planning consent for a municipal waste incinerator. The ruling in *Gateshead* preceded the coming into effect of the 1994 Waste Management Regulations[8] by which certain provisions of the EC Framework Directive on waste[9] are implemented in England and Wales. These Regulations motivated the first two of what was essentially a three-pronged attack by the local resident:

- —the local planning authority failed to address the threats posed by the atmospheric discharges but left these to be considered by the Environment Agency;
- —the authority misunderstood and failed to discharge its duties under the waste management regulations;
- —the authority failed to address the question whether the proposal for the incineration of waste represented the 'best practicable environmental option' (BPEO)[10] for the disposal of the waste in question.

Planning authorities are now required to fulfil specific obligations when determining planning applications for waste disposal sites; in particular, they must ensure the waste will be recovered or disposed of without endangering human health or the environment. By leaving the issue of atmospheric discharges (including dioxins) to the Environment Agency, which had indicated its acceptance in principle of the pollution control equipment, the planning authority had not fulfilled the duty imposed upon it by the Regulations. Similarly, the

[7] Above n.3.

[8] Waste Management Licensing Regulations 1994 (SI 1994, No. 1056).

[9] Directive 75/442/EEC [1975] OJ L194/39.

[10] In essence, an elaboration of BATNEEC applicable to processes where there is some choice of the medium (air, land or water) receiving the waste.

Regulations obliged the planning authority to consider the 'hierarchy' which ranked recycling above energy recovery as a preferred waste disposal option. The statutory waste management plan for Greater Manchester (GMWRA, 1996) had indicated a preference for recycling but, according to Carnwath J, there was nothing in that document which necessitated refusal of consent for the present incinerator. Finally, Bolton MBC had erred in failing to demonstrate that incineration constituted BPEO for the disposal of the wastes in question.

Compared with the High Court (where all three points were readily dismissed), the Court of Appeal was more sympathetic to the argument that the *Gateshead* principle could not justify any lessening of the duty on a planning authority to satisfy itself that a proposed waste installation could be operated without danger to human health or the environment. But, after considering the evidence originally put before Bolton MBC, Schiemann LJ was satisfied that its duty had not been breached in such a way as to make the planning consent unlawful. In contrast to the threat to the health of residents (the applicant included) in the vicinity of the incinerator, the other two points related to more general policy matters and Schiemann LJ expressed doubts about the *locus standi* of Mr Kirkman (or, for that matter, any other individual) to challenge them by judicial review.[11] But having reluctantly listened to the applicant's arguments, he was unprepared to disagree with the conclusions of Carnwath J. First, the Greater Manchester waste plan, with its presumption in favour of recycling, was a strategic document which could not oblige a planning authority to refuse planning consent in any given instance. Secondly, there is no statutory requirement on a planning authority to require a BPEO assessment and the waste plan could not be seen as creating a binding obligation to do so. However, BPEO was capable of being a material consideration, as Bolton had so treated it in this case. The weight to be attached to this consideration, and to any other, lay at their discretion. Equally, Bolton's indifference to the absence of figures comparing the cost of incineration with rival disposal options did not make its decision legally flawed.

The applicant's attempt to strengthen their case by invoking the doctrine of the 'direct effect' of an EC environmental directive was no more successful than an earlier occasion (see Miller, 1993) which involved the Framework Directive on industrial air pollution. The High Court was aware of the case in which the European Court held the Waste Framework Directive[12] to be insufficiently precise to be capable of 'direct effect' (Holder, 1996). Although it does not appear to have been pursued by the applicant in *Bolton*, the principle of indirect effect seems unlikely to have proved any more attractive to Schiemann LJ. By his construction of Article 3 of the Framework Directive, recycling happened to appear in the text before energy recovery, but that did not imply any binding priority to

[11] It was the ruling of Schiemann J (as he then was) in *R.* v. *Secretary of State for the Environment ex parte Rose Theatre Trust Co. Ltd* [1990] 1 QB 504 which, until a recent relaxation in judicial attitudes, restricted the role of individuals in pursuing public interest actions.

[12] Above n.9.

which Bolton should be sympathetic when exercising its planning obligations. But it is clear from policy statements, if not law, that both the European Community and the UK Government are committed to a waste management hierarchy which puts recovery subordinate only to reduction and avoidance. It could be argued that effective commitment to a strong notion of sustainability would require the empowerment of some state body to refuse to authorise a waste installation deemed to be operating at an unduly low level in the hierarchy. Under Part II of the Environmental Protection Act 1990, the Environment Agency currently has no power to refuse a waste management licence on those grounds. It is possible that the Pollution Prevention and Control Act 1999 might be interpreted as empowering the Agency to ensure that the authorisation of individual plants is consistent with overall waste strategy. Until a test case establishes this point, planning refusal (and the absence of an appropriate planning consent automatically entails refusal of a waste licence) could achieve that objective.

3. Secondary liquid fuels (SLF)

Hazardous waste incinerators come second only to nuclear installations in the LULU league of unpopularity. Cement kilns, although often a source of dust nuisance, have rarely been regarded in the same way. But kilns do seem to attract a similar level of opprobrium once they use, as part of their fuel, substances which would normally be disposed of by high temperature incineration.

Distillation followed by re-use is now accepted as the environmentally optimal option for dealing with contaminated industrial solvents like methanol. For solvents whose chlorine (or other halogen) content poses a special hazard re-use rather than disposal in the environment is particularly appropriate. However, the distillation process inevitably leaves some residues requiring disposal. The chemistry of cement manufacture requires the raw materials to experience high temperatures (in excess of 1400°C) for some time—precisely the conditions which are required to destroy organic wastes. Burning the residues from the solvent recovery process in cement kilns reduces the amount which goes to landfill—the least acceptable disposal option in terms of sustainability. Landfilling of organic material generates methane, which is about 20 times more potent as a greenhouse gas than carbon dioxide. International obligations to reduce methane emissions encourage an increased reliance upon incineration of waste and to co-incineration in cement kilns. Proponents of the use of solvent residues as an auxiliary kiln fuel argue that it also reduces the emission of sulphur dioxide as compared with total reliance upon coal or petroleum coke.

Merchant incinerator companies collect these contaminated solvents for a fee and burn them at high temperatures in purpose-built plant with no energy recovery and with very expensive emission control systems. They have been very concerned at the threat posed to their business by what, for the waste producers, is a much cheaper disposal option. They argue that the calorific value of solvent residues is needed in their incinerators to supply the energy to destroy toxic wastes in aqueous solution or sludges. They stress that these substances remain wastes, even though their calorific value can reduce the amount of coal or other primary fuel consumed in cement manufacture. As Purdue (1990) has demonstrated (prior to the SLF controversy), a legal definition of 'waste' is far from straightforward. On the second occasion that it considered the SLF issue, the House of Commons Environment Committee (HCEC, 1997) attempted to clarify the position but its report was far from conclusive. It identified four questions:

i. is SLF 'waste'?
ii. is the burning of SLF waste disposal or energy recovery?
iii. does the burning of SLF in a cement kiln constitute a 'material change of use' thereby necessitating planning permission?
iv. must an environmental assessment accompany any required planning permission?

which, it argued, could only be resolved in the courts. Indeed, it is precisely issues of this type—combining technical complexity with legal uncertainty—which have given rise to calls for an Environmental Court (see Chapter One).

Judicial reviews[13] of the Environment Agency's approval of applications—for variation of the authorisations of lime kilns in Durham and Derbyshire and a cement kiln in Lancashire—managed to avoid addressing these four questions. In summary, local residents failed to persuade Harrison J that such an application (to allow SLF to supply 25 per cent or, in one case, 40 per cent of the thermal input) necessitated a full BATNEEC/BPEO assessment of the whole process; it was sufficient to demonstrate that the substitution amounted to an improvement upon the originally approved process. Although without formally conceding the point, the operators accepted, for the sake of argument, that SLF was 'waste' and the Waste Management Regulations applied. In enforcing these Regulations, the Environment Agency is obliged to observe 'relevant objectives', which were to be interpreted as largely co-extensive with BATNEEC and BPEO controls. But there was one point on which the objectors were able to cause some embarrassment. If, following the prevailing orthodoxy as enshrined in *Gateshead*, planners must not encroach on the pollution control regime, then it follows that the latter must not prejudice planning's traditional protection of the 'amenity' of the locality. The regulations specifically exclude Environment Agency involvement in such matters where a relevant planning permission has been granted after 30 April 1994. But since planning permission for the kilns in question preceded this date, responsibility fell to the Agency. Despite some confusion, the judge was satisfied that evidence given at the inquiry established that

[13] R. v. *The Environment Agency and Redland Aggregates Ltd ex parte Gibson*; R. v. *The Environment Agency and Redland Aggregates Ltd ex parte Leam*; R. v. *The Environment Agency ex parte Sellers and Petty*, QBD, 8. May 1998 unreported.

the Agency had paid adequate attention to matters like noise and visual amenity.

A fourth challenge—against Lancashire County Council's concurrence with the operators of the cement kiln that SLF is a fuel not a waste and that its use did not require planning consent—was dropped before the hearing. Thus, apart from the minor issue on amenity, the important question for planners remained unresolved until June 2000 when, in a separate judicial review instituted by yet another local resident, the High Court ruled[14] that planning consent was not required for the use of SLF in the Durham lime kiln. Although this ruling makes further challenges unlikely, it does not entirely remove the possibility since the Court was at pains to point out that any 'change of use' is a matter of fact and depends upon the particular circumstances associated with the change in fuel content.

This discussion of the planning implications of burning waste-derived fuel is of more than academic interest when the position of third-party involvement in decision-making is considered. When planning permission is required, there arises the possibility of a planning inquiry (following 'call in' or an appeal over refusal or conditions) wherein local residents and environmental groups are able to participate. Comparable opportunities are not offered by the authorisation process under Part I of the Environmental Protection Act 1990. The latest regulations[15] allow any public representations, made in regard to an authorisation or an appeal, to be included in the public register, but private individuals are not entitled to take part in the appeal, to question any written submission or to cross-examine appellants or regulators at a hearing. Of course, judicial review by residents and others who can satisfy the 'sufficient interest' criterion is possible. But notwithstanding legal aid, the expense involved in this remedy—not least the possibility of having to pay the respondent's costs—amounts to a deterrent which far exceeds that which applies to third-party involvement in planning appeals.

It remains very likely that there are elected members of planning authorities who would have reversed their decision to grant planning consent for cement kilns had they been aware that these plant might subsequently burn substances which, because of their hazardous and toxic properties, would, in other circumstances, necessitate a range of stricter planning and pollution controls. This, it should be noted, differs significantly from the situation in *Gateshead* where the members of the planning authority were fully aware that it was an incinerator to which they were objecting so vehemently.

The EC Directive on landfill[16] aims to encourage recycling and to reduce the amount of organic waste. Landfilling of tyres has posed special problems and this disposal route for whole tyres will be closed from 2003 and for shredded

[14] R. v. *Durham County Council ex parte Lowther*, QBD 21 June 2000 unreported.

[15] Environmental Protection (Applications, Appeals and Registers) (Amendment) Regulations 1996 (SI 1996, No. 667).

[16] Directive 99/31/EEC [1999] OJ L182/1.

tyres from 2006. It is estimated that one hundredand eighty thousand tonnes *per annum* (about forty per cent of the UK arisings of used tyres) could be burnt in cement kilns (HLSCEC, 1999). In the light of the judicial reviews discussed above, it is difficult to imagine the assurances of technical agencies (whether UK or European) being sufficient to assuage the opposition which would undoubtedly attend such an increase on the current rate of 60,000 tonnes. Clarification of the status of co-incineration under planning law is likely to require further visits to the courts.

LOCAL AUTHORITY POLLUTION CONTROL

For certain industrial sources of air pollution, control is exercised by the local authority. With the exception of BPEO, the full range of powers and duties[17] applies to local authority pollution control (LAPC) as it does to IPC enforced by the central body. Control of the plant (for example, mineral works, foundries, animal rendering) falling within the remit of the former is reckoned to be technically less demanding. But odour from animal rendering works is notoriously difficult to eradicate even when the control measures are installed and maintained by co-operative management. Guidance issued by the Department of the Environment in 1991 envisaged that, as an interim measure prior to upgrading by April 1997 to the BATNEEC standard to be met by new rendering plants, existing plant should 'aim' to operate without causing odour; paragraph 13 states:

> The aim should be that all emissions are free from offensive odour outside the process boundary as perceived by the local authority Inspector [DOE, 1991b].

But when determining an appeal, brought by the operator of an animal rendering works, against such a condition, the Secretary of State relied upon some earlier general guidance (DOE, 1991c) to argue that conditions which specify the techniques to prevent odour should enable this aim to be met, and therefore a condition which simply replicates the aim is redundant. The Minister's decision in this (Bradford-upon-Avon) appeal was successfully challenged in a judicial review brought by the local authority.[18] But it was during the judicial review of yet another appeal decision[19] that the validity of a condition requiring no odour at the site boundary was considered at length.

During preliminary discussions with Torridge District Council over its application, Peninsular Proteins had accepted a 'no odour' condition. It was also accepted by the Inspector appointed to hear the appeal into the subsequent refusal of the North Devon renderer's application. But when the Secretary of

[17] As contained in Part I of the Environmental Protection Act 1990.

[18] R. v. *Secretary of State ex parte West Wiltshire DC* [1996] Env. LR 312.

[19] R. v. *Secretary of State for the Environment and Peninsular Proteins Ltd, ex parte Torridge DC* [1997] JPL 1106.

State upheld the appeal, this previously agreed condition was excluded from those which the local authority was directed to append to the authorisation. This exclusion was successfully challenged by the local authority. Following the inquiry and, in fact, after the Inspector had reported, a further (non-statutory) guidance note was published which urges authorities to apply a condition of this form 'only in exceptional circumstances' (DOE, 1995a). In the decision letter, the Secretary of State makes it clear that the close proximity of housing would constitute such circumstances but, with the nearest occupied dwelling being some five hundred metres distant, did not arise in this case. During the judicial review, Torridge DC argued that this implied presumption against the use of a 'no odour' condition arose only after the inquiry but, had the opportunity arisen, the authority would have vigorously demonstrated the 'exceptional circumstances' which applied in this case. McCullogh J accepted that this was sufficient reason to quash the Minister's decision.

This local/central debate over what may constitute a condition of an LAPC authorisation echoes earlier and longer disputes over conditions of planning consents. Indeed, the 'no odour' condition is comparable with model planning conditions, set out in a planning circular (DOE, 1973) and later a planning policy guidance note (DOE, 1994c), which specified maximum noise levels at the boundary of industrial premises. The references to the proximity of housing and the five hundred metre benchmark are far more familiar to planners than to chemical engineers. The Torridge case illustrates the difficulties in maintaining a rigid distinction between planning and pollution controls, at least in regard to the small-scale but more numerous LAPC sites (of which there will be more than twenty thousand in England and Wales when the Pollution Prevention and Control Act 1999 comes into effect[20]).

Any suggestion that a condition requiring 'no odour at the boundary' is unenforceable is readily countered by the observation that Dukinfield Magistrates' and Manchester Crown Courts fined a Tameside renderer more than £500,000 for its repeated breach. Moreover, this condition is not confined to rendering works: its application to the authorisation of a West Midlands foundry (the odour arises from the resins used to bind the sand forming the moulds) was upheld after an appeal by the operator (Anon, 1998) was quashed. The local authority in question has subsequently succeeded in enforcement action (Anon, 1999) against another foundry in default of this and other conditions of its LAPC authorisation. Since the inception of LAPC in 1991, local authorities in England and Wales have authorised more than 10,000 individual processes with around 60 appeals[21] (mostly against conditions), at least two judicial reviews and a judicial interpretation of the term 'persistency'.[22] Given their similarities, it is tempting to view the LAPC regime as becoming a miniature version of the planning system. This temptation was strengthened when the Planning

20 http://www.aeat.co.uk/netcen/airqual/info/labrief.html.

21 *Ibid.*

22 *Dudley MBC* v. *Henley Foundries Ltd*, QBD, 26April 1999.

Inspectorate was given responsibility for hearing LAPC (as well as IPC) appeals (DETR, 1997b).

LOCAL AIR QUALITY MANAGEMENT

APC together with their traditional duties over statutory nuisances[23] offer local authorities controls over individual, static sources of air pollution. In 1997, they acquired responsibilities relating to the overall air quality in their areas. The Environment Act 1995 requires district and unitary councils in England and Wales to carry out periodic reviews of the quality of the air (or, more accurately, of ambient concentrations of each of the seven pollutants specified in regulations: see Box 3.2) in their areas. Where a review indicates that an air quality objective will not be achieved by the prescribed date, then the local authority is obliged to declare an 'air quality management area' (AQMA) and it must produce, within one year, an 'action plan'[24] detailing how it proposes to ensure compliance with the objective. To this end, local authorities are urged to adopt an integrative approach, involving all relevant departments, especially planning, and collaborating with neighbouring authorities. In this connection, it should be noted that this regime of air quality management confers no new powers of control (over fixed or mobile sources) on local authorities.

In the latest guidance note (DETR, 2000b), the land use planning system is described as 'integral to improving air quality'. It later reiterates the theme of PPG23 in stressing the need to avoid duplication of technical controls more properly enforced by the Environment Agency. Where a proposed source of emission falls outside the remit of both IPC and LAPC, then a planning authority might contemplate the imposition of conditions, or even a planning obligation, 'to tackle the source's possible effect on land use or amenity'. In turn, planners are reminded that development plans should take account of any 'constraints on development as a result of the need to comply with any statutory environmental quality standards or objectives' including those concerned with air quality. Attention is drawn to the good practice guide on air quality and land use planning published by the Royal Town Planning Institute (RTPI, 1999a). This too stresses the importance of planning intervention especially in regard to development within an AQMA. But it advises against a policy of automatic refusal of planning consent for any source of the pollutant(s) which have caused an area to be designated as an AQMA. Given that some local authorities might choose to designate the whole of their areas, such a policy would cause blight of a clearly intolerable order. But air quality was recognised as a material consideration in circumstances which include:

i) the development could result in the designation of a new AQMA;

[23] Now contained in Part III of the Environmental Protection Act 1990.
[24] S.84 of the Environment Act 1995.

ii) the application would conflict with the proposals in the local authority's action plan;
iii) the application would render some elements the local authority's action plan unworkable [RTPI, 1999a, 6].

The DETR guidance notes makes the concession, which is important in the light of the *Gateshead* ruling, that:

> Where a development is likely to affect air quality significantly (i.e. where the air quality objectives are likely to be breached), then, provided the impact relates to the use and amenity of land, the local planning authority may refuse the application or mitigate its effects by imposing conditions [DETR, 2000b, 14].

To those familiar with Cheshire's attempt, nearly a quarter of a century ago, to include air quality standards in its structure plan (see Miller and Wood, 1983, 56), the above might seem a belated vindication of that county's approach. However, it was the industrial sources, especially those in the petro-chemical complex on the banks of the Mersey, which then formed the county council's principal concern. It is virtually impossible today to conceive of a newly commissioned incinerator or any another category of static source which, despite technical (BATNEEC) controls imposed under IPC or LAPC, could still be reckoned to affect ambient air quality *significantly*. The above advice is really of most relevance to transport sources.

PLANNING, TRANSPORT AND AIR POLLUTION

Apprehension of the effects of exhaust emissions was one of the many motivations of the first major study by planners into reconciling urban life with the motor car:

> The penetration of motor vehicles throughout urban areas is bringing its own peculiar penalties of accidents, anxiety, intimidation by large or fast vehicles that are out of scale with the surroundings, noise, fumes, vibration, dirt and visual intrusion on a vast scale [SGWP, 1963, 39].

At the time of the publication of the 'Buchanan Report', there were six and a half million private cars registered in the United Kingdom; thirty years later, registrations have more than trebled. Concern over the health effects of emissions has led to ever more stringent regulation, primarily in the form of product standards (for example, lead free petrol; catalytic converters, low sulphur diesel). But the role of land use planning, albeit less direct, is recognised in numerous official publications.

Planning Policy Guidance 13 on transport (DOE, 1994d) urges local authorities to carry out their land use policies and transport programmes in ways which help to:

—reduce growth in the length and number of motorised journeys;

—encourage alternative means of travel which have less environmental impact; and hence
—reduce reliance on the private car.

BOX 3.4: The Bath superstore

Although only in draft when Safeway plc appealed against the refusal of planning permission for their proposed supermarket in Bath, the circular on Air Quality and Land Use Planning (DOE, 1996c) conceded that the indirect consequences of a development, including traffic generation and the resulting impacts on air quality, were capable of constituting material considerations. No more detailed advice was given and the earlier guidance on planning and pollution control (DOE, 1994b) excluded consideration of 'indirect' causes of air pollution. However, PPG23 did suggest that '[w]here there are significant risks of damage to the environment, pollution controls will take into account the need to prevent or limit harm, even where scientific knowledge is not conclusive' (DOE, 1994b, para 1.12). But rather than rely upon 'pollution controls' to take account of the uncertainties posed by this particular development, the local planning authority itself had invoked the precautionary principle when refusing consent.

A formal environmental statement was not required for retail development of this size and none accompanied the application. In the subsequent appeal, the Inspector and, more especially, the Technical Assessor were still charged with the task of making sense of a number of unco-ordinated and conflicting submissions on traffic predictions, air quality, effects on public health and on stone buildings from interested parties (including the Bath Preservation Trust) as well as the appellants and the planning authority. The Assessor accepted that the development could lead to a greater number of exceedences of the proposed standard for fine particulates (PM_{10}: particles with a diameter below 10 microns). But the Secretary of State was later to place more emphasis upon HM Government's aim of halving vehicle PM_{10} emissions between 1995 and 2005 in compliance with the National air Quality Strategy. In addition, he was prepared to accept the estimate of 700,000 miles as the annual saving in overall car use within the store's catchment; but he was unable to adjudicate between the rival claims for the impact on mileage within the City itself. The submitted evidence on the rate of decay of the buildings (which are recognised in Bath's designation as a World Heritage Site) was equally inconclusive. All these considerations were material but, in the absence of arguments which established that any of the negative impacts outweighed the benefits which the development brought, the appeal was upheld.

Source: Planning Inspectorate File ref: APP/F0114/A/95/255444

PPG6 on town centres and retail developments (DOE, 1993a) seeks to complement the aims of PPG13 by recognising the need to avoid pollution in congested town centres and promoting the vitality and viability of town centres. Planning authorities are encouraged to ensure good access and to devise a comprehensive car parking strategy which, in favouring short-term parking, assists shoppers whilst deterring commuters. When the Royal Commission considered this issue in 1994, it recommended that a fresh grant of planning permission should become obligatory whenever a change of land use generated 'appreciably higher levels of traffic' (RCEP, 1994, para. 9.66). The effects on ambient air quality by vehicles visiting the store was the key issue in the determination of Safeway plc's planning application for a supermarket on the site of a former bus depot within the Bath Conservation Area (see Box 3.4).

In similar attempts to prevent new development attracting further traffic to areas of poor air quality, the London Borough of Greenwich refused consent for a petrol station near the Blackwell Tunnel and Ealing refused a McDonalds restaurant in its borough. Both developers were successful on appeal; in both cases, the fact that the development was not expected to cause an existing air quality objective to be exceeded was crucial. In granting consent for the Bath store, the Secretary of State imposed eighteen conditions, only one of which could have any influence on local air quality, *viz.* the installation of a traffic management system for the traffic light-controlled junctions by which access was gained to the site. The use of planning obligations, attached to consents for large shopping centres, to secure physical improvements in the adjacent road network is not uncommon. Planning conditions attached to development (offices, retail establishments) limiting car parking space clearly has an impact on traffic levels and therefore on pollution levels. But despite the recognition of the materiality of the 'indirect' impact of large retail (and comparable) development on ambient concentrations, we have yet to see an example of planners succeeding in preventing that impact by withholding planning consent for 'traffic magnets'.

Planning refusal for sensitive land uses (housing, schools, hospitals, day centres) in areas affected by existing pollution has always been far less controversial than planning intervention over sources. The 1972 draft circular urged that such development be 'kept well away from [polluting] industries already established or from land intended to be used for them' (DOE, 1972, 3). That official approbation now applies no less to development proposed in areas where high ambient concentrations are largely attributable to traffic. In the preparation of Surrey Heath's local plan for the borough, it was realised that traffic on the M3 would continue to cause breaches of the PM_{10} and the nitrogen dioxide objectives on a corridor of land on either side of the motorway until 2005 at least, thereby necessitating the designation of an AQMA. The land in question is designated for housing but the inspector conducting the local plan inquiry urged the planning authority to withhold consents until the exceeded pollutants levels drop below their respective objectives (Street, 2000).

The Surrey Heath case is unlikely to be an isolated example. In its enforcement of the local air quality management regime, a district council will become aware of the existence and location of pollution hotspots; it cannot ignore that information in the exercise of its planning functions (or, in the case of a non-unitary district, when advising the county planning authority). It will recognise that the designation of an AQMA could lead to the blighting of areas which, given their proximity to motorway interchanges, would, but for the ambient pollution, be prime development land. Loss of development value will prompt vigorously pursued appeals. In such a climate, two other factors, beside the attitude of the central executive, become important: the urgency with which local authorities implement any 'action plans' found necessary after the reviews of their areas; and the level (which, in theory, should be influenced by the precautionary principle) at which the various quality objectives have been set. In this connection, it should be noted that all but four of the twelve objectives now in force have a compliance date (see Box 3.2) earlier than that specified (*viz.* 31 December 2005) in the earlier regulations.[25]

The air quality objectives are motivated by a concern with the effects of air pollutants on human health. The Expert Panel on Air Quality Standards is at pains to stress the uncertainties in the many epidemiological studies which have been undertaken in various countries, but pollution episodes are known to be linked with increased cardio-vascular deaths and admissions to hospital (EPAQS, 1995). It recognises that high pollution during episodes is most likely to be simply the final element in a long chain of causes of the deaths of individuals with pre-existing cardio-vascular morbidity. But it cannot rule out the possibility that long-term exposure to air pollution may contribute to the development of these conditions. The Panel's recommended standard on particles therefore addresses the need to reduce both peak and average concentrations. Pollution episodes arise from a combination of poor dispersion and the spatial concentration of sources. Poor dispersion is associated primarily with meteorological (anti-cyclonic) conditions, but urban form (roads lined by tall buildings) can be a contributory factor. The spatial distribution of sources, especially traffic sources, is clearly something that can be addressed by land use planning. Congestion and delay at a busy road junction will lead to local pollution hotspots to the detriment of the health of nearby residents whilst a greater use of public transport will have a positive impact on ambient concentrations. 'Free flowing traffic and smooth driving techniques generally result in lower emissions and improved fuel consumption' and these are cited among the criteria against which a traffic management scheme should be judged (DETR, 2000c, para. 4.01).

In 1995, an action group of residents near Trafalgar Road (A206) in South-east London sought to persuade its 'traffic authority' (*viz.* the London Borough of Greenwich) to use its powers[26] to close roads whenever temperature

[25] Air Quality Regulations 1997 (SI 1997, No. 3043).

[26] S.14 of the Road Traffic Regulation Act 1984.

inversions raised concentrations of pollutants from vehicle exhausts to the point of exacerbating asthma suffered by children living in the vicinity. Acting on behalf of its children, this group applied to the High Court for a declaration that air pollution could amount to a 'danger to the public' justifying temporary road closure. MacPherson J had no hesitation in dismissing this application, arguing that the powers in question had to be construed in the context of 'road traffic matters' which, contrary to the claims of the applicants' counsel, could not be stretched so as to embrace occasional episodes of high pollution.[27] The Environment Act 1995 later extended the purposes for which these road closure orders can be made explicitly to include the pursuit of the air quality objectives. This extension applies without restriction in London; elsewhere orders made on air quality grounds cannot restrict access for more than eight hours in any 24 to premises on or adjacent to roads to which the restriction applies. However, the first guidance note on air quality and traffic management (DETR, 1997c, paras. 5.10–13) doubted whether these revised powers could be effective in providing the type of *ad hoc* remedy sought by the Greenwich parents. In the current note, these doubts have been replaced by an emphasis on the need for careful planning of such restrictions in order to avoid simply moving the congestion and pollution elsewhere (DETR, 2000c, para. 5.05).

DISCUSSION

The possibility of the emission of dioxins from any proposed installation invariably triggers vigorous opposition from neighbouring residents. Despite the rhetoric—the most toxic chemical known to man—which attaches to this group of substances, there remains uncertainty among epidemiologists and toxicologists over their effects on human health (USEPA, 1994). Scientific uncertainty of this kind has been one of the motivations of the 'precautionary principle' which has been part of the EC environmental policy[28] since 1992. Earlier, the willingness of the UK Government 'to take precautionary action to limit the use of potentially dangerous materials or the spread of potentially dangerous pollutants, even where scientific knowledge is not conclusive' was qualified by a proportionality condition—'if the balance of likely costs and benefits justifies it' (HMG, 1990, para. 1.18)—which the Environment Agency was later required to observe[29] when exercising its overall enforcement role. This reference to the precautionary principle in the White Paper, as well as another in the (then draft) guidance on planning and pollution control (DOE, 1992a, para.1.9), was cited by the planning authority during the inquiry into the Gateshead incinerator. This principle was also quoted in support of Bath's refusal of consent for the

[27] R. v. *Greenwich London Borough Council ex parte* W [1997] Env. LR 190, [1997] JPL 62.

[28] Art. 130r (now Art. 174) of the Treaty of Rome, as amended by the Treaty of Maastricht in 1992.

[29] S.39, Environment Act 1995.

superstore (Box 3.4). Benzene is a known carcinogen and 1,3-butadiene is one of a number of compounds found in car exhausts suspected of being capable of causing cancer. In view of the epidemiological evidence, albeit inconclusive, implicating particulates in the increasing prevalence of asthma among children, the Royal Commission (1991, para. 7.6) recommended that a precautionary approach be adopted towards particulate pollution, especially PM_{410} and smaller diameter particles originating, in the main, from diesel exhausts.

There is a clear temptation for third parties and environmental groups to cite the precautionary principle in any planning appeal to which it might be remotely applicable. But there is now English case law,[30] although not arising from a town planning case, which holds that the precautionary principle is incapable of 'direct effect'. The principle must be taken into account whenever the Council of Ministers considers environmental legislation (for example, on the harmonisation of national requirements on catalytic converters) but it is too imprecise to bind the Secretary of State (or any other emanation of a Member State) to a particular course of action and, by implication, planning refusal for any development posing uncertain environmental impacts.

Even if there were no health effects associated with exhaust gases, the relationship between urban form and the motor car would still be a major preoccupation of planners. An increased use of public transport is seen as desirable for many reasons, of which an improvement in urban air quality is but one. The Internet and the communications revolution generally might assist the emergence of spatial settlement patterns which are naturally sustainable. But until then, governments must maintain an interventionist approach. The Road Traffic Reduction Act 1997 obliges local traffic authorities to undertake a review of existing and forecast levels of traffic and to set targets for reductions. Road charging schemes are being studied as a means of reducing the demand for car journeys (MVA, 1996). Higher parking charges and fiscal methods (especially the excise levied on petrol) are used as deterrents to private motoring. But until both supply and demand side measures demonstrate more effectiveness, both central and local government must continue to hope that more direct controls over exhaust emissions (increased reliance on clean fuels, catalytic converters, stricter emissions standards in the 'MOT' tests) will serve to reduce violations of the air quality objectives.

None of these various policy instruments is without its political cost, but they do not offend the powerful interests which are threatened when planning consent is withheld for superstores or for prime housing sites, especially in the south-east of England. Nevertheless, the ministerial reasoning in the Bath and similar cases is uncomfortably redolent of the *Tragedy of the Commons* (Hardin, 1962): the atmosphere above the UK is already contaminated by the products of countless car journeys made by millions of people to numerous destinations; but to use that fact to justify denying some people the benefits

[30] R v. *Secretary of State for Trade and Industry ex parte Duddridge* (1995) 7 JEL 224.

associated with driving to one, new location is perverse as well as an infringement of liberty. But just as Hardin argued that the (then) feared population explosion justified infringement upon the right to reproduce, then so too the alleviation of urban air pollution will not be achieved without some violation of the modern interpretation of the right to liberty, *viz.* to drive and park wherever and whenever we choose.

4

Risk, Land Use Planning and Major Accident Hazards

GORDON WALKER

INTRODUCTION

SINCE 1999 MEMBER States of the European Union have been required to have in place land use planning policies and procedures which take account of the major accident threat posed by the use and storage of hazardous materials. This represents a further development of the EU role in land use issues (Walker, 1991) and in some parts of Europe is presenting problematical challenges to current practice. However, in the UK, the implementation of the latest EU legislation[1] is building on nearly 30 years of pre-existing policy and practice which has recognised that the land use planning system has an important role to play in protecting against and preventing catastrophic harm. Indeed, one of only a handful of fundamental planning statutes[2] in force in the UK is devoted entirely to dealing with 'hazardous substances'—a fact that is often overlooked even in some of the established planning texts.

Many industrial installations present day-to-day pollution impacts from 'normal operations' and, in Chapter 3 above, Miller discusses the planning role in this context. However, some of the same installations, along with many others across the country, present a greater potential hazard resulting from accidents or abnormal operating conditions leading to fires, explosions and/or releases of toxic gas. These are classic high-consequence, low-probability threats, where accidents happen very rarely, but when they do the consequences can be quite devastating. Examples of previous accidents include Flixborough (UK) in 1974, Seveso (Italy) in 1976, Bhopal (India) in 1984, Enschede (Netherlands) 2000 and in the UK in smaller scale incidents at a range of sites including refineries and chemical stores (see the list in Box 4.1).

The land use planning system can help contain this threat by acting alongside other regulatory systems which have evolved in parallel and which need to interface, sometimes uneasily, with the planning function. As will be made clear in this chapter, the planning role is important, but at the same time constrained

[1] Directive 96/82/EC [1997] OJ L10/13.

[2] Planning (Hazardous Substances) Act 1990.

BOX 4.1: Some recent incidents at major accident hazard sites in the UK

Site and location	Date	Description
Allied Colloids, Bradford	July 1992	Major fire involving a cocktail of chemicals; 30 people received hospital treatment after smoke inhalation
Hickson and Welch, Castleford	Sept 1992	Fireball ripped through chemical plant, killing 5 people on site
Associated Octel, Ellesmere Port	Feb 1994	Leak of ethyl chloride and subsequent major fire
Texaco Pembroke Refinery, Milford Haven	July 1994	Explosion and fires, injuring 26 workers on site and damaging property up to two miles away
Albright and Wilson, Avonmouth	October 1996	Fire leading to toxic smoke plume. At least 12 people temporarily hospitalised with respiratory and eye problems

and sometimes ineffectual in achieving the goal of protecting against harm. As with so many other aspects of land use planning, the public good of protecting against disaster is in practice balanced against the economic imperative of allowing businesses to get on and 'do business'. Increasingly however 'doing business' is being recast in shades of green, and voluntary risk reduction measures adopted independently of formal regulatory intervention are providing new channels for achieving desirable land use outcomes.

This chapter begins with an attempt to offer some insight into the role for planning in protecting people's lives and the environment from major accident hazards. It then provides a discussion of the roles and positions of different stakeholders in major accident hazard issues—the Health and Safety Executive (HSE), local planning authorities, industry and the public. The increasingly important role for risk reduction measures achieved outside formal regulatory intervention is finally examined together with the motivations pushing industry towards voluntary action.

There is a range of terminology used to refer to the threats that form the focus of this chapter. Sometimes the term 'major hazard' or 'major accident hazard' is used, sometimes 'hazardous installations', 'hazardous substance' or 'consent sites'. In each case the reference is to installations where, in the event of a major accident and release of toxic, explosive or flammable materials, local people and the nearby environment could be seriously affected. For the remainder of this chapter the term 'major accident hazard' will be utilised. This does not however include nuclear risks which are regulated separately. Explosive stores holding blasting explosives, fireworks or gunpowder are also dealt with under distinct legislative[3] but related procedural arrangements, and are not discussed in detail in this chapter.

THE LAND USE PLANNING ROLE: POLICY AND PRACTICE

The land use planning role involves applying controls over both the location of major accident hazard sites and development near to these sites. Hazardous sites are dealt with by the Planning (Hazardous Substances) Act 1990 and the associated regulations[4] (referred to hereafter as the P(HS) legislation). Under this legislation operators of sites holding above designated quantities of specified hazardous substances have to apply to hazardous substances authorities (HSAs)—largely local planning authorities—for a specific hazardous substances consent. This consent is in addition to any application for planning permission, which, for new sites, would normally be made simultaneously.

The P(HS) legislation was introduced to enable planning authorities to apply specific controls over the location of hazardous storage, to a degree that could not be achieved through the use of established planning powers (Walker, 1994; DOE, 1992b). The consents specify which hazardous substances can be held and the maximum inventory on-site at any one time. Quite powerful conditions can also be applied to the consents, for example, specifying where within a site hazardous substances are to be held in order to keep hazardous storage away from site boundaries. However, the conditions have to relate to essentially locational issues rather than the day-to-day operation of the plant (see below). Modifications to existing consents have to be applied for, if, for example, a company wants to increase the level of storage above the specified maximum level or move the storage locations from those initially agreed. Just as with planning applications, there are requirements to consult outside bodies when HSAs receive consent applications, with the HSE specified as the key source of expert advice.

New applications for consents are received comparatively infrequently. However, when the P(HS) legislation was first introduced a large number of existing site operators were able to claim a 'deemed consent'. Until changes to threshold inventory levels were made in 1999 (see below) there were about eleven hundred installations holding consents around the country. Among these installations are major chemical and petrochemical plants, but also many that are less obviously hazardous, such as brickworks using liquefied petroleum gas (LPG) as a fuel, water treatment plants holding chlorine and warehouses storing ammonium nitrate fertiliser. As shown in Box 4.2, sites presenting a

[3] Explosives Act 1875, as amended.

[4] Planning (Hazardous Substances) Regulations 1992 (SI 1992, No. 656).

BOX 4.2: The distribution of sites with hazardous substances consent in England and Wales (pre-Seveso II Directive amendments)

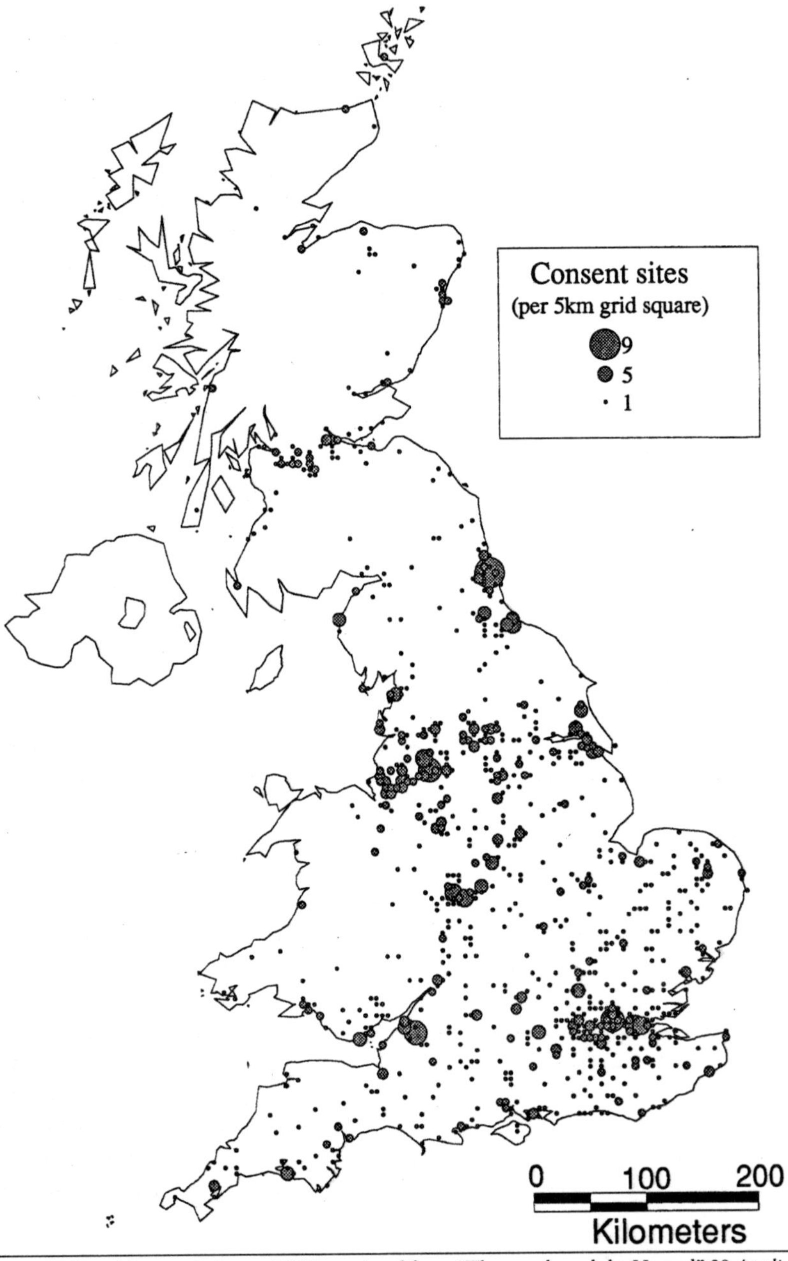

Source: Walker, Mooney & Pratts (2000) reprinted from "The people and the Hazard" 20 *Applied Geography* 199–34 with permission from Elsevier Science.

potential major accident hazard are broadly spread across the UK, although there is distinct clustering in areas which have a concentration of the chemical and/or petrochemical industry (Walker and Draycott, 1996; Walker, Mooney and Pratts, 2000).

The control of development in the vicinity of existing hazardous sites is also informed through consultation with the HSE. The questions of what counts as 'in the vicinity' and which development proposals are significant enough to warrant expert advice are dealt with by the specification of 'consultation zones' around sites and lists of types and sizes of relevant proposed developments. Site-specific consultation zones are specified by the HSE around all of the sites with hazardous substances consent. These zones vary substantially in size and shape extending from only a one hundred metres up to one and a half kilometres from storage locations. Consultation with the HSE on planning applications within these zones is no longer optional; it is obligatory for all relevant development proposals such as new housing, schools, hospitals or large retail or entertainment developments. By far the major part of the consultation activity dealt with by the HSE relates to applications for development in the vicinity of hazardous sites (see the case studies in Miller and Fricker, 1993 for examples).

A European Directive,[5] promulgated in 1982 in the wake of the accident at Seveso, did not recognise a role for land use planning, despite including provisions for all other aspects of risk management (Walker, 1991). However, a new version of the Directive (COMAH or Seveso II[6]) has now introduced a number of general land use planning provisions, including requiring procedures for gaining expert technical advice and public participation in decision-making—see the details in Box 4.3 (Christou and Porter, 1999). This Directive has been implemented in the UK largely through the existing legislation and structures described above. Some changes have however been necessary and have been implemented through modifications to the P(HS) legislation.[7] Most significantly the number of sites coming within the consents regime has doubled (up to an estimated two and a half thousand), a key aspect of the transitional deemed consent arrangements has been removed (see below), expectations of policies in structure and unitary development plans have been tightened (through amendments to PPG12 and development plan regulations) and risks to the environment from accident events have now to be considered and consulted on alongside risks to people (HSE, 1989).

Whilst the above description of current legislation presents the policy position, there is, as ever, the question whether intentions match deeds. A number of studies examining the practice of HSE consultation and scrutiny of hazard issues in planning applications undertaken in the 1980s found that action 'on the ground' was slow to emerge and revealed some basic problems with information, procedures and control powers (Miller, 1988; Petts, 1988; Walker and

[5] Directive 82/501/EEC [1982] OJ L230/1.

[6] Above n.1.

[7] Planning (Control of Major Accident Hazards) Regulations 1999 (SI 1999, No. 981).

BOX 4.3: Land use planning provisions within the Seveso II Directive

Article 12 Para 1	Member states shall ensure that the objectives of preventing major accidents and limiting the consequences of such accidents are taken into account in their land use policies and/or other relevant policies. They shall pursue those objectives through controls on: a) the siting of new establishments b) modifications to existing establishments c) new developments such as transport links, locations frequented by the public and residential areas in the vicinity of existing establishments, where the siting of developments are such as to increase the risk or consequences of major accidents Member states shall ensure that their land-use and/or other relevant policies and the procedures for implementing those policies take account of the need, in the long term, to maintain appropriate distances between establishments covered by this Directive and residential areas, areas of public use and areas of natural sensitivity or interest, and, in the case of existing establishments, of the need for additional technical measures in accordance with Article 5 so as not to increase the risks to people.
Article 12 Para 2	Member states shall ensure that all competent authorities and planning authorities responsible for decisions in this area set up appropriate consultation procedures to facilitate implementation of the policies established under paragraph 1. The procedures shall be designed to ensure that technical advice on the risks arising from the establishments is available, either on a case-by-case or on a generic basis, when decisions are taken.
Article 13 Para 5	Member states shall ensure that the public is able to give its opinion in the following cases: —planning for new establishments. . . —modifications to existing establishments . . . —developments around such existing establishments

Macgill, 1985). The P(HS) legislation and associated clarification of HSE consultation procedures addressed some of these problems, but evidence of implementation difficulties remains. For example, a study of the early implementation of the P(HS) legislation undertaken for the DOE (Walker, 1994) found that there was poor understanding of the regulations and the planning role within LPAs and inconsistencies in the application of exemptions, enforcement action and tracking of non-compliance. Only a few of the twenty-five recommendations for improvements in policy and practice arising from this study have since been implemented. A survey of LPAs also found limited inclusion of policies on hazardous industry in development plans, despite strong policy guidance from central government that such concerns should be explicitly addressed (Walker and Bayliss, 1997).

Beyond the details of policy and practice, it is necessary also to recognise the major limitations on the land use planning system in the UK achieving any substantial mitigation of hazard impacts. However well-informed planning decisions may be about risk concerns, there is a long legacy of poor siting that the planning system can do very little about. The majority of sites in the UK which are now identified as hazardous have been in place for many years. They were established long before planning controls took any specific account of risk concerns and hence substantial populations often accumulated in their vicinity (Walker, Mooney and Pratts, 2000). For example, Fawley near Southampton was established as a 'company town' alongside an oil refinery dating from 1921, which expanded into a major petrochemical complex in the 1950s. Over twelve and a half thousand people now live within the risk zones defined for toxic and flammable incident scenarios.

Whilst in theory the planning system can intervene to remove current land uses and the P(HS) legislation can be used to revoke existing consents, in practice these steps are enormously expensive and difficult to take, and hence very rarely used (Petts, 1988; Miller and Fricker, 1993). The survey of LPAs referred to above established that very few development plans policies included relocation of hazardous sites as a policy aim (Walker and Bayliss, 1997). Furthermore, when the requirement for specific 'consents' to be held for all hazardous storage was first introduced in 1992 (see above), the P(HS) legislation granted 'grandfather rights' for all existing site operators preventing the refusal of any consents for pre-existing hazards, however badly these may have been located. Indeed the 'deemed consents', which were offered to existing operators, required them to claim for double the inventory of hazardous substances they already held, effectively opening the door to an uncontrolled intensification of risk at some very badly located sites.

Whilst the P(HS) legislation was in some ways quite striking in its appearance at a time when the broader emphasis within government was on deregulation, the priority within the enactment of the legislation was clearly one of protecting the existing rights of industry rather than intervening to reduce risks. Seveso II similarly refers to the 'long term' goal of separating hazards and populations (see Box 4.3) rather than any more immediate rationalisation of land use patterns—although under the modifications to the P(HS) regime implementing the Directive the doubling inventory requirement has now been removed.

BOX 4.4: Risk contours around a hazardous installation

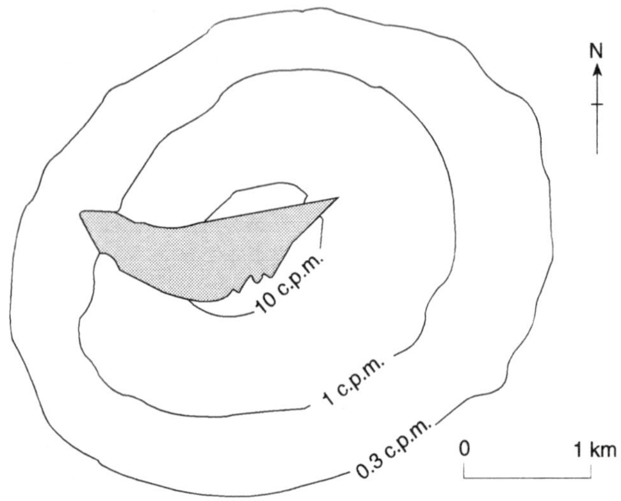

Hence in the majority of situations the role for planning is limited to one of restricting additional population in areas significantly at risk and, if possible, preventing any further intensification of risk at the hazard source (i.e. to prevent a bad situation from getting even worse). Even in these respects the possibilities for action can be limited—the existence of, for example, a housing estate close to a chemical site can establish a strong precedent for allowing further incremental additions to the housing stock, as each addition on its own may appear relatively insignificant.

That there are constraints on the planning role in this context is clearly not surprising or unique. It is a fundamental characteristic of the UK planning system that pre-existing development rights are protected and that established land uses possess enormous inertia. With changing values and priorities, there are inevitable dislocations between past planning decisions and current standards of acceptable development locations. What is important in this context is that opportunities for intervention and improvement (both formal and informal) are identified, that decisions are well-informed and that relevant stakeholders have the opportunity to exercise influence over these decisions. It is to these different stakeholders and to the decision-making processes within which they operate that attention now turns.

STAKEHOLDERS, RISKS AND PLANNING INTERVENTION

The analysis of interest groups, actors or stakeholders can play an important role in understanding the practice and outcomes of land use planning (Rydin, 1998). This chapter has already introduced a number of key players: the planning or hazardous substances authority as decision-maker, the HSE as expert adviser, industry as risk creators and the public as risk-takers. Some of the complexities of the relationships between these different stakeholders have been hinted at in the preceding discussion. Further to illuminate roles, relationships and political contexts, it is useful to examine each of the stakeholders in greater depth. This discussion draws on a number of research projects undertaken for the DETR and the HSE during the 1990s.

1. HSE: providing advice

The Health and Safety Executive has a number of different roles in the control of major accident hazards. In each of these it is cast as the technocratic 'risk expert' largely providing advice and guidance, but on occasions directly intervening to ensure that safety standards are maintained. In order to give advice to LPAs the HSE has to estimate the level and spatial distribution of risk arising from potential accident events. It does this by using computer models to simulate accident events and estimate the likely consequences of these accidents on people and the probability of them taking place (HSE, 1989). The end products of the computer models are risk contours drawn around a hazardous site. Risk contours show how levels of estimated risk around a hazardous installation are distributed and decline with distance (see the example in Box 4.4). Once these risk contours are in place the HSE is able to use them to estimate the level of risk involved at particular proposed developments near to a hazardous site—or to estimate the level of risk that a new hazardous site will present to existing populations.

Rather than simply providing the LPA with the calculated risk statistic, the HSE judges the *significance* of the level of risk, basing this on two key factors; the calculated level of risk judged against specified threshold 'tolerability' criteria; and for development near to hazardous sites the type of development that is involved (industry, housing, community facilities etc.). Based on this judgement of significance, the HSE advises the LPA whether on safety grounds the proposed development should be allowed or refused. In practice the criteria for judging the significance of levels of risk are translated into inner, middle and outer zones specified around each site (see Box 4.4). Box 4.5 shows how different types of development are typically considered in relation to these zones. In the inner zone where the level of individual risk is highest only industry, warehousing and very limited housing development are normally recommended for construction and other types of development are recommended for refusal. In

BOX 4.5: A decision-making matrix used by the HSE

DEVELOPMENT CATEGORY	INNER ZONE	MIDDLE ZONE	OUTER ZONE
Industry, warehousing, farm buildings and housing developments involving < 10 dwellings	ACCEPT	ACCEPT	ACCEPT
Retail, community and leisure facilities, large industrial parks	MAYBE	MAYBE	ACCEPT
Housing developments > 10 dwellings and large hotels	REFUSE	MAYBE	ACCEPT
Developments involving especially vulnerable populations such as schools, hospitals, sheltered housing; developments involving more than 1000 people out of doors (theme parks, sports stadia)	REFUSE	MAYBE	MAYBE

the outer zone where the risk is lowest, all developments except those containing especially vulnerable populations are normally deemed acceptable. In the middle zone 'maybe' responses predominate. Here a more detailed assessment would be undertaken by the Major Hazards Assessment Unit.

The HSE thus has a well-developed approach to dealing with requests for advice. Whilst the assessment work they undertake is technically complex, the advice initially communicated to the LPA is very straightforward—recommending refusal or acceptance of the application—although in more complex situations more involved and detailed information is provided. The HSE has sought over the years to make sure that it is consulted on a consistent basis and that its advice is carefully considered. It has in particular been keen to be consulted early on in the formulation of local plans so that it can influence the more strategic land use decisions that are made around hazardous sites—all the more important since the move towards 'plan-led' planning following the Planning and Compensation Act 1991. In some cases a decision-matrix, such as shown in Box 4.4, has in effect been translated into zonings in local plans so that there is a strategic guide to where the HSE is likely to recommend refusal.

HSE advice is deliberately limited to considering only the safety implications of the proposed development (rather than any other planning considerations). The HSE attempts to provide advice consistently and on an 'objective' basis—although in practice, as with any risk assessment work, there is considerable qualitative judgement incorporated into both the estimation of risk levels and the interpretation of the results (HSE, 1999). As discussed in the next section, it is then in most situations up to the LPA to decide how to respond to the HSE advice and to determine the outcome of the planning or hazardous substances consent application.

2. LPAs: taking decisions

LPAs rarely contain risk 'experts'. Professional planners and elected planning committee members have to deal with a whole mass of 'land use' issues, which include meeting social and economic needs alongside protecting environmental quality and community safety. Some LPAs with concentrations of chemical and petrochemical sites will come up against major accident hazard issues on a regular basis and consequently develop some level of familiarity and understanding of risk and the approaches developed by the HSE for giving advice. The majority will have to contend with major hazard issues far less frequently and consequently can find it very difficult to deal with the safety implications of the decisions they have to take.

Partly for this reason, a minority of planners have argued that LPAs have an unnecessary and inappropriate role in dealing with major accident hazards, suggesting that instead the HSE as the expert body should take decisions about what 'is and isn't safe'. Such views were particularly prevalent when the introduction of the P(HS) legislation increased the responsibilities of LPAs in the early 1990s (Walker, 1994).

The institutional relationship between the HSE and LPAs has been debated throughout the development of the land use planning role. The policy position was clearly laid out by the Advisory Committee on Major Hazards in 1984:

> It has been suggested that when safety is involved the planning decision should in effect be taken by the HSE on the grounds that planning authorities are not experts in the assessment of risk. We have rejected this in the past and continue to do so [HSC, 1984].

As noted earlier, the standard advice provided by the HSE does not include any discussion of statistical estimates of risk, but provides an interpretation of the significance of risk levels and a recommendation on whether or not there are sufficient grounds for objecting to the planning application because of hazard concerns. The way in which such advice is dealt with by the LPA to an extent depends on the advice the HSE provides (Miller, 1994):

1. *HSE response of 'no objection on hazard grounds'*—where the HSE raise no objection it is almost universally the case that LPAs then consider safety

issues no further. It is very rare for LPAs to attempt to exercise a greater level of protection than recommended by the statutory expert body. This is in part at least because an applicant refused permission on hazard grounds would have a very good chance of winning an appeal against this decision where the HSE did not back up the LPA's concerns about safety. Where an appeal was made the LPA would need to employ consultants to give alternative expert advice, often involving considerable expense. In addition guidance from the DOE stated that LPAs 'should not substitute their own interpretations of risk assessments for those of the expert authorities' (DOE, 1994b).

Pressures on the LPA therefore have to be very great for them to act more cautiously than the HSE recommends—involving either high levels of local public concern or major implications for other development plans in the area. An example of the latter situation arose in Middlesborough where the LPA refused permission for a tank storing ammonium nitrate (which presents a toxic and explosive risk) even though the HSE considered the risks this presented to be acceptably small. The applicant then appealed, but failed to get the decision overturned. In this case the assessment of risk made by consultants employed by the council was accepted by the inquiry Inspector as superior to that of the HSE. This was however an exceptional rather than typical outcome, although Miller and Fricker (1993, 226) describe a similar example. The major inquiries into gas and petrochemical developments in Scotland in the early 1980s (Snowball and Macgill, 1984) were also forums for vigorous debate over safety and the rights of participation by the public at risk.

2. *HSE response 'advising refusal on hazard grounds'*—the HSE advises refusal of planning applications comparatively rarely but where it does it can present major dilemmas for planning authorities. Again there is pressure on LPAs to follow the HSE's advice. Circular 11/92 guides LPAs that if the HSE advises refusal of planning permission (or hazardous substances consent), this should not be overridden 'without the most careful consideration'. LPAs also have to inform the HSE if they are minded to go against its advice to refuse applications, with sufficient time to allow the HSE to consider whether or not to request the Secretary of State for the Environment to call in the application for his determination and effectively take the decision out of the LPA's hands.

Thus it is comparatively rare for LPAs to grant permission where the HSE has recommended refusal. Research has found that most cases where this has happened relate to the control of development in the vicinity of existing major hazard sites. Two predominant and interrelated reasons are generally given for this course of action; development need and risk comparisons. For development need the argument is made that the particular context of the development in terms of plans for economic regeneration, or its role in serving the needs of the local community, outweigh the gains to public safety that could be achieved by restraining development. Risk comparison arguments revolve around the significance of the risks when compared to either other types of everyday risk or the level of risk from the major accident hazard already tolerated by people already living in the local area (which the HSE sees as irrelevant to the advice it gives on new development proposals: HSE, 1989).

In a few LPAs such reasoning has been translated into explicit development plan policies. For example, in an area of St Helens where there had been a major demand for new housing development close to a hazardous site the development plan states that 'strict adherence to HSE guidance in all cases is not compatible with the aims of urban regeneration' (St Helens MBC, 1995, 212). Halton Borough Council, which covers the two towns of Widnes and Runcorn and a major concentration of chemical sites, stands out as having an often critical perspective on HSE advice and a clear set of principles on which to assess HSE risk assessments. Consultants are used to provide alternative assessments of risk and a set of local risk criteria have been developed to inform decision-making which are less stringent than those applied by the HSE. The blighting effect of following HSE advice has been a major concern for planners in Halton, who argue that a consequence of stopping new development in the area on hazard grounds would be 'widespread urban blight and degeneration' (Brough, 1993). In the mid-1980s Halton's Assistant Director of Planning[8] estimated that applying the HSE policy of development restraint in Halton would have resulted in a loss of urban land to the value of £6 million and a net job loss of over two thousand.

Despite there being a number of examples where LPAs have gone against HSE refusal advice, the call-in power has been used very little by the HSE. The first and most publicised case related to an application for a large addition to a housing estate (consisting of four hundred and fifty houses, shops and a school) in the vicinity of an ICI plant in Poulton-le-Fylde in 1981 (Lewis and Hayns, 1989). Here the inquiry Inspector decided in favour of the LPA concluding that the 'prudence' sought by the HSE was inappropriate. A second controversial case involved an application in 1993 for the conversion of an old canal-side warehouse into a hotel very close to the boundary of a chemical site in Accrington, Lancashire. Here the council members felt that the need for redevelopment of the warehouse as part of a general policy of rejuvenation along the canal was so strong that it outweighed safety concerns. The HSE in this case decided that the risk to the proposed occupants of the hotel was so high that they used their influence to ensure that the application was 'called in' and a public inquiry held. At this inquiry the applicants argued that the HSE assessment was overly theoretical and that a more pragmatic view, taking account of the good safety record of the firm and comparability of the level of risks with others such as death from road accidents, should be emphasised. The Inspector however concluded, in contrast to the Poulton case, that the HSE view should prevail, arguing that:

> given the careful analysis of risk factors . . . and the level of risk compared with the norm, there is no justifiable reason to disagree with the HSE assessment. On the contrary I believe that the level of risk at up to 300 chances per million, must in the context of considering a development proposal in the vicinity of a hazardous installation

[8] C. Brough, personal communication.

be taken very seriously. To assume a lower level arrived at more pragmatically would, in my view be irresponsible at this site.[9]

The pattern of responses to HSE advice discussed above indicates that it is very rare for safety issues to be discussed in any depth in local planning decisions. Typically it is not safety or levels of risk that are debated by planners and planning committees; at least implicitly, it is the expertise and credibility of the HSE and the threat of appeals or call-ins which are the key underlying factors.

3. Industry: producing risks

The traditional position for industry is to oppose regulatory intervention and 'interference' from government. To some extent the introduction of the hazardous substances consent system in 1992 produced such 'typical' reactions. For example, the Independent Tank Storage Association argued that the legislation was unnecessary, would pose an unreasonable administrative burden and allow inexpert local councillors to get involved in issues they did not understand (Walker, 1994). The deemed consent provisions of the hazardous substances legislation requiring the claiming of double current inventory levels were also the result of strong pressures applied from parts of industry concerned about protecting their operational flexibility. In many situations, where applying for new hazardous substances consents or plant extensions, industry adopts the 'expected' arguments emphasising the low levels of risk involved, the good track record of the chemical industry and the improbability of accidents arising.

However, it would be wrong to characterise industry as universally or typically opposed to regulation and playing down the significance of risks. Indeed, particularly where the control of development in the vicinity of hazardous sites is concerned, companies have realised that their interests lie in the application of tight planning controls. If development near to their sites is not restricted then the numbers of people at risk may increase, leading to tougher restraints being placed on any planned expansion of the hazardous site, and ultimately a greater number of people hurt or killed if an accident does take place (with greater financial and political implications). Such concerns about population accumulation have been evident in responses made by site operators to draft development plans and individual development proposals where substantial encroachment, or the precedent of encroachment, was seen to be taking place. For example, in Stoke on Trent, the operators of a hazardous site went to the lengths of employing risk assessment consultants to support their objection to the draft local plan allocation of land near to their site for residential development.

[9] Inspector's report: Application for change of use of warehouse to restaurant function rooms, Accrington Lancashire. PNW/5291/219/7 (25 March 1993).

Perhaps more fundamentally many of the site operators have been seeking to develop better relationships with their local communities, encouraging dialogue and co-operation with LPAs and the HSE, rather than confrontation. The significance of such shifts in encouraging voluntary risk reduction are discussed below.

4. The Local Public: taking risks

Members of the public in communities around existing or prospective hazardous sites are intended to be the main beneficiaries of the application of planning controls over industrial hazards. On occasions they become actively involved in the process of making decisions, particularly where major new hazardous developments are involved and there is substantial publicity in the local and sometimes national press. In such cases vociferous and well-informed opposition to developments can materialise. However, these are comparatively rare situations when considered in the context of the far more numerous developments proposed in the vicinity of existing sites and dealt with in a more mechanistic fashion by LPAs and with very little publicity or public involvement.

A recent research project provides some useful insights into the views of local people living near to hazardous sites about the full scope of planning intervention (Walker et al. 1998; Simmons and Walker 1999). This research utilised extended focus group discussions in communities around seven hazardous sites in order to explore perceptions of risks and attitudes to a range of policy issues. The application of planning controls was explored through the use of two hypothetical planning scenarios as part of the focus group discussions. These scenarios asked the participants to make and discuss decisions about the location of a new hazardous development and housing near to an existing site.

The discussion taking place in the focus groups clearly displayed the relevance and salience of planning control to members of the public. Participants were, without prompting, critical of the failures of planning decisions made in the past, leading to sites being located far too close to housing and other developments. As a consequence people were having to live with day-to-day nuisances from odour and perceived health risk, alongside worrying about the risks of a major accident. In this context there was widespread support for the application of planning controls.

Some participants adopted a distinctly moral stance, arguing that no people should have a risk imposed on them. They therefore opposed the construction of any housing where an accident could potentially cause harm. The majority were less dogmatic and accepted the need to exercise some form of compromise and balance between the needs for housing and other facilities and protecting public safety. A minority however challenged the need for any planning controls by arguing that people could decide for themselves where to live. Through relying on informed consent and the operation of market forces, the local authority could allow houses to be built anywhere, rather than having to prohibit building where the hazards were deemed to be too high. The following quotation from a focus group discussion is illustrative of this position

> *Female 4*: I'd allow all of the sites to be built on. . . I mean as me living in that sort of area I make a conscious decision to live there. Okay, again I'm young. I can move out if I want to. I know okay the foolproof computer can one day break down. I can be blown to smithereens. It's the choice I have. You have to give people that choice. . . . There's a risk everywhere so as long as people were aware of the risks I'd allow them to build on all of the sites [Langley, West Midlands, Group 5 (2)].

This reliance on individual 'informed consent' was strongly contested by others in the groups who argued that there was neither choice nor information necessarily available to people, and that relying upon choice was inequitable. The strongest and most repeated challenge made was that choice was not available to council tenants and people renting from housing associations, who often have to accept accommodation they are allocated.

> *Male 1*: You haven't got a choice.
> *Male 2*: It's a case of take it and like it and lump it. Shut your mouth and get on with it.
> *Male 1*: Me and my family were in bed and breakfast and then half-way housing and then this house come up and they said, well, take it.
> *Male 2*: That's right, you've got no choice anymore. [Fawley, Hampshire, Group 6 (2)]

Such discussion was interesting in the way that it mirrored debates over both the role for individual choice and government intervention in responses to other risks issues (for example, BSE and beef on the bone) and the balance between private and collective interests in land use planning. Throughout the groups however the majority position clearly favoured the protection of collective interests through the use of planning powers, and in other respects, such as the criteria used by the HSE to give advice to LPAs, the outcomes of the planning scenario discussions were broadly supportive of current policy.

Where attitudes were more critical was in the expectations of how decisions would in practice be made by LPAs, with a widespread feeling that public safety concerns would have little priority for local decision-makers. There was widespread cynicism about the motives of local authorities, with planning decisions identified as examples of where site operators and developers were in a powerful position to influence local authorities. Similarly whilst strong arguments were made in favour of the principle of public participation, there was little expectation that this would have any impact on decisions made. A typical viewpoint was as follows:

> *Female 5*: There not gonna listen to us are they.
> *Male 4*: We've not really got much of a say anyway, you know.
> *Female 5*: No.
> *Male 4:* You can air your views but I don't think they really take you seriously [Llandudno, North Wales, Group 2 (2)].

The new Seveso II Directive includes rights of information provision and participation in planning decisions for local people (Walker et al. 1999). Whilst these are important and help people become aware of the risks involved, there are clear problems of distrust and disempowerment which may limit their significance and utilisation. There are also questions of timing, with information not necessarily provided for members of the public when they can act upon it to make an input into planning decisions. To an extent the concerns expressed by local residents about the extent to which their views would in practice have influence on planning decisions is borne out by the DOE guidance that:

> the perception of risk should not be material to the consideration of the planning application unless the land-use consequences of such perceptions can be clearly demonstrated [DOE, 1994b].

Despite arguments that a number of legal cases have established a more important role for public perceptions, the expert opinion of the HSE and of other parties to decisions remains of primary importance. However, as discussed in the next section, there are informal and less explicit ways in which public opinion and community relations are in practice having an influence on land use conflicts.

BEYOND STATUTORY INTERVENTION

It was emphasised in earlier discussion that there are fundamental constraints on the scope for LPAs to influence or change what already exists. Planning powers over hazardous sites are almost entirely focused at the point of development decision—intervention can potentially take place on new site proposals but is far more problematical for existing installations. Conditions on new planning permissions[10] and hazardous substances consents provide the only means by which LPAs can formally influence the ongoing operation of plants and have been successfully used in some cases to reduce the risks from new proposed hazardous installations. However, such intervention by LPAs is not encouraged by the DOE with guidance on the use of conditions on consents directing that LPAs are 'not to pursue objectives more appropriate to health and safety legislation' (DOE, 1992b, 29). For existing sites it is not feasible to 'add in' conditions to established planning permissions, or to require risk reductions under the hazardous substances consent regulations (indeed as discussed earlier the deemed consent provisions allowed exactly the opposite!).

It is not only LPAs whose hands are to an extent tied in dealing with badly located hazardous sites. The HSE is also limited in its power to intervene. The HSE is responsible for the scrutiny of operational safety at hazardous installations, but can require only safety measures that are considered 'reasonably practicable' to be

[10] Or s. 106 planning obligations.

taken. Whilst this reduces the risks presented off-site to a 'residual level' (HSE, 1989), the HSE cannot force companies to adopt further risk reduction measures beyond those that are 'reasonably practicable' solely on the grounds of their location and proximity to population, or to prospective development sites.

For these reasons hazardous sites remain poorly located and conflicts appear between the need for development in the vicinity of existing sites and concerns over the safety of people to be based at these developments. The only formal response that can be made is to control development in the vicinity of sites with, in some situations, the blighting effects and lost development value referred to earlier. However, recent research has identified a growing trend towards informal and co-operative responses by industry to such situations with on-site risk reductions measures employed on a voluntary basis (Walker, 1999). These risk reductions have led to reductions in the size of consultation zones around hazardous sites and the alleviation of sometimes significant development restraints.

In each case identified risk reductions were made on a voluntary basis without the use of statutory powers by LPAs. Actions taken by companies included (i) cutting storage levels by the introduction of 'just-in-time' delivery systems, moving to on-site chemical production rather than storage, and the removal of surplus storage tanks; (ii) the installation of extra safety technology beyond that required under standard industry practice; and (iii) the movement of storage tanks away from site boundaries thereby also moving the consultation zone external to the plant. Several cases also involved companies agreeing formally to reduce the levels of storage they were permitted to hold under the hazardous substances consent regulations by seeking a variation to their consented inventories.

A number of factors explaining this move towards voluntary action by companies can be identified:

(i) *discussion and negotiation*—in most of the cases identified discussions and negotiations outside the formal planning process took place, usually involving the company, the LPA and the HSE. Whilst discussions outside formal application approval and plan making have always taken place, land use planning in general has shifted towards a greater use of bargaining and negotiation as a means of achieving desired planning outcomes (Healey et al. 1988). HSE also has become more open to dialogue outside formal LPA consultation procedures, realising the benefits that can be gained through pre-application and more strategic discussion.

(ii) *economic incentives*—in a number of cases economic factors were important to the risk reductions made. In one particularly problematical situation involving protracted negotiations and ministerial level representations, a company in the West Midlands whose consultation zone covered much of the area of an Urban Development Corporation (UDC) was given a £2.5 million repayable grant by the UDC to facilitate the introduction of a 'just-in-time' chlorine delivery system. The resulting decline in chlorine storage at the site more than halved the size of the consultation zone and enabled major flagship development projects in the UDC area to go ahead. In other cases companies were at least in part motivated by the commercial benefits they could gain from the development of land in their ownership. For example, a privatised water company storing chlorine at a water treatment works pursued a means of reducing inventory levels so that empty land close to the site owned by the company could be zoned for housing by the LPA and sold to generate profit.

(iii) *local 'political' factors*—a contributory factor stressed by many interviewees was the pressure on companies to be seen to be responding to local community concerns as transmitted either through representations from the LPA or in some cases through active media coverage and local opposition to the plant. Such sensitivity is symptomatic generally of the recent decline in public support for the chemical industry, particularly in the wake of the Bhopal accident (Jasanoff, 1994). This has prompted a range of community initiatives under the Chemical Industry Association's 'Responsible Care' programme—including the setting up of local public liaison committees, the holding of open days and the production of community newsletters (Chemical Industries Association, 1993, 1995; Tombs, 1993).

(iv) *auditing and voluntary compliance*—alongside local factors, general trends in industry towards more formally assessing and auditing environmental impacts and risks have more readily enabled site operators to identify opportunities for risk reduction (Orell and Cryan, 1987), sometimes in collaboration with regulatory agencies. The notion that industry may take action to address environmental impacts and risks on a voluntary basis through negotiation has also become more widely accepted with, for example, the Chemical Industries Association agreeing targets for emission reductions at a national level and some companies formulating site level environmental commitments and targets (Tombs, 1993).

(v) *regulatory avoidance*—site operators have also looked favourably upon risk reductions where they can lead to the lessening or avoidance of related 'regulatory burdens'. For example, by cutting inventory levels and reducing the size of consultation zones, the requirements on some hazardous sites operators to distribute information to the public and pay for the preparation of off-site emergency plans can also be reduced in scale (Walker et al. 1999). Indeed, by reducing inventories below key threshold levels, these requirements can be avoided altogether.

CONCLUSION

The UK now has, at face value, a mature and developed framework for addressing the threats posed by major accident hazards through the land use planning system. The UK's experience has enabled it to take the lead role in shaping the EC legislation before it was finalised. The Seveso II Directive has provided an opportunity to extend and tighten various aspects of the legislative framework, but has not fundamentally challenged existing UK practice. The potentially difficult relationship between the HSE and LPAs is now in a relatively settled state, benefiting from the evolution of consultative procedures and a greater understanding of respective roles—an understanding which, as Miller and Fricker (1993) noted, has had to transcend the largely divergent epistemologies of risk assessors and town planners. Tensions undoubtedly remain in defining the respective boundaries of the planning and health and safety systems and in the treatment of expert advice, but the lines of demarcation are now reasonably clear and agreed. To an extent these tensions are also being addressed by the trend towards co-operative and voluntary risk reductions by industry, circumventing the limitations of institutionalised coercive regulation. This is an important development fitting with wider developments in approaches to co-operative environmental governance (Glasbergen, 1998) and challenging conventional modes of analysis of corporate interests. As Pearce and Tombs (1996) suggest in relation to trends within the US chemical industry, this does not mean that site operators have been motivated by a 'new humanitarianism'; rather a recasting of what is seen as in their own economic and strategic interest has taken place, alongside pragmatic responses to a range of external social and political pressures.

Co-operative and informal responses to conflicts between hazardous installations and other existing or proposed land uses cannot, however, be seen as a panacea. In some circumstances what appears to be an absolute risk reduction may in fact amount to only a risk transfer (for example from on-site storage to greater inventories transported by road). There will also undoubtedly be many situations in which site operators will be unwilling or unable to make anything more than marginal reductions in risk levels. As Smith (1990) and Tombs (1993) both stress, the chemical and petrochemical industries wield considerable corporate power, and it would be naïve to suggest that commercial interests are now universally in line with or subservient to those of local communities.

The balance between different interests and stakeholders is a theme which runs through much of the discussion in this chapter. In some situations the balances are being made explicitly, for example, in planning inquiries where there is extensive debate of safety concerns and how they should weigh against development benefits. In other contexts the balances being made are less explicit. For example, the advice the HSE provides on surrounding development, whilst in some senses only technical in character, contains an implicit judgement that nearby industrial activities need not be constrained by safety concerns. Whilst this can be explained by the assumption that workers are fit and organised when compared to other categories of populations (and thus more able to respond to an accidental release in an effective manner), it also clearly provides a route for maintaining the overall priority to be given to employment generation and business development. The deemed consent provisions of the original P(HS) legislation also provide an example of where there were 'hidden' judgements being made about the balance between private and public interests, with risk intensification taken out of the control of local decision makers. The question of balance between interests also emerged from the analysis of the views of members of the public living near to hazardous sites. Whilst the principle of balancing between different planning considerations was generally accepted, how this balance should be achieved, the extent to which local people really have a voice in these decisions, how they obtain information and the extent to which it should impinge on the review of past as well as new decisions were more contested.

Looking to the future it is likely that such questions will be raised more often and in a greater range of contexts. This is for three main reasons. First, more sites are now to come within the remit of the P(HS) legislation, in some cases raising issues of safety in the vicinity of such sites for the first time. Secondly, there is also likely to be more pressure for development near to established hazardous sites, particularly in the older urban-industrial areas. The renewed focus on urban development and regeneration arising from sustainability concerns is emphasising the need for compact settlements and the use of brown field rather than green field land to accommodate projected new housing demand (Breheny and Hall, 1996). For this reason, land previously accepted as effectively sterilised by the presence of a hazardous site, or zoned for industrial or commercial development, may come under increasing pressure for residential use. Thirdly, the greater general sensitivity to risk across society, deepening distrust of expert reassurance and concerns about the equity and justice of risk distributions (Walker and Bickerstaff, 2000), is also likely to challenge the technocratic rationales on which the framework of major hazard control has been built. In this context it is all the more important that issues of regulatory implementation are addressed, and that opportunities for open debate, discussion and co-operation between stakeholders are developed.

5

Planning and Nature Conservation: Law in the Service of Biodiversity?

CHRISTOPHER RODGERS

THE THEORETICAL BASIS OF NATURE CONSERVATION LAW

THE PROTECTION OF wildlife habitats has been the focal point of nature conservation law in the UK since 1947, when the landmark recommendations made by the Wildlife Conservation Special Committee were accepted (Huxley Report, 1947). The National Parks and Access to the Countryside Act 1949 implemented the central recommendations of the Huxley Committee, and provided for the designation (based on scientific and ecological criteria) of Sites of Special Scientific Interest and Nature Reserves. Partly as a consequence of the need to implement the requirements of the Berne Convention and the EC Wild Birds Directive,[1] the domestic legislation was considerably strengthened in Part 2 of the Wildlife and Countryside Act 1981, and habitat protection in UK law is now based on the network of Sites of Special Scientific Interest (SSSIs) notified under the 1981 Act. The latest available statistics reveal that there are currently nine hundred and sixty-three notified SSSIs in Wales (Countryside Council for Wales, 1999) and four thousand and eighty-eight in England (English Nature, 2000).

The legal regime for protecting wildlife sites in the UK is founded in the general principles of property law. The earliest statutory measures in this field, such as the 1949 Act, were primarily based in planning law. The emergence of a discrete body of 'nature conservation law' is a development of more recent provenance, in which the passing of the Wildlife and Countryside Act 1981 is of central importance (Rodgers, 1996). The changes introduced in the Wildlife and Countryside Act 1981 placed greater emphasis on the role of the landowner in conservation law, and reinforced the key role he plays in delivering nature conservation in protected sites. The 'command and control' approach to environmental regulation is not appropriate in the law of nature conservation. The principal reason for the development of a distinctive approach in matters of nature conservation lies in the basic tenets of English property law. The starting point for any discussion of the rights and obligations of the property owner in

[1] Directive 79/409/EEC [1979] OJ L103/1.

English law is the well known maxim: *cuius est solum eius est usque ad coelum et ad inferos*. In English law the property owner owns everything to the centre of the earth and up to the limit of the sky, and enjoys absolute powers of enjoyment use and management of his land. The legal rights of the property owner are, in English law, theoretically absolute, and are not conditioned by any limitation based on notions of environmental stewardship. Although abrogated and statutorily modified in many situations (not least by the post-war planning legislation) the *cuius est* principle remains the starting point for a discussion of the theoretical basis of nature conservation law. It explains why the legal protection of SSSIs, and other wildlife sites, rests primarily upon the so-called 'voluntary' principle, *viz*. that the promotion of nature conservation requires the voluntary co-operation of landowners, farmers and other site owners to deliver sympathetic land management tailored to preserving the conservation interest in protected sites.

The law governing the protection of SSSIs has a number of distinctive features. The most fundamental is the regulatory dichotomy in the legal framework for controlling potentially damaging development in SSSIs. Both planning law and nature conservation law have a role to play. The regulatory framework is complicated by the fact that many damaging activities likely to injure the conservation interest in wildlife sites are not subject to planning control. This is particularly the case with agricultural and forestry operations, most of which do not constitute 'development' within the meaning of planning law,[2] and are not therefore subjected to the requirement of planning permission. Similarly, many agricultural and forestry operations which *do* require planning permission are granted automatic consent under the General Permitted Development Order.[3] Damaging development in these categories is subjected to a separate regulatory system applied by the Wildlife and Countryside Act 1981. The latter imposes a statutory consultation procedure before potentially damaging operations can be carried out in an SSSI, administered by the Nature Conservancy Council.[4] Where planning consent is required for a potentially damaging operation, on the other hand, special controls are applied through planning law. Statutory consultation requirements are imposed here by the General Permitted Development Order, which requires the planning authority to consult the Nature Conservancy Council and take its views on the development into account when making a decision on planning permission, and special principles of planning policy guidance are set out in Planning Policy Guidance Note 9 to assist in the decision making process (DOE, 1994e).

The existence of dual administrative consent procedures for operations in SSSIs complicates the administration of the law, and also explains a number of

[2] Ss. 55(2) (e) and (f) of the Town and Country Planning Act 1990.

[3] Sched. 2 Parts 6 and 7 to the Town and Country Planning (General Permitted Development) Order 1995 (SI 1995, No.418).

[4] English Nature, Scottish Natural Heritage or the Countryside Council for Wales, as the case may be (hereafter referred to collectively as 'the Nature Conservancy Council').

weaknesses in the legal framework for protecting wildlife sites. There is also a wider issue, concerning the participatory nature of land use regulation and the 'democratic deficit' in nature conservation law. An important facet of planning law is the introduction of a measure of democratic control of land use proposals and development. The introduction into UK planning law of the concept of environmental impact assessment has, in particular, introduced a strongly participatory ethos into the consideration of environmentally damaging development proposals. The legal regime for protecting wildlife sites is only partially based, however, on the 'participatory' planning model. The consultation procedures for damaging operations in SSSIs are set out in Part II of the Wildlife and Countryside Act 1981. Although considerably strengthened by measures introduced in the Countryside and Rights of Way Act 2000, the consultation process here remains a largely 'closed' one, involving only the Nature Conservancy Council and the landowner or occupier. The 1981 Act makes no provision for wider public participation in the evaluation of potentially damaging proposals. Where a proposal requires planning consent, on the other hand, the planning procedures for regulating development in SSSIs offer the possibility of wider public participation in decision-making on land use issues. Many development proposals in SSSIs and other protected sites will require EIA (Environmental Impact Assessment) before planning consent can be granted, and this offers greater scope for public participation in the decision-making process. The more restrictive consultation provisions in the Wildlife and Countryside Act reflect the fact that modern conservation law is ultimately grounded in notions of property law, and not the more participatory ethos introduced by the post-war planning legislation. The Countryside and Rights of Way Act 2000 has introduced a number of changes to nature conservation law to strengthen the legal protection of SSSIs, but this has been done by building on the established legal framework and does nothing to alter the basic legal structures or ethos of the 1981 Act.

SITES OF SPECIAL SCIENTIFIC INTEREST

1. Notifying sites of special scientific interest

The focus of the Huxley Report's recommendations, on which our modern SSSI system is based, was primarily scientific. SSSIs should be designated on the basis of scientific criteria where a site was of special scientific value because it hosted rare or endangered flora or fauna, or unusual geological features. This is reflected in section 28 of the Wildlife and Countryside Act 1981, which requires the relevant Nature Conservancy Council to notify land as an SSSI where it is of special interest by reason of any of its flora, fauna or geological or physiographical features. In principle, the SSSI series should comprehensively cover the major conservation interests in the UK, in terms of the best examples of the full range of natural and semi-natural ecosystems with their essential natural processes.

It should also encompass the full range of nationally and internationally important geological and physiographical sites, and include sites necessary to support viable populations of endangered and vulnerable species of flora and fauna (see generally DETR, 1998b, 16). The SSSI network of protected sites has also been the chosen medium for transposing into domestic law the UK's obligations under a variety of international treaties and EC Directives—principally the Wild Birds Directive,[5] the Habitats and Species Directive of 1992,[6] the Ramsar Convention[7] and the Berne Convention.[8]

The criteria for selecting SSSIs for formal notification are scientifically based, and the Nature Conservancy Council carries out site selection without formal public consultation prior to notification. A consultation process of limited scope is carried out following notification, for the purpose of confirming or modifying the notification, but this allows for little direct involvement by the public. The Wildlife and Countryside Act 1981 requires[9] the Nature Conservancy Council to serve the SSSI notification on the owners and occupiers of all land affected by that notification, on the local planning authority, and the Secretary of State. The notification must also be published in at least one newspaper circulating locally. The notification must specify not only the land subject to notification and the flora, fauna, geological or physiographical factors by reason of which the land is of special interest, but also any operations likely to damage the conservation interest. The carrying out of proscribed operations is subject to legal controls once the notification is made.[10] A period of at least three months following the formal site notification must be allowed for objections or representations to be made. The manner in which representations may be made, and the time scale for making them, are for the Nature Conservancy Council to decide and specify when making the SSSI notification.[11] The Nature Conservancy Council must confirm the notification within nine months.

This process is unusual in a number of respects. It primarily allows for objections by affected landowners or occupiers, and representations from the planning authority, but rarely generates wider public consultation on SSSI notifications. Moreover, the notification procedure—whereby the Nature Conservancy Council must consider representations before issuing confirmation (or modification) of the notification—falls short of conferring a formal right of appeal. Indeed, the current procedures involve the Nature Conservancy—the notifying body—in reconsidering the scientific basis of a notification it has itself

[5] Above n. 1.

[6] Directive 92/43/EEC [1992] OJ L206/7.

[7] Ramsar Convention on Wetlands of International Importance especially as Waterfowl Habitat (Cmnd. 6465, 1976) as amended by Protocol of 3 December 1982.

[8] Berne Convention on the Conservation of European Wildlife and Natural Habitats (Cmnd. 8738, 1979).

[9] S. 28(1) of the Wildlife and Countryside Act 1981, as amended by Sched. 9 to the Countryside and Rights of Way Act 2000.

[10] Under ss. 28C and 28D of *ibid.*

[11] S. 28(3) of *ibid.*

made. There is no right of appeal to an independent body, neither is there a right to have the notification reassessed periodically to ensure the site's conservation interest still merits its notification as an SSSI.[12]

This is to be contrasted with the arrangements in Scotland, where a right of appeal against notification exists to an independent committee, and where notifications can be periodically reviewed at the landowner's request. Provision is made under section 12 of the Natural Heritage (Scotland) Act 1991 for representations made by a landowner affected by an SSSI notification to be referred to an independent advisory committee. The advisory committee is independent of Scottish Natural Heritage (SNH), and its members must have appropriate scientific expertise and training. Its role is limited to considering the scientific basis for the notification, and it cannot (for example) consider the appropriateness or otherwise of the land use restrictions contained in the site notification. SNH must consider its recommendations when deciding whether to confirm or vary the initial notification of the SSSI. Its findings are not binding on SNH, however, though a decision to ratify which ignored the committee's clear recommendations may be open to judicial review in the courts.

The 1991 Act also gives the advisory committee a limited role in periodically reviewing SSSI notifications in Scotland. An affected landowner may make representations to SNH that the original grounds for notification of the SSSI have ceased to be valid. In this event the matter is referred to the advisory committee for its view. Normally, a landowner can require a review only after ten years, and thereafter at ten yearly intervals. The only exception is where he made relevant representation at the time of initial notification, in which case a reference can be made within the initial ten years following notification. The committee's views must be taken into account before SNH decides to vary or revoke the notification.

The introduction of an independent appeal procedure for England and Wales would undoubtedly introduce greater transparency into the operation of the notification provisions, and may provide a more effective mechanism for reconciling conflicts between property rights and the public interest in nature conservation. There is evidence that land managers and farmers, who resent interference with their managerial prerogative, poorly understand the SSSI notification provisions. Seventy per cent of the participants in a recent research survey reported that the SSSI notification provisions were poorly understood by farmers and landowners, and eighty-eight per cent favoured the introduction of an independent review procedure, possibly modelled on the Scottish system, for dealing with appeals (Rodgers and Bishop, 1998, chapter 2). Were a similar right of appeal to be introduced in England and Wales, however, there is a compelling case for saying that appeals should be limited (as in Scotland) to a consideration of the scientific basis for the notification. Given that the recent Consultation

[12] The Countryside and Rights of Way Act 2000 introduces a power for the Nature Conservancy Council to review SSSI notifications and de-notify sites where appropriate. This does not give the landowner a right to a periodic review of its status, however.

Paper on SSSI protection (DETR, 1998b, para. B.11) rejected proposals to introduce an appeal system in England and Wales based on the Scottish model, it is unlikely that the notification procedures will be amended in the foreseeable future to introduce either a wider right of appeal against notification or wider public consultation on notification proposals. The DETR's (1998b) Consultation Paper recognised the need to widen support for the designation of SSSIs, but the government intends to do so by asking the Nature Conservancy Councils themselves to devise new procedures for securing the widest possible support for their decisions 'both from the appropriate scientific communities, and from land managers and other local people' (DETR, 1998b, proposal 5, 19).

2. Nature conservation orders

Prior to the implementation of the Countryside and Rights of Way Act 2000, the basic legal framework for the protection of SSSIs was supplemented by provision for the making of nature conservation orders. These were made by the Secretary of State under section 29 of the 1981 Act, following consultation with the Nature Conservancy Council. Nature conservation orders could be made only on SSSI land which had flora or fauna, physiographical or geological features that were of national significance, or for the purpose of securing the survival in Great Britain of any kind of animal or plant or complying with international obligations. The DETR (1998b) Consultation Paper on the SSSI legislation proposed abolishing the distinction between SSSIs of national importance, to which section 29 formerly applied, and other SSSIs, on the basis that all SSSIs should be regarded as of national importance. This recommendation was implemented in the 2000 Act (DETR 1998b, B5 and Proposal 2).

In practice the power to make nature conservation orders (NCOs) was used to confer additional protection on sites subjected to threatened development, in order (for example) to give the Nature Conservancy Council greater time to negotiate a management agreement to protect the wildlife interest. Nature conservation orders were very sparingly used, however. In Wales there are only six extant orders (Countryside Council for Wales, 1999), and in England sixteen (of which four are 'special' NCOs, see below) (English Nature, 2000). Unlike the notification provisions for 'ordinary' SSSIs, the making of a nature conservation order obliged the Nature Conservancy Council to pay compensation to affected property owners for any depreciation in land values flowing from the additional restrictions on land use imposed by the order.

3. Managing SSSIs for nature conservation

Once a site has been notified, legal restrictions on the occupier's land use are applied to protect the site from unsympathetic development that might harm the conservation interest. Some are applied through planning law, others through nature conservation law. Different legal controls are applied to development or land use proposals of different types. If a land use proposal in an SSSI requires planning permission, the relevant controls are applied through planning law and planning procedures. If it does not require planning approval, the relevant controls are applied through nature conservation law, and this imposes consultation procedures and legal controls in many respects different from those familiar to planning lawyers.

As we have seen, because they are largely outside the scope of development control, damaging agricultural and forestry operations in SSSIs are subjected to a separate regulatory system by the Wildlife and Countryside Act 1981. This imposes a statutory consultation procedure that requires a landowner to give prior written notice to the Nature Conservancy Council if he wishes to carry out an operation that has been specified in the SSSI notification as potentially damaging to the nature conservation interest of the site.[13] Prior to changes introduced in the Countryside and Rights of Way Act 2000, there was then a four-month period during which it was a criminal offence for him to carry out the operations in question without operational consent from the Nature Conservancy. Once the four-month 'consultation' period had elapsed, however, he was entitled to carry them out without hindrance, whatever the implications for the nature conservation value of the site.[14] This curious provision was a compromise, intended to balance the competing interest of property rights and the conservation interest. It was intended to give the Nature Conservancy Council time to assess development proposals and negotiate a management agreement for the site, in order to protect its nature conservation value. The Countryside etc. Act 2000 considerably tightens the consent procedures for potentially damaging operations in SSSIs. The Nature Conservancy Council will henceforth have power to refuse consent for an indefinite period, subject to the landowner's right of appeal against a refusal (or against the imposition of conditions) to the Secretary of State.[15]

There is no requirement for a formal environmental impact assessment of potentially damaging agricultural or forestry operations under the 1981 Act. Moreover, many types of agricultural and forestry development which would otherwise require planning consent (for example the erection of buildings or private roads) are given automatic planning permission under the General Permitted Development Order 1995.[16] This means that there is no administrative consent procedure *applied by planning law* within which an environmental impact assessment of agricultural or forestry operations can be carried out. This was recognised as a gap in the UK's implementation regime for the 1985 Directive on Environmental Impact Assessment ('EIA').[17] Many forestry operations have now

[13] See s. 28 of the Wildlife and Countryside Act 1981, discussed further below.

[14] For judicial criticism of this 'toothless' regime see *Southern Water* v. *Nature Conservancy Council* [1992] 3 All ER 481, especially at 484 (Lord Mustill).

[15] S. 28E and 28F of the Wildlife and Countryside Act 1981, inserted by Sched. 9 to the Countryside etc Act 2000.

[16] Above n.3, Sched. 2 parts 6 and 7.

[17] Directive 85/337/EEC [1985] OJ L175/40.

been brought within the EIA regime, under amendments introduced to comply with the requirements of the 1997 EIA Directive.[18] This required Member States to institute development consent procedures for projects within the scope of EIA, if none existed in their domestic legal order. Instead of bringing forestry operations within full planning control, however, the necessary procedural changes have been made by creating a new consent procedure under which many types of forestry works now require prior consent from the Forestry Commissioners and the submission of an environmental statement. The new consent procedure applies to forestation, deforestation, forest road works and forest quarry works, and indicative thresholds have been laid down to identify forestry operations requiring EIA.[19]

No parallel provision has been made for EIA to be applied to agricultural operations that may damage an SSSI. Some additional types of agricultural development have been brought within the scope of EIA by the changes introduced following the 1997 EIA Directive, but these are all categories of operation which already constitute 'development' for the purposes of the planning legislation. The majority of agricultural operations still fall outside the scope of planning control, and are regulated instead under the consent procedures set out in the Wildlife and Countryside Act 1981. The conversion of previously uncultivated land to intensive agricultural use with greenhouses and buildings is now a Schedule 2 matter requiring screening for possible EIA, as is development involving intensive livestock rearing facilities above the indicative thresholds set out in the EIA regulations (DETR, 1999a, Annex A). Additionally, special rules apply to agricultural operations in sites that have also been designated under EC Wildlife Directives, in respect of which many rights conferred by the General Permitted Development Order are withdrawn. These are discussed below, but do not apply in 'ordinary' SSSIs.

In marked contrast to the consultation procedures applicable to planning applications, where a formal environmental impact assessment may be required, participation in the statutory 'consultation' for agricultural operations under the Wildlife and Countryside Act 1981 is limited solely to the Nature Conservancy Council and the landowner or occupier. There is no requirement for the Nature Conservancy Council to carry out an environmental assessment of the proposal's implications for the site, akin to that required under the latest EIA regulations.[20] There is no requirement for the landowner to produce an environmental statement, still less that his proposals be open to public scrutiny. Indeed, the 1981 Act merely requires him to notify the Nature Conservancy Council of the nature of the operation and the land on which he proposes to carry it out.[21] In many cases this may be insufficient to enable the Council to

[18] Directive 97/11/EEC [1997] OJ L73/5, amending Council Directive 85/337/EC.

[19] See the Environmental Impact Assessment (Forestry) (England and Wales) Regulations 1999 (SI 1999, No. 2228).

[20] Town and Country Planning (Environmental Impact Assessment) Regulations 1999 (SI 1999, No.293).

[21] S. 28E(1)(a) of the Wildlife and Countryside Act 1981, as amended.

carry out a proper assessment of the proposal's implications for the site (see Rodgers and Bishop, 1998, at paragraph 2.6 for criticism of the adequacy of the existing arrangements for notification and consultation on potentially damaging operations in SSSIs).

In practice, the Nature Conservancy Council's officers will carry out a risk assessment of individual proposals, encompassing both the likely damage to the conservation interest if they are carried out and the likelihood of the project going ahead. This may lead to an informally negotiated compromise whereby the project goes ahead in amended form, minimising the damage to the site. Or they may decide that no damage will ensue and give consent. Alternatively, the landowner may be offered a management agreement regulating his land use, and providing for sympathetic management in return for payment. Whichever outcome ensues, there is no provision for subjecting the exercise of administrative discretion to public scrutiny and possible challenge. Similarly, as there is no formal environmental assessment *per se*, there is no scope for public participation in the decision-making process. This is arguably inappropriate, as compensation paid to 'buy out' damaging land use proposals under a management agreement will be provided from public funds through the Nature Conservancy Council. Decisions on development proposals likely to damage wildlife sites should arguably be subject to public scrutiny, whether the proposals are for agricultural or forestry operations (and thus exempt from planning control) or for projects requiring planning permission—for example, housing or infrastructure projects.

Where development in an SSSI requires planning consent it will be subjected to wider scrutiny under the planning system. In the case of projects requiring planning permission, a statutory consultation requirement is imposed through the planning process, which requires the planning authority to consult the Nature Conservancy Council before granting planning consent for projects with implications for a notified SSSI (DOE, 1994e, paras. 30–32). The Nature Conservancy Council has power to designate a 'buffer zone' of up to two kilometres around a notified SSSI, and must be consulted on all planning applications within this extended consultation zone. Planning guidance indicates that the consultation area should normally not extend beyond 500 metres from the boundary of an SSSI, but may extend to the full two kilometres in the case of important sites, for example those designated in accordance with international treaty obligations or EC wildlife law (DOE, 1994e, para. 31). The planning authority must, moreover, consult the Nature Conservancy Council on all development likely to affect an SSSI, even if outside the boundaries of the notified consultation zone around the site (DOE, 1994e, para. 30). Under changes introduced by the 1999 EIA regulations, all development proposals affecting an SSSI, or within the consultation area around such a site (where one has been notified), must also be 'screened' to ascertain whether a full EIA should be carried out.[22] An EIA is likely to be required where development is in, or near

[22] All development within sensitive sites, as defined by reg 2 of the 1999 EIA Regulations (above n.20), is 'EIA development', and must accordingly be screened to ascertain whether it will have

to, such sites, especially if they are international wildlife sites designated for protection under European or international treaty obligations (DETR, 1999a, paras. 36–37).

Notwithstanding the EIA and consultation provisions, however, the conservation interest of the site is not given a special weight over other material planning considerations when deciding whether or not to grant planning permission. Provided the advice of the Nature Conservancy Council (and where relevant the environmental information provided by the EIA) is considered, and weighed alongside other material planning considerations, a decision to grant planning consent cannot be impugned even if it will have a seriously detrimental effects on the site.[23] This is viewed by many as a serious weakness in the legal order protecting SSSIs.

THE IMPACT OF EC ENVIRONMENTAL LAW

The European Community has adopted several measures requiring Member States to designate wildlife sites for protection, and to protect endangered or vulnerable species of bird or animal. Principal among these are the Wild Birds Directive[24] of 1979 and the Habitats Directive[25] of 1992. The scientific criteria to be applied by Member States when identifying and then designating sites are laid down in considerable detail in the EC Directives. Unlike the Wildlife and Countryside Act 1981, under which the selection criteria for SSSIs are widely drawn, and neutral in terms of the flora and fauna to be protected, the EC Directives are habitat- and species-specific. The types of habitat to be protected are specified in detail in the Annexes to the Habitats Directive, as are the vulnerable animal and bird species that the two Directives are aimed at protecting. The administrative procedures for identifying and designating these sites therefore require the application of advanced scientific knowledge and skills.

There is therefore little scope for public consultation on the identification and selection of candidate sites for legal protection. Such public consultation as has been provided for takes place once sites have been identified, and is limited to the merits of the inclusion (or non-inclusion) on the draft list of specific sites, and in particular their proposed boundaries. It is nevertheless important that the selection procedures adopted by Member States be open to public scrutiny, and the European Court of Justice has been active both in ensuring strict compliance with the Directives' requirements, and in limiting the administrative discretion available to Member States wishing to minimise the Directives' impact by side-stepping the designation process. The critical question here is usually whether

significant environmental impacts and require EIA. SSSIs and international wildlife sites are 'sensitive sites' for this purpose.

[23] See *R.* v. *Poole BC ex parte Beebee* [1991] JPL 643.

[24] Above n.1.

[25] Above n.6.

the omission of specific wildlife sites from the designation process is open to legal challenge, and whether pressure groups and the public can challenge the restrictive drawing of site boundaries.

1. The Wild Birds Directive

The Wild Birds Directive of 1979 places a general obligation[26] on Member States to take measures to maintain a sufficient diversity and area of habitats for the one hundred and seventy-five species of bird listed in Annex 1 to the Directive. Furthermore, article 4 of the Directive requires Member States to designate 'special protection areas' (SPAs) for the conservation of the vulnerable and endangered species listed in Annex 1 and all regularly occurring migratory species. One of the key provisions is Article 4(4), which requires Member States to take steps to avoid pollution or deterioration of the habitat in a special protection area, or disturbance of the birds within the area. All SPAs designated in the UK are already SSSIs, or will be notified as such under the 1981 Act prior to adoption under the Directive. The selection and designation of SPAs is an ongoing process. Wales currently has thirteen SPAs covering eightyfive thousand, nine hundred and eighty-two hectares (Countryside Council for Wales, 1999). In England there were, at 31 May 2000, in total eighty SPAs covering five hundred and nine thousand, nine hundred and sixty-four hectares (English Nature, 2000). The criteria for the selection of SPAs under the Directive are entirely scientific, and premised on the need to identify candidate sites hosting species listed in Annex 1 to the Directive which are resident or regularly occurring migratory species (for the guidelines used to identify and assess candidate SPAs in the UK see Joint Nature Conservation Committee, 1999).

The Wilds Birds Directive has been considered by the European Court on several occasions, in rulings with significant implications for the wider law of nature conservation. The case law has been primarily concerned with the duties of Member States when designating SPAs, and the drawing of the boundaries of protected sites. The Court's rulings have drastically limited the discretion available to Member States to omit wildlife sites from designation. They have also limited their ability to draw site boundaries restrictively, so as to minimise their potential impact on development proposals on adjacent land.

In R. v. *Secretary of State for the Environment ex parte RSPB*[27] the European Court of Justice ruled that the only criteria that could be used by Member States when designating SPAs, and defining their boundaries, are the ornithological criteria in the Directive. Economic or social reasons cannot be used to justify the exclusion of an area from a designated SPA if, applying the Directive's ornithological criteria, it should be included. Accordingly, the UK government's

[26] Art. 3, above n.1.
[27] (1997) 9 JEL 168.

decision to exclude the Lappel bank from the proposed Medway Estuary SPA because of the need for expansion of the Port of Sheerness was unlawful. The Court followed the earlier ruling in *Commission* v. *Spain*,[28] which had established that economic factors were not a relevant consideration when designating or fixing the boundaries of an SPA (in this case the Santona Marshes, an important wetland habitat for migratory wildfowl). In the earlier *Leybucht Dykes* case,[29] the German government had proposed to allow development in an SPA on the grounds of public health and safety. The Court ruled that a reduction in the area of a special protection area, once designated, could be allowed only on very narrow grounds (which included public safety or public health factors), and that works could not be permitted for economic or recreational reasons. In another of its recent rulings on the Birds Directive,[30] the ECJ has now held that Member States are obliged to classify as SPAs all sites which, applying the ornithological criteria in the Directive, appear to be the most suitable for the conservation of Annex 1 birds. This is important, as it enables pressure groups and others to challenge the omission of any key site meeting the Directive's criteria from a Member State's list of designated sites.[31] The obligation to designate all suitable areas cannot be avoided by taking alternative special nature conservation measures.

2. The Habitats and Species Directive

The objective of the 1992 Habitats and Species Directive is the creation of an ecological network of special areas of conservation, to be known as *Natura 2000*. Member States are required to contribute to the *Natura 2000* network by designating 'European Sites' in accordance with criteria set out in Article 4 and Annexes 1 and 2 to the Directive.[32] The network will consist of sites of three types: those which host the natural habitat types listed in Annex 1 to the Directive, those which comprise the habitats of the rare species listed in Annex 2 to the Directive, and Special Protection Areas designated under the Wild Birds Directive (discussed above). Each Member State is required to contribute to the creation of the *Natura 2000* network in proportion to the representation within its territory of the natural habitats and habitats of species specified in the Directive. The Directive divides the territory of the European Union into five

[28] Case C–355/90, [1993] ECR I–4221.

[29] Case C–57/89, *Commission* v. *Germany* [1991] ECR I–883.The immediate effect of the Leybucht Dykes decision was mitigated by Art. 4 of the 1992 Habitats Directive, which brings the law on development in SPAs into line with the much less restrictive provisions for special areas of conservation designated under the Habitats Directive.

[30] Case C–3/96, *Commission* v. *Netherlands* [1999] Env. LR 147.

[31] E.g., the Netherlands had classified 23 SPAs by the end of 1989 with a total area of 327,602 ha, whereas a study published by the International Council for Bird Preservation listed no fewer than 70 sites in the Netherlands covering 797,920 ha. as satisfying the Directive's ornithological criteria: *ibid.*, at para. 23 of the AG's Opinion.

[32] Above n.6, Art. 3.

bio-geographical regions for the purpose of assessing the ecological importance of proposed sites.[33] The UK lies in the Atlantic bio-geographical region.

When selecting sites for designation the overall objective of the Directive and *Natura 2000* must be the guiding criterion, *viz.* 'to enable the natural habitat types and the species habitats concerned to be maintained or, where appropriate, restored at a favourable conservation status in their natural range'.[34] Clearly, the identification and classification of possible sites requires the application of detailed scientific criteria and expertise, and was therefore the sole responsibility of the conservation agencies. The criteria applied in selecting UK sites for possible inclusion in *Natura 2000* were developed by the Joint Nature Conservation Committee, and closely follow and apply the scientific criteria in the Directive itself (Joint Nature Conservation Committee, 1995). A number of general principles were applied in the site selection process, reflecting the conclusions reached at the meeting of the Atlantic bio-geographical region held in Edinburgh in 1994 (Joint Nature Conservation Committee, 1995, Appendix 4). These included the presence of an identified priority habitat type or species, rarity of habitat type in the European context, and whether a high proportion of the extant habitat type species was present.

The draft list of candidate special areas of conservation in the UK has been amended on several occasions, having originally been published in March 1995. The implementation process for the Directive is complex, as is the timetable for implementation. To complete the process the European Commission is required to draw up two further lists—one of sites hosting priority species or habitats (identified by reference to criteria in Annexes 1 and 2 of the Directive), and another of 'Sites of Community Importance' under Annex 3. Not surprisingly, the legislative timetable is running behind schedule. Once the list of Sites of Community Importance has finally been agreed, however, following consultation between Member States and the Commission, the Directive requires Member States to designate the sites as 'special areas of conservation' as soon as possible, and by the end of six years at most.[35] In principle, therefore, the full list of special areas of conservation should be designated, and *Natura 2000* completed, by 5 June 2004.

3. Implementing the Habitats Directive

The Habitats Regulations[36] and Planning Policy Guidance Note 9 (DOE, 1994e) seek to transpose the Habitats Directive into UK law by building upon the

[33] Art. 1(c)(iii) of Directive 92/43/EEC. The areas are the Alpine, Atlantic, Continental, Macronesian and Mediterranean bio-geographic regions.

[34] Art. 3.1 of Directive 92/43/EEC, above n.6.

[35] *Ibid.*, Art. 4(4).

[36] Conservation (Natural Habitats &c.) Regulations 1994 (SI 1994, No. 2716), hereafter referred to as "the Habitats Regulations". Both the Habitats Regulations and PPG9 (Nature Conservation, 1994) are to be reviewed in the wake of the passage of the Countryside and Rights of Way Act 2000. Public consultation on proposed revisions to both is expected during 2001.

regulatory model developed in English law for protecting SSSIs. They make provision for the designation in the UK of 'European Sites'.[37] These sites comprise:

(i) special areas of conservation designated under the Directive,
(ii) sites of Community importance identified by the European Commission,
(iii) sites hosting a priority natural habitat type or priority species in respect of which consultation has been initiated between the UK government and the Commission, and
(iv) 'special protection areas' already designated under the Birds Directive.

The Habitats Directive requires Member States to ensure that any plan or project likely to have a significant effect on a site is subject to 'an appropriate assessment of its implications for the site in view of the sites conservation objectives'. The Directive places a general duty on Member States to take appropriate steps to avoid, in special areas of conservation, the deterioration of natural habitats as well as disturbance of the species for which the areas have been designated 'insofar as such disturbance could be significant in relation to the objectives of the Directive'.[38] Thus, after carrying out an assessment of a project's implications for a site, it can be authorised by the competent authorities only after they have ascertained that it will not adversely affect the integrity of the site concerned 'and, *if appropriate*, after having obtained the opinion of the general public'[39] (emphasis added).

The European Commission has recently published non-binding guidance on the content of these obligations for Member States (CEC, 2000). There is, as yet, little judicial guidance from either the European or domestic courts on the content of the duty to protect sites. However, the concept of site integrity has recently been considered in the Scottish courts, in relation to the grant of licences by the Secretary of State for Scotland to kill barnacle geese on Islay. The Court of Session held that the impact of the project under consideration must be considered in relation to its impact on the species not only in its natural range, but also in relation to the population in the special protection area itself. The decision to grant licences to destroy geese within the SPA was therefore open to challenge because of the impact on the bird population within the SPA (the relevant point of reference)—the fact that it would not threaten the overall population of barnacle geese in relation to the species overall was not relevant.[40]

The Directive gives Member States wide scope to decide the extent of public consultation in the environmental assessment process, and the criteria for assessing the 'appropriateness' of public consultation are left open. This is a major weakness in the legal order established by the Directive, and gives wide discretion to Member States' administrative bodies concerning the manner in which the environmental assessment of damaging proposals affecting European

[37] Conservation (Natural Habitats &c.) Regulations 1994 (SI 1994, No. 2716) reg.10.
[38] Art. 6.2 of Directive 92/43/EEC.
[39] *Ibid.*, Art. 6.3.
[40] *RSPB* v. *Secretary of State for Scotland*, [2000] Env.L.R. 168 (Court of Session).

sites is to be carried out. This has been exploited to the full in the procedures adopted for implementing the Directive in the UK. These simply adapt existing administrative consent procedures for regulating both development and agricultural activities, without significantly extending the scope for public participation or public scrutiny of administrative decision-making. A more purposive interpretation of the Directive's requirement for the environmental assessment of potentially damaging projects could have yielded considerable advances in increasing the transparency and openness to scrutiny of administrative decision-making—both by the nature conservation agencies and by those local planning authorities with responsibility for overseeing the management of European sites.

MANAGING EUROPEAN SITES FOR NATURE CONSERVATION

Rather than apply a bespoke and unified consent procedure for projects affecting European sites, the transposing regulations adapt the existing consultation mechanisms and administrative consent procedures applicable to 'ordinary' SSSIs. As we have seen, these are fragmentary and in some respects unsatisfactory. This means that the dichotomy between regulation via the planning process and regulation via provisions modelled on the Wildlife and Countryside Act 1981 also underpins the rules applicable in European sites. This has resulted in an unnecessary complication of the procedures for applying the environmental assessment of plans and projects required by the Directive in all European sites. A plan or project likely to significantly affect a European site may be subjected to an environmental assessment under either the EIA Directive or the Habitats Directive. Indeed, some projects may be subject to EIA under both, as the EIA requirements under the two Directives are not mutually exclusive and to some extent overlap. The scope of EIA under each Directive, and the Directives' respective potential for introducing greater public participation in land use planning, will be analysed separately.

1. Environmental impact assessment in European sites

British lawyers have struggled to assimilate the new culture of openness and participation in administrative decision-making following the adoption of the Environmental Impact Assessment Directive in 1985. The Directive's objective was to subject all private and public projects likely to have a significant effect on the environment to a process of environmental assessment before project approval is granted by the relevant public authorities.[41] Importantly, however, the Directive also requires Member States to introduce procedural rights to

[41] Art. 1(1) of Directive 85/337EEC.

public consultation and requires that appropriate information be provided in a comprehensible form to promote public awareness of environmental implications and the opportunity to express opinions, which must be taken into account at the decision stage.[42]

Environmental assessment under the EIA Directive is *project-based*, whereas environmental assessment under the Habitats Directive is *site-based*. Where a development is an infrastructure project requiring planning permission, and is also within Schedule 1 to the 1999 EIA regulations, an environmental assessment is mandatory, whereas for those types of development listed in Schedule 2 it is required only where the project is likely to have significant effects on the environment. Planning guidance indicates that an EIA would normally be required for any Schedule 2 project likely to have significant effects on the special character of an SSSI (DOE, 1994e, para. 39). Where sites are also designated for protection under the EC Wild Birds and Habitats Directives, however, an EIA must be carried out *in all cases*—including all proposed Schedule 2 projects—before planning permission can be granted.[43] In these cases the project will also be subject to a separate environmental assessment under the Habitats Regulations, although information collated for the purposes of the EIA can be used for the purposes of the (second) environmental assessment conducted under the Habitats Directive (DOE, 1994e, Annex C).

The ethos and focus of the environmental assessments under the EIA and Habitats Directives are somewhat different. The focus of the EIA Directive is on increased public participation and openness in decision-making, whereas the environmental assessment under the Habitats Directive is somewhat technocratic, requiring the application of scientific criteria to safeguard the conservation interest of high value nature conservation sites. Where an EIA is required under the 1999 regulations, an environmental statement must be submitted by the developer, and will be available for public scrutiny. There is no parallel requirement under the Habitats Directive, and the process is not premised on public participation in the same way. Moreover, the assessment criteria are much broader under the 1999 Regulations, whereas the criteria for granting consent under the Habitats Directive are tied closely to the concept of 'site integrity' and its protection. The introduction of environmental assessment as a procedural tool was intended to enable administrative bodies to improve the protection afforded to habitats and biodiversity by improving the awareness and assessment of ecological criteria. Unfortunately, the EIA Directive has failed to meet these expectations, a situation which has been attributed to the use by Member States' administrative bodies of their discretionary power to arrive at a political conclusion that an environmental impact assessment need not be made for Schedule 2 projects, even where they clearly affect a wildlife habitat (Krämer, 1997, 248). The introduction of a rather 'technocratic' form of

[42] Art. 1(1) of Directive 85/337EEC Arts. 6, 8 and 9.

[43] Reg. 48 of the Conservation (Natural Habitats etc) Regulation 1994, above n.36.

environmental assessment for wildlife sites by the Habitats Directive (see below) is unlikely to improve this situation, as decision-making here is based upon the application of scientific criteria, with little room for public participation.

The courts have, in the UK, always adopted a restrictive interpretation of the EIA Directive's requirements in cases involving wildlife habitats, and in so doing have undermined its effectiveness in opening decision-making to wider public scrutiny. They have consistently viewed the environmental assessment provisions in strictly procedural terms, instead of viewing EIA as a participatory process which involves the production of information and consultation intended to influence the decision-making process at every stage (Macrory, 1992). The courts have tended to view the environmental assessment process and the requirement for submission of an environmental statement as synonymous (see generally Stallworthy, 1998). Thus in *Beebee*,[44] Schiemann J adopted the restrictive view that the purpose of EIA is simply to bring to the local planning authority's attention all material relevant to making a decision. If the substance of the environmental information likely to emerge from the procedures under the 1999 Regulations was already in their possession, no formal environmental statement having being submitted, then no remedy would lie to quash a decision to grant planning consent. Similarly, in *Wychavon*[45] the court held that if all the relevant information was available to the planning authority, but not in the form of an environmental statement, then it would be an abuse of the court's discretion to grant a remedy. This ignores the wider question of public participation in the decision-making process, and the right to information implicit in the environmental assessment process itself. In a landmark decision, the House of Lords in *Berkeley* v. *Secretary of State*[46] has now ruled that the environmental statement must be an accessible document (or compilation of documents) provided by the developer. It is not possible to treat a disparate collection of documents (some not provided by the developer) as satisfying the Directive. This represents a considerable tightening of the procedural requirements for EIA upon which the courts will insist, and should foster greater public participation in the decision-making process by making environmental information more widely available. It remains to be seen what effect the decision will have on wider judicial attitudes to environmental assessment as a tool for promoting public participation in decision-making.

Restrictive judicial interpretation has undoubtedly had a limiting effect on the role of EIA in safeguarding designated wildlife sites. A recent example is provided by the decision in *World Wide Fund for Nature and RSPB* v. *Secretary of State for Scotland*.[47] WWF and RSPB applied for judicial review of the Highland Council's decision to grant planning permission for the replacement of the existing ski lift on Coire Cas, in the Cairngorms, with a funicular railway. The site

44 Above n.23.
45 *Wychavon DC* v. *Secretary of State ex. parte Velcourt* (1994) 6 JEL 351.
46 [2000] 3 All ER 897 (HL).
47 [1999] Env.L.R. 623. (Court of Session).

of the proposed railway was adjacent to both a Special Protection Area designated under the Wild Birds Directive, and a Special Area of Conservation designated under the Habitats Directive. Scottish Natural Heritage withdrew its objections after a planning agreement and visitor management plan were drawn up, which met its concerns for the protection of the nature conservation value of the two sites and (in its view) minimised the potential impact of the railway development. One of the issues concerned the Council's failure to make the final draft of the planning agreement and visitor management plan available for public consultation before the agreement was concluded and planning consent given. Previous drafts of both had been made available, but the final draft was not put out to consultation. The relevant regulations implementing the EIA Directive in Scotland[48] required further consultation only when the planning authority required an applicant to provide 'further information'. The final draft of the agreement was not considered to be further information in the required sense, and the court also held that (in any event) the project had moved beyond the consultation stage to the implementation phase. While the decision was doubtless predictable, given the extensive consultation which had taken place on the earlier drafts of the agreement, the supposed distinction between 'consultation' and 'implementation' phases in the environmental assessment process is open to question, and again belies a tendency by UK courts to over-emphasise the centrality of the environmental statement in the environmental assessment process. The process is intended to promote public participation and scrutiny of proposals at every stage of the decision-making process, and not simply on the environmental statement put forward by the developer. If followed, this approach could further limit public participation and scrutiny of development proposals (see Last, 1999).

The courts' approach to environmental assessment since its introduction in 1988 displays a traditional deference to administrative discretion and a tendency to a literal reading of domestic rules without reference to the objectives of the Directive (Alder, 1993). This narrow approach has been facilitated by the absence in English law of a notion of environmental rights. As Alder notes, the 'Directive has been absorbed into the traditional framework without apparent recognition of the distinctive nature of environmental concerns or of the participatory character of environmental assessment' (Alder, 1993, 219). A good illustration is provided by the first instance decision in the litigation[49] over the 'Lappel Bank' SPA in the Medway Estuary. Here it was held that whether a project fell within Schedule 1 or 2 of the EIA Regulations (and therefore required an environmental assessment) was exclusively a matter within the planning authority's competence to decide, and that the exercise of its discretionary decision-making power was open to challenge only under the *Wednesbury*[50] principle of unreasonableness. This is also a clear example (see Krämer, 1997) of the courts

[48] Environmental Assessment (Scotland) Regulations 1988 (SI 1988, No.1221), reg.22(1).
[49] *R.* v. *Swale BC ex parte RSPB* (1991) 3 JEL 135.
[50] *Associated Provincial Picture Houses* v. *Wednesbury Corporation* [1948] 1 KB 443.

sanctioning the use of administrative discretion to side-step the requirement for environmental assessment, even where a project will clearly impact adversely on a designated wildlife site. The use of EIA under the Environmental Assessment Directive has, therefore, had a limited impact in terms of promoting the protection of habitats and biodiversity.

2. Site-based environmental assessment and the Habitats Directive

1: Proposals requiring planning consent

The relative failure of project-based EIA to deliver the required level of protection for wildlife sites throws greater emphasis onto the need for the site-based assessment required by the Habitats Directive to be rigorously applied. Unfortunately, the procedures adopted in the UK give little cause for confidence—either that they will deliver an enhanced level of protection for these sites, or that they will promote greater public participation or transparency in the decision-making process. It is doubtful whether the rules introduced by the 1994 Regulations will prove workable or effective in practice. Neither do they satisfactorily provide for the public scrutiny of the public agencies' exercise of administrative discretion in dealing with them. The planning rules applicable to development proposals in a European site are, in principle, more stringent than those applicable in an ordinary SSSI. The combined effect of Part IV of the Conservation etc. Regulations 1994 and planning policy guidance in PPG 9 (DOE, 1994e) is to raise a presumption against development within a European site. Permitted development rights under the General Development Order, for example for agricultural and forestry operations, are also restricted in European sites. The same requirements are also applied by the 1994 Regulations to other regulatory authorisations or consents with implications for European sites, for example, the grant of discharge consents,[51] pollution authorisations[52] and consents for electricity works or pipelines.[53]

The regulations also require the competent authorities to review existing decisions and consents affecting a European site as soon as reasonably practicable after it is designated. Existing permissions and consents will be reviewed as if they have just been applied for. The authorities must undertake an assessment of the implications of an existing consent for the site's conservation objectives, applying the same criteria as those outlined above. They have power to modify, revoke or affirm any relevant permission, authorisation or consent as appropriate. This will prove a time-consuming task for the various governmental agencies with responsibility for granting regulatory authorisations, such as the Environment Agency, and for planning authorities reviewing planning consents.

[51] I.e. under the Water Resources Act 1991, by the Environment Agency.
[52] E.g. under Part 1 of the Environmental Protection Act 1990.
[53] E.g. under the Electricity Act 1989 or Water Industry Act 1991.

It may also prove very expensive, as compensation will be payable in respect of consents and authorisations withdrawn under the 1994 Regulations.

The Habitats Regulations[54] restrict the granting of planning permission, or any other regulatory consent, for any plan or project which is likely significantly to affect a special protection area or special area of conservation, and which is not directly connected with the management of the site. The 'competent authority' with responsibility for granting the consent (for example, the planning authority in the case of a planning application, or Environment Agency in the case of a discharge consent) must consult the Nature Conservancy Council before arriving at a decision to grant or refuse consent. If it considers that the proposed plan or project is likely to have a 'significant' effect on the site, after taking advice from the Nature Conservancy Council, it must itself carry out an environmental assessment of the project's implications for the site.[55] The project must be assessed in terms of its implications for the integrity of the site, judged by reference to the ecological criteria specified in the site notification.

Where a plan or project requires planning permission, the criteria by which the environmental assessment must be carried out are specified in greater detail in Planning Policy Guidance Note 9 (DOE, 1994e). These require the project's implications to be assessed in view of the site's conservation objectives, so as to ascertain whether it will prejudice the *integrity* of the site. *Site integrity* is the key concept applied by the regulations and PPG9. By this is meant 'the coherence of its ecological structure and function, across its whole area, that enables it to sustain the habitat and/or the levels of populations of the species for which it was classified' (DOE, 1994e, 17). The Nature Conservancy Council will advise on the technical aspects of the assessment, for example on the impact of land-take issues or hydrology. If the planning authority decides that the integrity of the site will be adversely affected it must not grant planning permission. Planning permission cannot be granted unless it is satisfied that there are no alternative solutions for the proposed development, for example alternative sites for the development, or in the case of major road or infrastructure projects, alternative routes that will entail reduced disturbance of the site.

If there is no alternative solution, permission cannot be granted unless the proposed development has to be carried out for imperative reasons of overriding public interest. The 1994 Regulations offer no definition of the 'overriding public interest' criterion, merely transposing in literal terms the phraseology of the Directive itself and reciting the fact that they may include considerations of a social or economic nature.[56] The overriding importance of the public interest in development must clearly be such, however, as to override the ecological importance of the designation—and the 1994 Regulations require the planning authority to consult with and consider the views of other competent authorities

[54] Regs. 48, 49 and 54, above n.36.
[55] *Ibid.*, reg 48(1).
[56] *Ibid.*, reg 49.

before agreeing to the development.[57] If the site hosts a 'priority' habitat or species type, the grounds on which consent can be granted are narrower. The only considerations of overriding public interest which can justify a grant of planning permission are those relating to public health or safety, or beneficial consequences of primary importance for the environment.[58] If there are other grounds, their status as imperative reasons must be confirmed by the European Commission in consultation with the government.

The 1994 Regulations[59] also prohibit the exercise of any permission granted by the General Permitted Development Order (the 'GDO') that would breach the requirements of the Habitats Directive. Any development authorised by the GDO which would have a significant effect on a European site must not be begun until the developer has received written notification of approval from the local planning authority. Landowners wishing to carry out improvements or development in or near a designated European site, on the assumption that it benefits from GDO approval (for example, for the erection of farm buildings under Schedule 2, Part 6, of the General Permitted Development Order 1995), should therefore first consult the local planning authority. If they do not, they could be the subject of enforcement proceedings. The planning authority will consult with the Nature Conservancy Council to ascertain whether the proposed development will adversely affect the integrity of the site. If in their view it will, then the development cannot be carried out without planning permission. The criteria for assessing the impact on the site, and on 'site integrity', will then be applied. In the context of a site-based environmental assessment on the subsequent planning application, the rules restricting the grant of planning consent unless there is an overriding public interest in development will also apply. These have already been discussed. Planning permission can be granted only in the limited circumstances provided for in the Habitats Regulations and PPG9.

2: Environmental assessment outside the planning system

As we have seen, many operations likely to damage a protected site will not require planning permission, for example a change in the use of existing buildings or land from a non-agricultural to an agricultural use, or from one type of agriculture to another, or an intensification of an existing agricultural land use. These are not 'development' within the meaning of the planning legislation. In these cases the legal controls required by the Habitats Directive are to be found in statutory consultation provisions laid down in the 1994 Habitats Regulations.[60] These mirror those for 'ordinary' SSSIs set out in section 28 of the Wildlife and Countryside Act 1981, but with significant additional restrictions

[57] *Ibid.*, reg. 52(4).
[58] *Ibid.*, reg. 49(2).
[59] *Ibid.*, regs. 60–63.
[60] *Ibid.*, reg. 19(1) and (2).

intended to guarantee the higher level of protection afforded to European sites under the Directive.[61] As with other SSSIs, a landowner or occupier must give written notice of his intention to carry out a potentially damaging operation, and there is then a four-month period for negotiation during which it is a criminal offence to carry it out without the Nature Conservancy's consent. There is no provision for public participation in the consultation process on applications for operational consent to damaging proposals. A number of additional controls are applied in European sites:

—any notification already in force under the 1981 Act has effect for the purpose of the 1994 Regulations, but the existing notification can be amended by the Nature Conservancy at any time. Notice of amendment must be given to the owner or occupier of the site, and takes effect only when notice has been given.[62] All European sites will already have been notified under the 1981 Act, and this provision allows for the renotification of sites with additional operations specified as potentially damaging to the conservation interest, where this is necessary to comply with the conservation objectives of the Directive. A renotification could also amend the existing SSSI notification under the 1981 Act as to the flora, fauna or physiographical/geological features by reason of which the site is of special interest, if this is necessary to secure compliance with the Habitats Directive.

—When the Nature Conservancy Council receives an application for operational consent which is likely to have a significant effect on a site, it must carry out an environmental assessment of its implications in view of the site's conservation objectives. They can consent to the operation only after having ascertained that it will not adversely affect the integrity of the site.[63] The environmental assessment is not open to public participation, neither is the project proponent obliged to produce an environmental statement. The exercise of the Nature Conservancy's administrative discretion is not, moreover, open to public scrutiny, and the environmental information on which the assessment is based is not publicly available. Indeed, there is no obligation on the agency even to give reasons for refusing consent. This is an 'environmental assessment' of a more restricted kind than that required on planning application.

—If, having been notified by the owner of his intention to carry out a potentially damaging operation, the Nature Conservancy considers there to be a risk that it will be carried out before the expiry of the four-month

[61] See especially, Art. 6.2 of Directive 92/43/EEC. The provisions discussed here are to be amended to bring them into line with the amendments to the regime for "ordinary" SSSIs made by the Countryside and Rights of Way Act 2000 (above n.15). In particular, the four month consultation period on notified operations will be removed to bring the consultation arrangements into line with the new s.28E to the 1981 Act. Until this has been done there will be discrepancies in the regimes for SSSSIs and European sites.

[62] Reg. 18 of SI 1994, No. 2716.

[63] Reg. 20(1)–(2) of *ibid*.

consultation period, it must take appropriate steps to notify the Secretary of State. This must be done at least one month before the expiry of the statutory four-month consultation period under the Regulations.[64] This is intended to enable the Secretary of State to make a Special Nature Conservation Order protecting the site. Once a Special Nature Conservation Order has been made, the legal prohibition on carrying out notified operations becomes indefinite. This procedure is open to the objection, however, that it presupposes that the Nature Conservancy can anticipate the landowner's actions and take steps before the site is damaged.

—Where a site is made subject to a Special Nature Conservation Order, the Nature Conservancy's ability to grant consent is further limited. It must carry out an environmental assessment of the plan or project proposed, and can give consent only if satisfied that the project will not adversely affect the integrity of the site. In this case, moreover, it must give reasons for refusing consent. The environmental assessment is still a 'closed' one, however, with no provision for public participation or public scrutiny. The provisions for Special Nature Conservation Orders mirror those for nature conservation orders in SSSIs, formerly contained in section 29 of the 1981 Act.

The landowner can require a reference to the Secretary of State in two situations—within two months of receiving the Nature Conservancy Council's notice of refusal of consent to the operation (i.e. if he wishes to challenge the decision), *or* within three months of an application being made if no notice of decision has been received within that time. There is no provision for the wider public to challenge a decision either to grant or refuse consent.

The circumstances in which the Secretary of State can override the Nature Conservancy's discretion are defined in terms that closely follow the criteria laid down in the Directive itself for safeguarding European sites. He can direct the Council to give consent to a potentially damaging operation only if he is both satisfied that there is no alternative solution, and that the plan or project must be carried out for 'imperative reasons of overriding public interest'. Where the site does not host a *priority* habitat or species type, the public interest consideration dictating consent *can* include reasons of an economic or social nature. Where, however, the site hosts a priority habitat or species type, the overriding reasons of public interest justifying consent are restricted to reasons relating to public health, public safety or 'beneficial consequences of primary importance to the environment'.[65] If a damaging operation is allowed on appeal to the Secretary of State he is under a duty to ensure that compensatory measures are taken maintain the overall coherence of the *Natura 2000* programme. The scope of this duty is not specified, but it could, clearly, encompass designating an alternative site with similar habitat characteristics to replace that whose conservation status has been compromised as a consequence of the consent.

[64] Reg. 20(4)–(5) of *ibid.*
[65] Reg. 24(5)–(6) of *ibid.*

CONCLUSION

The current structures of UK planning law are problematic when applied to the protection of wildlife sites and biodiversity. A clear example is provided by permitted development rights under the GDO, which create a particular problem in tailoring suitable measures to implement international treaty obligations to protect high nature-value sites. In the case of the EC Habitats Directive, in particular, it must be doubted whether the domestic procedures for subjecting GDO rights to environmental assessment will be effective in practice. They require a measure of goodwill from potential developers in notifying the relevant authorities before commencing projects which would otherwise have automatic GDO consent. They also presuppose that developers will be aware that the exercise of previously applicable GDO rights is now subject to prior verification before being exercised. The absence of suitable administrative consent procedures for evaluating the exercise of GDO rights was, at an early stage, identified as a weakness in the UK's implementation of the 1985 EIA Directive (Grant, 1991). The subjection of GDO rights in European wildlife sites to prior verification closes the 'gap' for the purposes of implementing the Habitats Directive, but the administrative consent procedures applied by the transposing regulations are cumbersome and may prove ineffective. It would surely have been preferable to have removed all GDO rights within designated European sites, rather than impose a cumbersome procedure for the prior assessment of projects or plans benefiting from GDO rights.

Planning law has an important part to play in protecting wildlife sites. However, the realisation of its full potential as a tool for promoting biodiversity will require the development of simplified administrative procedures for assessing development proposals in SSSIs and European wildlife sites. The legal framework for regulating land use in protected wildlife sites is currently fragmentary and unsatisfactory. This is a direct consequence of the exemption from planning control of most agricultural and forestry operations, and the consequent need for a separate consent procedure outside the planning system for these types of land use activity. Its failure to give adequate legal protection to our most important wildlife sites is evident from the statistics for damage to SSSIs produced annually by the regional Nature Conservancy Councils. A study by the National Audit Office found that between 1987 and 1993 over twenty per cent of SSSIs in England suffered loss or damage (National Audit Office, 1994). Sadly, the number of SSSIs suffering damage annually has remained at roughly this level, with English Nature reporting, for instance, that sixty-nine SSSIs suffered new damage in the year to 31 March 1998 (English Nature, 2000). A similar picture emerges in Wales, where overgrazing by livestock is perceived to be a particular problem, particularly in upland SSSIs (see Countryside Council for Wales, 1999).

Many of the obstacles to the efficient use of planning law to protect biodiversity could be removed with the adoption of a unified, and simplified, development consent procedure applied to all plans or projects affecting protected sites, whatever their nature. This would also make the full implementation of EC Wildlife Directives immeasurably easier. The challenge for reform would be to produce a system which can reconcile a number of seemingly irreconcilable interests and principles. The law must balance the promotion of greater public participation in official decision-making with both the protection of legitimate property rights and the need to ensure that the scientific expertise of the Nature Conservancy Council retains a central role in the management of wildlife sites. The current law, as we have seen, fails to deliver on a number of counts. Although planning law is a better vehicle for promoting public participation in land use planning, no special weight is currently given in planning law to the scientific expertise of the Nature Conservancy Council, when assessing applications for planning consent other than in European sites. On the other hand, the consultation arrangements for non-planning matters (such as agricultural operations) give the Nature Conservancy Council considerably greater control over land use matters, but provide for little public participation in decision-making. Any reformed administrative consent system for dealing with land use matters should be based on the 'participatory' planning law model, with safeguards to ensure that scientific expertise is brought to bear in tailoring appropriate land management regimes for protected wildlife sites. Devising a suitable legal framework within which this could be done will be challenging, and will require an explicit recognition that the promotion of nature conservation in the UK cannot be based solely on the voluntary principle, as hitherto.

6

Derelict and Despoiled Land—Problems and Potential

JOHN HANDLEY

STATING THE PROBLEM

THE TRANSITION FROM an agrarian to an industrial economy in the eighteenth century brought with it a fundamental change in the nature of land use. Rather than a resource to be husbanded so as to sustain productivity and fertility for future generations, land was, within the industrial economy, a commodity to be exploited for the mineral wealth beneath it and for accommodating the residues of industrial production and mineral extraction.

One of the consequences, as graphically expressed in a pioneering review of the problem by the Civic Trust, is derelict land:

> Where there's muck there's money, was the glib cliché that comforted our forebears' consciences. Today we are beginning to see that dirt, dereliction and decay are major obstacles to the future prosperity of our older industrial centres. We have undertaken to abate the pollution of the atmosphere in these 'black areas'. We have made up our minds progressively to purify their streams and rivers. But as yet we have made no systematic effort to tackle the mess that sullies the earth [Civic Trust, 1964].

Thirty years later a national MORI poll (sample: 2050 adults aged 15+) concluded that sixty-five per cent of people considered that derelict and despoiled land was still 'commonplace in most regions of Britain' and seventy-one per cent that 'derelict land reduces the quality of people's lives' through its social, economic and environmental impact (MORI, 1995). It was the blighting effect on the landscape that concerned people most, closely followed by rubbish dumping and, at lower intensity, a range of health concerns, especially for children.

It is interesting to compare perceptions of the general public with those of local authority professionals involved in land reclamation (see Box 6.1). Information on the principal adverse effects of dereliction, as perceived by the local authorities prior to reclamation, was taken from grant application forms, supplemented by discussion with local authority officers (Arup Economics and Planning, 1994). In common with the general public, the local authority officers saw the adverse effect on amenity (i.e. on the visual environment) as the most widespread negative influence of derelict land (eighty-one per cent of sites).

BOX 6.1: Adverse effects of dereliction as stated by local authorities

	Number of sites	*% of total*
Adverse impacts on amenity	130	81
Danger to the public	70	44
Dirt & pollution	50	31
Disincentive to investment	127	79
Depression of land values	90	56
Prevents access	25	16
Contamination	26	16
Fly tipping	27	17
TOTAL	160	—

Source: Arup Economics & Planning, 1994. *N.B. Categories are not mutually exclusive*

However, they gave much greater prominence to the disincentive to investment (seventy-nine per cent of sites). This may reflect the intended 'hard' end-use for housing, industry, commerce etc of the sites in this particular survey.

Some indication of the prevalence of environmental hazards may be obtained from a survey in England and Wales of fifty-two 'wasteland' sites with potential for community uses (Handley, 1996, 12) using a standard survey methodology proposed by Land Capability Consultants (LCC, 1989). On the basis of this survey (see Box 6.2) the concerns of the public are well founded, especially the tendency for damaged and neglected land to attract bad neighbour uses (see also Box 6.3).

Dereliction arises from the 'failure' of the development process in the recycling of developed sites because development costs exceed the potential value of completed development (Arup Economics and Planning, 1995). A variety of factors are at work here but, at its most basic, the economics of property development can be summarised as:

development cost < value = (re)development
development cost > value = no development

Government has used a variety of instruments to overcome the disincentive to development and promote land recycling; the most effective of these historically was the Derelict Land Grant (DOE, 1990).

At first, Derelict Land Grant[1] was made available only in selected areas but in 1966 the Local Government Act extended grant coverage throughout England. Derelict land is defined as 'land so damaged by industrial or other development that it is incapable of beneficial use without treatment'. Although non-statutory, this definition has stood the test of time and has been widely accepted and used

[1] Derelict Land Grant was subsumed within English Partnership's Investment Fund in 1994; comparable grant regimes exist in Wales and Scotland.

BOX 6.2: Frequency of negative impacts of wasteland on 52 prominent sites in England and Wales

Site characteristic	Negative Impact (%)		
	YES	NO	UNKNOWN
Contaminated land[1]	53	26	21
Groundwater pollution	49	24	27
Airborne pollution	24	37	39
Instability[2]	60	18	22
Safety[3]	79	9	12
Bad neighbour uses[4]	93	5	2

Notes

1 Land so toxic as to inhibit natural colonisation

2 Risk of slumping, subsidence, accelerated erosion etc.

3 Presence of uncapped mine shafts, deep water, unfenced culverts, railway lines etc.

4 Motor cycle scrambling, 'joy' riding, fly tipping, burning stolen cars, wire stripping, drug abuse, criminal activity etc.

by both central and local government (Kivell, 1987); most recently it has been endorsed by the Report of the Urban Task Force (Urban Task Force, 1999).

It should however be recognised that derelict land is only one category of land in and around urban areas which is of environmental concern, other categories include:

Operational land: land in active use (especially for mineral working, waste disposal and larger scale industry) which may not be realising its full potential and be detrimental to the environment.

Vacant land: land on which some previous productive use has ceased for a significant period of time.

Contaminated land: land which represents an actual or potential hazard to health or the environment as a result of current or previous use.

Operational land can have a very significant impact on the environment, particularly when uses include mineral working, waste disposal and heavy industry. Mineral working is especially important as about half the dereliction in the Derelict Land Survey was originally from this source. Vacant land may or may not have been developed in the past and only part of previously developed land is derelict; it was quantified for the first time in 1990 in a National Sample Survey of Vacant Land in Urban Areas in England known as 'VLS' 90' (DOE, 1993b). The extent of contaminated land depends very much on how the definition is interpreted; current estimates range from fifty thousand to two hundred thousand hectares (RCEP, 1996). The Royal Commission estimates that 60 per cent of derelict land is also contaminated. The relationship between vacant, derelict and contaminated land is illustrated in Box 6.4.

BOX 6.3: Public perception of the ten most detrimental features of derelict land to quality of life

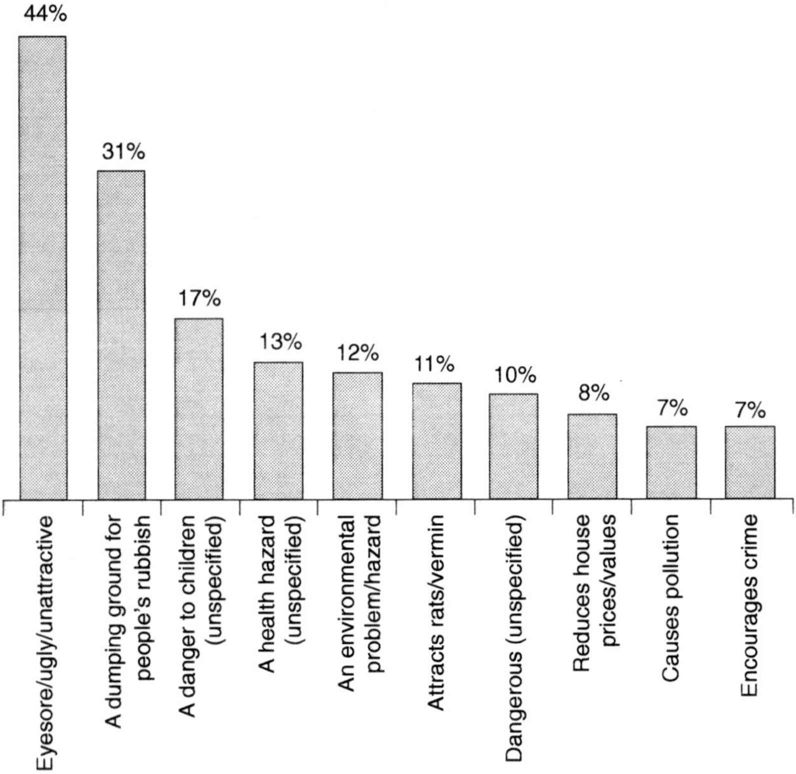

Source: MORI, 1995.

This chapter will focus on derelict land but needs to take account of all damaged and neglected land; the 'urban industrial wasteland' of Burt and Bradshaw, 1986. It will explore the origin and nature of derelict and despoiled land, including contaminated land. Is this an inevitable by-product of an industrial society or can the planning system stem the flow or redirect it to positive ends? In fact, when it comes to land recycling, we shall find that 'brown field land' is itself a contested resource with competing claims between housing, industry and commercial development on the one hand ('hard' end-use) and agriculture, forestry, nature conservation and recreation on the other ('soft' end-use). The situation is further complicated on contaminated land where remediation to make good inherited pollution may put at risk the environmental capital (amenity, landscape and biodiversity) that has accrued through time. Realising the full potential of derelict and despoiled land and reconciling competing claims upon it

BOX 6.4: The relationship between vacant, derelict and contaminated land

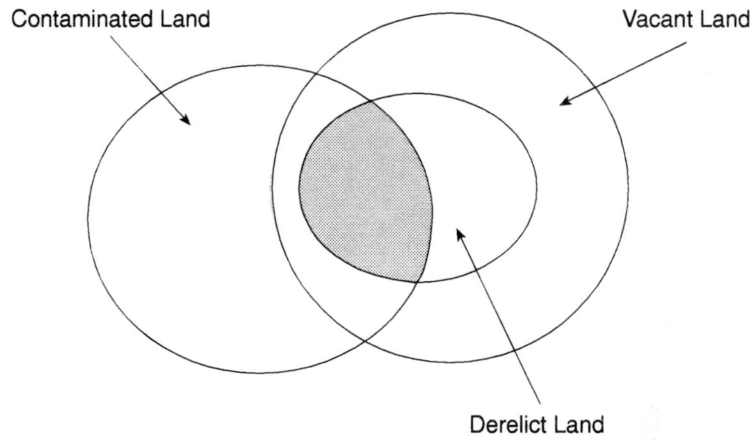

Source: Reisen, 1998.

demand a strategic approach. The development of such strategies within the changing context of national, regional and local governance will be briefly reviewed.

THE ORIGINS AND CHANGING NATURE OF DERELICT LAND

Derelict land, as defined above, includes:

—spoil heaps;
—excavations and pits;
—derelict railway land;
—military dereliction;
—mining subsidence;
—general industrial dereliction.

As implied by the definition, the condition of derelict land is such as to demand intervention. Whether that intervention is justified depends partly on the cost of treatment in relation to realisable value (Gilchrist, 1991) and partly on judgement about the extent to which natural recovery has healed the scars of development and begun to transform the site into an environmental asset (DOE, 1995b).

Periodic surveys of derelict land have been carried out in England on a more or less consistent basis from 1974 to 1993. Surveys have also been carried out in Wales and Scotland, but not in Northern Ireland. The results of the 1993 survey in England are shown in Box 6.5.

BOX 6.5: The amount of derelict land and the area justifying reclamation by type of dereliction—1 April 1993.

	Derelict Land		*Area Justifying Reclamation*		*% Justifying Reclamation*
	Hectares	*%*	*Hectares*	*%*	
Spoil Heaps	9,191	23%	7,382	21%	80%
Colliery Spoil Heaps	4,109	10%	3,904	11%	95%
Metalliferous Spoil Heaps	3,003	8%	1,738	5%	58%
Other Spoil Heaps	2,079	5%	1,740	5%	84%
Excavations & Pits	5,807	15%	4,599	13%	79%
Military Dereliction	3,275	8%	3,060	9%	93%
Derelict Railway Land	5,615	14%	4,749	14%	85%
Mining Subsidence	674	2%	653	2%	97%
General Industrial Dereliction	9,749	25%	9,313	27%	96%
Other Forms of Dereliction	5,289	13%	4,809	14%	91%
TOTAL	39,600	100%	34,566	100%	87%

Source: DOE, 1995b.

General industrial dereliction was the largest category in DLS93 (twenty-five per cent) closely followed by derelict spoil heaps (twenty-three per cent). The greater part of industrial dereliction (ninety-six per cent) and colliery spoil heaps (ninety-five per cent) was reported as justifying reclamation. By contrast only fifty-eight per cent of land covered by metalliferous spoil heaps was said to justify reclamation; this category includes the often picturesque former tin mining landscapes of Cornwall, one of which, at Kerrier is designated as a 'World Heritage Site'.

Despite the availability of Derelict Land Grant to facilitate reclamation, successive surveys have shown that, in England, the stock of derelict land justifying treatment has remained stubbornly constant at around thirty-nine thousand, four hundred hectares, plus or minus five hundred and seventy-nine hectares during the latter part of the twentieth century (see Box 6.6).

The picture in Scotland and Wales, where the attack on derelict land was spearheaded by National Development Agencies, is rather different, with significant reductions in the total stock being achieved over the same period (Wales more than twenty-five percent, Scotland more than forty-five per cent: see Handley, 1996). Despite calls for a national agency for England as early as 1969 (Hunt Report, 1969) it was not until 1994 that the Urban Regeneration Agency (English Partnerships) was established in England, and subsequently, in 1997, Development Agencies for the English Regions were created.

During the period covered by the surveys there was extensive land reclamation activity in England and, latterly, investment via Derelict Land Grant exceeded £100 million *per annum* (Arup Economics and Planning, 1995). It is therefore surprising that the stock of derelict land justifying treatment has remained so constant. The explanation can be found in Box 6.7, which shows the dynamics of land reclamation from 1988–93; here 'new dereliction' arising is estimated as a residual by combining land reclaimed over the period with net-change in the stock.

We can draw three conclusions from this:

1. The rate of land reclamation more or less equals the rate at which new dereliction is created;
2. There must be significant turnover within the stock of derelict land; and
3. The make-up of derelict land will change through time.

Because of problems of compatibility between data sets the long-term comparison (1974–93) must be restricted to four categories:

—spoil heaps;
—excavations and pits;
—military dereliction;
—other forms of dereliction.

Data from successive surveys over this period are presented in Box 6.8.

BOX 6.6: The changing stock of derelict land in England 1974–93.

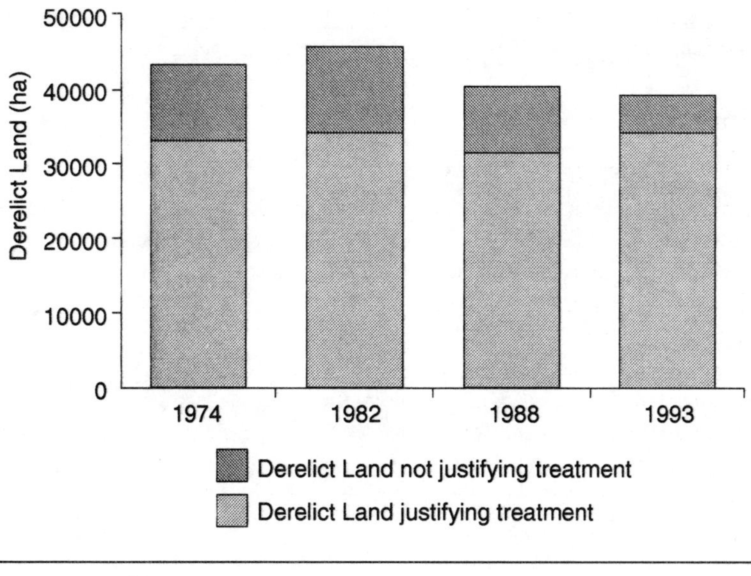

Source: DOE, 1995b.

BOX 6.7: The dynamics of derelict land 1988–1993 (area in hectares)

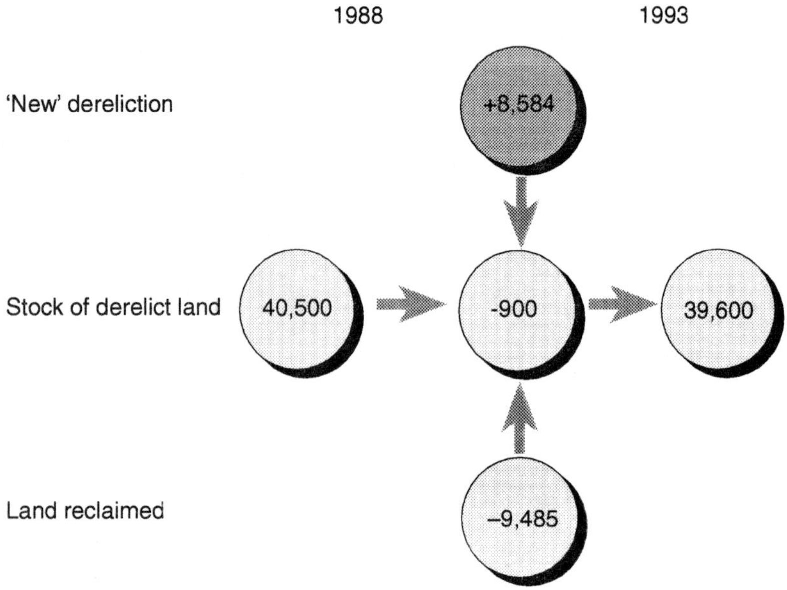

Source: DOE, 1995b.

BOX 6.8: The changing spectrum of derelict land 1974–93

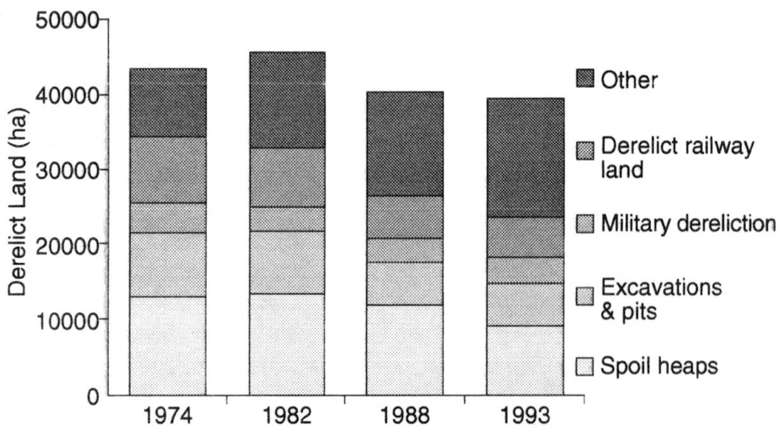

Source: DOE, 1995b.

The following trends are evident:

i. a steady decline in the extent of spoil heaps, excavations and pits from 1974–93;
ii. a reduction in military (mostly wartime) dereliction until 1988 with a sharp upturn to 1993;
iii. a progressive reduction in derelict railway land from 1974–93;
iv. a marked increase in 'other forms of dereliction' from 1974–93 with 'general industrial dereliction' a key component from 1988 onwards.

The changing spectrum of derelict land reflects deep-seated economic changes within society during the latter part of the twentieth century:

—the closure of traditional heavy industries as we move into a more knowledge based post-industrial era;
—the privatisation of public utilities which may have further accelerated the demolition of old industrial stock;
—the 'peace dividend' which, for the first time since the second world war, is contributing to an increase in military dereliction.

It is important to consider whether these trends have continued through the 1990s and into the twenty-first century. The evidence should be provided by the National Land Use Database (NLUD) which in 1999 superseded the Derelict Land Survey (DLS). NLUD was set up at the request of the Urban Task Force to provide an inventory of vacant and derelict sites, and vacant buildings in England. The primary objective is to quantify the scale of the land resource which may be available to meet the government's aspirational target that sixty per cent of future housing demand in England should be met on recycled land (Urban Task Force, 1999). The acknowledged strengths and weakness of the NLUD are set out in Box 6.9.

The NLUD survey results indicated a reasonable match between the estimate for previously developed vacant land of sixteen thousand, two hundred hectares and comparable vacant land (in urban areas only) in VLS'90 (about fifteen thousand hectares), notwithstanding complications about vacant land dynamics and the extent of vacant land in rural areas. However, the estimate for Derelict Land, using the same definition as for previous surveys, implied a significant reduction from thirty-four and a half thousand hectares in 1993 (DLS) to seventeen thousand, three hundred hectares in 1999 (NLUD). Work is continuing to clarify whether this is a real or apparent reduction. A preliminary comparison of the two data sets by DETR suggests an apparent absence from the NLUD results of a large amount of 'spoil heaps, excavations and pits, railways and military land'. It seems that the local authority surveyors may have excluded such sites from their NLUD return because of their very limited development potential (Urban Task Force, 1999).

Notwithstanding the statistical debate, it seems likely that the economic trends identified above will have continued into the twenty-first century and

BOX 6.9: The National Land Use Database: strengths and weaknesses of data collection approach

Strengths

Based upon a very large sample of planning authorities, sites and buildings

Tight specification will have helped ensure consistent use of definitions and collection methods.

Teams of surveyors working alongside local authorities will have improved consistency of approach

Independent validation of results.

Combined expertise of DETR, Local Government Management Board, English Partnerships and Ordnance Survey co-ordinating the exercise.

Work on supply availability is being counter-balanced by detailed demand studies.

Weaknesses

It was a time-limited exercise.

A national survey to compile consistent statistics will not cover the variety of local circumstances that can be addressed in a locally defined urban capacity study.

Given the difficulties of data collection over a short period of time, it is likely to under-estimate the potential contribution from the existing stock of buildings.

It is a snapshot only of land supply which does not take into account the dynamics of brownfield development.

There are some signs of inconsistencies with other data sources, for example the Derelict Land Survey.

There is likely to have been serious under-counting of small infill sites which, for example, form a very significant percentage of the recycled land potential in London.

Windfall projections of local planning authorities over the next few years provide only a very limited basis for considering land availability over a 25 year period.

Source: Urban Task Force, 1999.

informal discussion with key industrial sectors, for example the Chemical Industries Association, indicates substantial 'latent dereliction' within their extensive land holdings. Moreover, as the potential for industrial obsolescence is further accentuated by the pace of technological change in a globalised economy, we should perhaps begin to think of 'dereliction' *as a process to be managed rather than a problem to be solved.*

DERELICT LAND PREVENTION AND THE PLANNING SYSTEM

For environmental planning to be effective in tackling dereliction appropriate measures need to be in place which can tackle both the underlying stock of derelict land and the continuing flow of sites into dereliction. Clearing the stock is considered in the next two sections; here we are concerned with derelict land prevention. The case for action was clearly set out by the Department of the Environment in 1994 when specifying research into the problem:

> The scale of the derelict land problem and the cost of the DLG programme have prompted interest in finding mechanisms to prevent dereliction from arising in the first place. The National Audit Office 1988 report 'Department of the Environment: Derelict Land Grant' found that the closure of major industrial activities other than mineral operations (e.g. large factories, steel works and chemical plant) could be a significant cause of dereliction, and questioned the justification that these have to be restored by the public purse rather than at the owners' or operators' expense [Arup Economics, 1995, 49].

This reflected a new policy emphasis in the Environment White Paper (HMG, 1990), which states firmly that, on the basis of the polluter pays principle, 'those causing contamination and dereliction should pay for putting it right. Placing more responsibility on those who cause damage could reduce the amount of derelict land more quickly, and make it available for development or other use to benefit the community'. Selman (1992) has suggested that, in general terms, a range of mechanisms (see Box 6.10) may be available to the environmental planner. He argues that we must select from the options available and that the art of skilful planning 'lies in the imaginative combination of legal remedies, negotiation, mediation and persuasion'.

In preventing dereliction the approach in the White Paper signals a significant shift in the existing principles of development rights and opens the way for a more interventionist approach. Indeed the range of Government options included consideration of the scope for market-based instruments to discourage those who currently hold land derelict and vacant for long periods without seeking to recycle it for beneficial uses (HMG 1990, 93). It is in this area that the strongest form of intervention, compulsory purchase, has been used by the Development Corporations, not to pre-empt dereliction, but to acquire derelict land from recalcitrant owners for the purposes of urban regeneration, most notably through 'vesting orders' in the London and Liverpool docklands.

By contrast, less heavy-handed forms of environmental planning have been remarkably effective in both reducing the stock of derelict land and pre-empting new dereliction within the minerals industry. The role of the planning system in England in achieving reclamation of mineral workings has been reviewed by Simpson (1998). He emphasises the seminal role of the Committee on Mineral Planning Control (Stevens Committee, 1976), which identified the

BOX 6.10: Spectrum of community powers over the use of land

Education of landowners: provision of information and advice

Financial incentives and penalties (especially taxes and grants)

Restraints on undesirable uses: Planning consents, site licences etc

Removal of property rights on the open market

Removal of property rights by compulsion (compulsory purchase and nationalisation)

Source: after Selman. 1992.

following measures for preventing dereliction and securing an effective after-use of land:

1. the need for local authorities to have access to a sufficient number of properly qualified staff capable of assessing the impact of mineral working, competent on land restoration and able to agree mineral working and restoration programmes and to monitor their progress;
2. amendments to planning law enabling the review of planning conditions and to improve their enforcement;
3. the inclusion of strategies for the after-use of areas of development plans;
4. an increased use of progressive restoration where feasible;
5. a greater readiness of operators to accept planning for restoration as an integral part of mineral working; and
6. empowering planning authorities to impose conditions requiring after care.

These recommendations were progressively incorporated into law through the Town and Country (Minerals) Act 1981, the Town and Country Planning Act 1990, the Planning and Compensation Act 1991 and the Environment Act 1995. This legislation is interpreted and translated into practice through a comprehensive set of Minerals Planning Guidance Notes (MPGs). Since 1974 some sixty-eight thousand hectares of mineral workings have been restored and the proportion of sites covered by aftercare conditions has increased from sixteen per cent in 1988 to thirty-three per cent in 1994 (DOE, 1996d).

The reduction in both the absolute amount and relative quantity of dereliction due to mineral working (see Box 6.7) is due not simply to a progressive tightening of planning control but to an effective partnership between government, local planning authorities, industry and other agencies. This is especially evident in research and development programmes to improve the effectiveness of restoration where industry has been a willing partner or research sponsor in supporting innovation (see for example Environmental Advisory Unit, 1988; Giles, 1992; Gunn et al., 1997).

Of course problems remain, especially on operations governed by older planning consents such as those under the Interim Development Order (IDO) in the period 1943–8. Here the planning conditions may be weak, inappropriate or almost non-existent. These IDO consents were addressed through the Planning and Compensation Act 1991 and the Environment Act 1995 extended these provisions to sites granted permission between 1948 and 1982. The requirement to update permissions is fairly new and it remains to be seen how effective the legislation will be in achieving effective restoration and avoiding dereliction on these older consents. However, so far as new operations are concerned it is current government policy that unless the operator can demonstrate to the satisfaction of the mineral planning authority that its proposals will achieve the successful reclamation of the site, and that appropriate mechanisms are in place to fund the restoration, then the development should not proceed (DOE, 1996e).

A fundamental reason for the effectiveness of the planning system in pre-empting minerals dereliction is that development is, by its nature, temporary. A finite mineral resource means that there is a fixed time horizon for the operation, albeit in a hard rock quarry this may be more than sixty years. The reason non-mineral developments have not been more widely subject to rehabilitation conditions is that such developments have usually been regarded as 'permanent' (Arup Economics and Planning, 1995). Some types of non-minerals development, for example residential, are indeed unlikely to result in dereliction, but others such as petro-chemicals, telecommunications and the utilities (with specialist construction for specific uses) and others which may be vulnerable to changing market forces, for example superstores, out-of-town shopping complexes and holiday parks may all contribute to dereliction in the twenty-first century.

In 1992 the Department of the Environment issued a consultation paper 'Proposals to Prevent Land Becoming Derelict' (DOE, 1992c) which basically set out two options:

(a) Applying restoration conditions to new planning permissions for industrial or commercial use, similar to those routinely attached to mineral workings;

(b) Extending local planning authority powers to require owners and occupiers of land to reclaim derelict land, for example by building on existing powers under section 215 of the Town and Country Planning Act 1990.

The proposals were given 'a lukewarm welcome by local authorities and amenity bodies, whilst industry was worried that these proposals might add to their costs and deter new investment' (Arup Economics and Planning, 1995, 49). There were also practical problems such as defining when land had become derelict and specifying an appropriate restoration standard.

Government was, however, sufficiently encouraged by the response to consultation that it commissioned Arup Economics and Planning, in association with Clark Whitehill Berwin Leighton, to undertake research with a view to:

(a) assessing the effectiveness of the various options for using the planning system to ensure that restoration takes place, and the costs that they would impose upon industry; and
(b) advise the Department of the Environment on how any such options might be implemented.

In responding to the Department's research brief Arup Economics and Planning drew an analogy with the Environmental Protection Act which uses chemical thresholds relating to specified levels of contamination to trigger remedial action; they sought physical criteria to do with the condition of land and buildings which could be used to trigger action to prevent dereliction. Such action might be undertaken voluntarily by the site owner in compliance with a condition, through enforcement action by the local authority against non-compliance with the condition, or as default action against the state of the site (Arup Economics and Planning, 1995). A range of potential mechanisms were identified and tested through structured interviews and case study analysis. The results of this evaluation are summarised in Box 6.11.

The study concluded that the three options with the most potential to prevent dereliction and which did not appear to have overriding practical or political constraints to their implementation were:

—rehabilitation conditions on certain types of activities;
—a new section 215 provision;
—carry-back provisions to provide tax relief on rehabilitation expenditure.

The concept of rehabilitation conditions has been discussed above, and is in many ways the preferred approach.[2] The 1990 Town and Country Planning Act includes default powers[3] which justify local authority action on grounds of preserving amenity. At the time of the review, these had limited applicability to

[2] Arup Economics and Planning preferred the term 'rehabilitation condition' for non-minerals development because 'restoration condition' has a specific meaning within Sched. 5 to the Town and Country Planning Act 1990.

[3] S.215 of the 1990 Act.

BOX 6.11: Comparative evaluation of measures to assist derelict land prevention

	Rehab. Conditions	Financial Guarantees	New LA Power	Tax Relief	Tax
Impact	✓				(✓)
Practicality	✓		✓	✓	
Incentive		✓			✓
Flexibility	✓	✓	✓	✓	✓
Does Not Deter Investment	(✓)			✓	
No Call on Public Funds		✓			(✓)
Minimal Legislative Change	✓	✓		✓	

Source: Arup Economics & Planning, 1995.

derelict land prevention but the consultants considered that they could be strengthened and extended to make them more effective. The ability of *mineral operators* to offset restoration expenditure against income provides an incentive for rehabilitation following completion of operations; an extension to other industries could help prevent dereliction. Arup Economics and Planning suggested a suite of policy changes which could be implemented in short, medium or longer timescales (see Box 6.12).

The Government's response was to publish Environment Circular 02/98 'Prevention of Dereliction Through the Planning System' (DETR, 1998c). The Circular encourages local planning authorities to use their section 215 powers and to serve notices on the owners and occupiers of land in their area if it appears to them that amenity is being prejudiced by its condition. The government strengthened the default powers under section 215 by introducing new regulations[4] empowering local planning authorities to recover costs for carrying out such work. The Circular emphasised the potential for proper use of planning conditions to pre-empt dereliction, especially for 'high risk' development which is temporary, specialised or located in sensitive areas.

It remains to be seen how effectively the local planning authorities respond and whether further measures are necessary to stem the flow of derelict land. The likelihood is that without the minerals sector, the economic drivers in society will continue to produce significant areas of derelict land. We must therefore examine the process of derelict land reclamation beginning with land recycling for 'hard' end-use.

[4] Town and Country Planning General (Amendment) Regulations 1997 (S.I. 1997, No. 3006).

BOX 6.12: Recommended policy changes for prevention of dereliction and their associated timescales

	TIMESCALES		
Action/ Provision	**Short**	**Medium**	**Long**
'Restoration Condition'	• Apply more widely to specified activities on time-limited permissions	• Issue planning guidance cross referenced to Circ 1/85 • Extend scope of activities to be covered	• Consider amending GDO in respect of utilities development
Financial Guarantees		• Monitor levels of default on 'restoration' conditions	• If default a problem consider ways of introducing a system of guarantees
s.215 and New LA Power	• Introduce Regulations for LAs to put a charge on the land to recover their costs under existing s.215	• Amend legislation to introduce new section allowing prevention of dereliction as an objective for LA action	
Tax Provisions	• Amend legislation in respect of capital allowances and carry back provisions		• Consider tax on derelict land

Source: Arup Economics & Planning, 1995.

LAND RECLAMATION TO 'HARD' END-USE

Land reclamation for residential, commercial and industrial use has much to commend it. Land recycling for 'hard' end-use may release pressure for development on green field sites as well as contributing to urban regeneration by stimulating development and improving environmental quality. The twin objectives of minimising the use of scarce land resources for development and maximising the efficiency with which previously developed land is recycled both contribute to the principle of sustainable urban development. Government has set a target of sixty per cent of additional households in England to be built on previously developed land, or provided through conversions, by 2008 (DETR, 1998d); it is one of the 'headline indicators' for sustainable development (DETR, 1998e).

By the early 1980s the contribution that land reclamation could make to urban renewal was clearly recognised; DLG resources were substantially increased and priority was given to reclaiming land for 'hard' end-uses in urban areas, particularly the inner cities. Environmental improvement schemes continued to be encouraged where dereliction was extensive since they would help to make these places more attractive to investors. Grant was also made available direct to the private sector to enable it to play a greater role. The principal intention of the programme was to bring the land up to a 'green field site' standard. Grant rates varied being one hundred per cent of eligible costs for local authorities and English Estates, and eighty per cent for other applicants, in priority areas (Assisted Areas and Derelict Land Clearance Areas). Outside these areas the grant rate was fifty per cent for all applicants, except that in national parks and 'areas of outstanding natural beauty', local authorities could receive grant at seventy-five per cent. There were claw-back arrangements on disposal of the land to recover the added value of the site attributable to the DLG aided works.

Government commissioned research on the effectiveness of the DLG programme in the mid-1980s (Roger Tym and Partners, 1987). The consultants found that the environmental and safety objectives of schemes were successfully met in most cases, but the objectives related to provision of development land were less so. A third of sites intended for industry or commerce and a fifth of the sites intended for housing remained vacant for periods in excess of three years following reclamation. Furthermore, in practice, only twenty-seven per cent of the twelve thousand, six hundred hectares of land reclaimed and brought back into beneficial use was to 'hard' end-uses (Mabey, 1991), and the South East was the only English region where reclamation to hard end-use exceeded that to soft end uses. These findings prompted a review of DLG policy:

> The priority given to hard end use reclamation has brought benefits from the private sector investment which has subsequently been generated. However, dereliction is not solely confined to inner city areas and the cost of reclaiming land to a hard use standard is often high. The Government has therefore decided that the priorities of the DLG Programme should be revised to allow a greater degree of flexibility in project selection within the context of locally developed reclamation strategies. This will enable the worst dereliction to be treated first wherever it is found and for it to be reclaimed for the most appropriate end use (including environmental improvement) [DOE, 1991d].

This policy statement is important not only because it marked a shift in priorities at the time, but because, despite subsequent changes in agency structure and grant regime, it is still substantially in force today. The balance between hard and soft end-use and the key players in land reclamation over the period

1988–93 are shown in Box 6.13. The effectiveness of land reclamation to hard end-use has been reviewed for the DoE by Arup Economics and Planning (Arup Economics and Planning, 1994). They examined one hundred and sixty schemes completed between 1989 and 1990 and found that, by the time of the study in 1992, forty-eight per cent of the sampled schemes had been fully developed, nineteen per cent partially developed and thirty-three per cent remained undeveloped. A site was less likely to be developed if it was very small (less than half a hectare), recently reclaimed or in an area of low land values. The principal reason for non development was low demand.

BOX 6.13: Derelict land reclaimed and in use (1988–93) and reclamation agencies

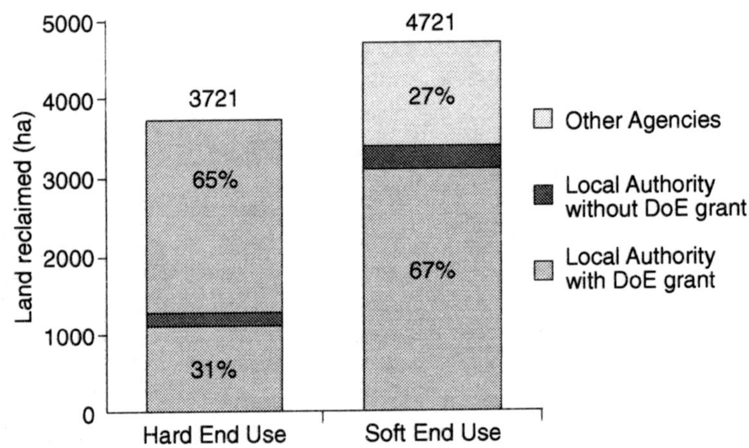

Source: DOE, 1995b.

Low demand is one of a number of factors which inhibit land recycling for hard end-use and which will make government targets for re-use of brownfield land difficult to achieve. They include:

i. the physical and chemical condition of the land demands a significant development premium in grant aid; £54,000 per hectare was the net cost of development and £7,128 per residential unit in the aforementioned study (Arup Economics and Planning, 1994);
ii. land recycling is much more effective in regions with high demand; in the period 1988–93 new dereliction was being created more rapidly in the South East than in the North West but, because of differences in demand, there was a net reduction in the stock of derelict land in the South East and a further increase in the North West, which already had the largest stock of any English region;

iii. the geographical distribution of land *within* a region may not be conducive to land recycling; a significant proportion of derelict land is in rural locations (Box 6.14), often with Green Belt status, and derelict land tends to be concentrated in older industrial areas where social deprivation is high and the private sector is loathe to invest.

BOX 6.14: Urban versus rural distribution of derelict land

	Urban		Rural		Total	
	ha	%	ha	%	ha	%
Derelict land	20,479	52	19,121	48	39,600	100
Area justifying reclamation	19,759	57	14,807	43	34,566	100

Source: DOE, 1995b.

It follows that the recycling of derelict land needs to be considered in the broader context of regional development and that well focused urban regeneration programmes are required at the local level. The most effective land recycling in local authority programmes was where the scheme formed part of a wider area-based strategy managed by a well organised local authority team, often co-ordinating a range of funding sources of which DLG was one (Arup Economics and Planning, 1994). 'Other agencies' played an important role in reclamation to hard end-use during this period (see Box 6.13), especially the Development Corporations. Other more flexible public/private partnerships emerged during the 1980s, such as in the reclamation of Salford Quays (Struthers, 1997) and Ravenhead Renaissance, St Helens (Ashworth, 1991).

In November 1993 the Government established a new urban regeneration agency for England—English Partnerships—to spearhead the attack on derelict and despoiled land. It was to promote the regeneration of areas of need through the reclamation, development or redevelopment of land (DOE, 1994f). There was to be a strong emphasis on partnership working and Derelict Land Grant was subsumed into a new Investment Fund. English Partnerships (EP) devolved much of its regeneration activity to regional offices and many of these functions, and the associated grant regimes, have now been taken over by the newly established Regional Development Agencies. It will be some time before an objective judgement can be made about the effects of these administrative changes on the effectiveness of land recycling and whether EP's projects have achieved sustainable regeneration in the areas on which they are located (PA Consulting, 1999). In the meantime the Urban Task Force has proposed a series of measures for reforming the planning process and managing the land supply which, if implemented, may significantly improve the prospects of success (Urban Task Force, 1999). However, the Urban Task Force also recognised that derelict and despoiled land has the potential to make an important contribution to urban environmental quality as a wildlife, landscape and recreational resource:

> We also need to promote the idea of the ecologically sensitive city in which humans recognise that they cohabit with nature. Trees, woodland and other open space are all important in fostering biodiversity, in enhancing human health and well-being, and in reducing noise and pollution. We can use some of our previously developed land to create new areas of green space [Urban Task Force, 1999, 43].

It is to land reclamation for 'soft' end-uses that we now turn.

LAND RECLAMATION TO 'SOFT' END-USE

Reclamation to 'soft' end-uses has always been an important feature of the derelict land reclamation programme and this received renewed emphasis in the Derelict Land Grant Advice Note of 1991:

> These new priorities will allow a greater level of grant aid to be given to schemes intended to improve the environment. Schemes for other environmental purposes such as those designed to improve facilities for public relaxation or recreation, or aimed at nature conservation will also be supported [DOE, 1991d].

Support was also to be given to 'historic conservation' and to tree planting and woodland establishment in association with the Community Forests. Historically the DLG Programme for 'soft' end use had been dominated by agriculture and public open space (see Box 6.15).

BOX 6.15: Land reclaimed to soft end uses and in use 1988–93

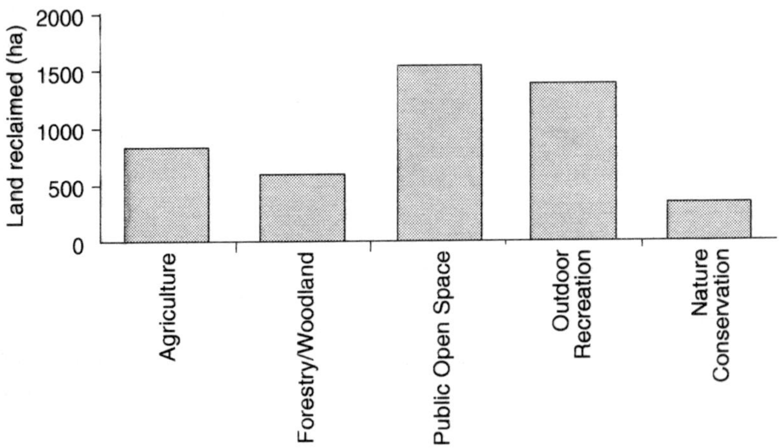

Source: DOE, 1995b.

The new priorities reflected research findings which emphasised that schemes with nature conservation and forestry objectives were not only cheaper to establish and maintain, especially beyond the woodland establishment phase, but that they also performed well against a range of benefit criteria including safety, land-use compatibility, visual benefit, amenity use and nature conservation value (Land Capability Consultants, 1989).

During the 1990s local authorities were hard pressed to manage traditional parklands, let alone an expanding estate of 'public open space' on reclaimed land (HCETRAC, 1999). The emphasis in land reclamation schemes for soft end-use therefore shifted towards working with the grain of natural recovery so as to maximise biodiversity whilst minimising both capital and revenue costs (Handley, 1996; Land Use Consultants, 1996). In fact many sites designated for their nature conservation interest in Unitary Development Plans are also included in local authority registers of derelict land. The importance of brown field land as a wildlife habitat and the need to balance competing claims for development and conservation are recognised by the UK Biodiversity Steering Group (UK Steering Group Report, 1995). It identifies two key issues in urban areas:

(1) how to ensure that development does not adversely affect environmental resources, so that where new development must take place, loss of biodiversity is avoided, reduced to a practical minimum or reversed; and
(2) how to enhance biodiversity in existing open space and in new development.

The way in which environmental planners can contribute to addressing these issues has been set out very clearly by the Royal Town Planning Institute in its publication *Planning for Biodiversity: A Good Practice Guide* (RTPI, 1999b) and Box (1998) has provided guidance on objective setting for ecological restoration and habitat creation.

Woodland cover in England and Wales is low by European standards at seven point two per cent and eleven point six per cent respectively compared with a European average of twenty-eight per cent. Although Great Britain has doubled its woodland cover from five per cent in 1920, there is a broad consensus that this area of woodland is still insufficient. This view stems from the many benefits that trees and woodland provide. Perry and Handley (2000) reviewed the potential for woodland on 'urban and industrial wasteland' and concluded that opportunities exist to increase the woodland cover significantly on operational land, vacant land, derelict land and even contaminated sites. The new Forest Strategy for England (Forestry Commission, 1998) recognises that forestry has an important role to play within urban regeneration, especially through the Community Forest programme. There is of course the potential for conflict with competing land-uses such as nature conservation. Experience within the Community Forest projects suggests that, provided good quality survey information is to hand, conflict can be avoided and, with proper design these two uses are often complementary (Hodge, 1995).

When the public was asked what should be done with derelict land (MORI, 1995) it expressed clear preferences. The top six answers were:

—parkland and recreation	28%
—housing and secure accommodation	28%
—play areas and safe play grounds	27%
—landscaped open space and green areas for walking	18%
—tidy, clean it up, make it look nice	12%
—industrial areas	10%

If this response was unsurprising the answer to a question about *who* should have a role of deciding what is to be done with such areas was striking. The established role of local authorities was recognised here (seventy-three per cent) but there was marginally stronger support for an input by local people (seventy-five per cent). Local community organisations were cited by fifty-nine per cent of respondents. The potential for community involvement in land reclamation is considered next.

THE POTENTIAL FOR COMMUNITY INVOLVEMENT

The benefits of community involvement have long been recognised:

> in particular, local communities must be much more involved from the early planning stage to the final maintenance stage. In the end it is the needs of the community and the value of the environment which should guide us [Burt and Bradshaw, 1986, 103].)

However, Kivell (1987) in reviewing land reclamation policy and practice observed that community involvement has been minimal, and that whilst this may be understandable on some large and technically complex sites, there are smaller sites, for example in inner city residential areas, which lend themselves to a participative approach. All too often land reclamation has been thought of as a complex technical activity, the legitimate province of the civil engineer and environmental scientist, and community interests have been marginalised in the process; so reinforcing feelings of loss, exclusion and resentment (Handley, 1996; Starkings, 1998). Starkings, in a perceptive review, emphasises the importance of 'sense of place' and that places carry subjective meanings for people living and working in and around them. She points out that, as places evolve and change, people's perception alters accordingly. Usually this change in the landscape takes place slowly, within a human timescale, but land reclamation has the power to alter a place beyond recognition in a short period of time.

Social scientists have pointed out that decisions about buildings or the landscape are often made by outsiders who do not understand or value them in the same way as local people. Starkings (1998) adapted a model developed by Bourassa (1991) which sets up a two by two matrix according to existential and professional status (see Box 6.16).

BOX 6.16: The land reclamation community bridged by community development

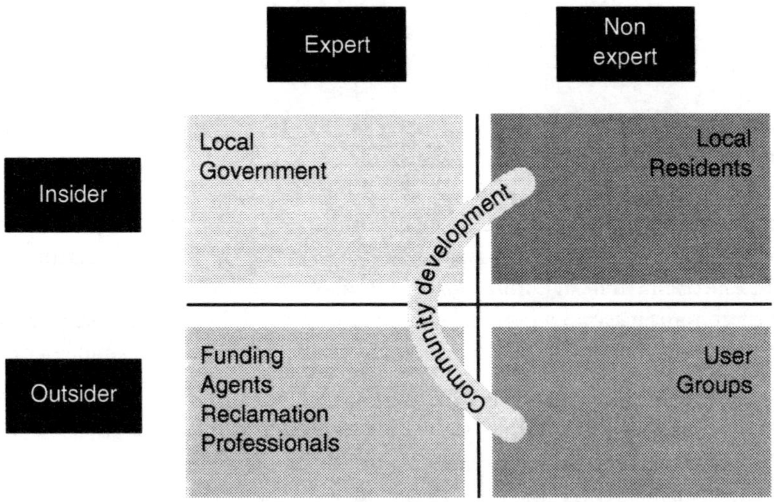

Source: Starkings, 1998, adapted from Bourassa, 1991.

The model emphasises that the reclamation community as 'expert outsider' is often well removed from both local residents and the user community. A reclamation scheme which seeks to overcome, rather than reinforce, social exclusion needs to develop a proper awareness of the priorities of these different communities of interest and preferably engage people in a meaningful way in planning, implementation and after-care. The case study for testing the model was Bold Moss, St Helens, a large colliery spoil heap owned and managed by the Groundwork Trust, an environmental charity. This project is important because it demonstrates that an ecologically informed and participative approach to land reclamation can be pursued successfully even on a large and hostile site (Handley et al., 1998). Starkings concluded that the early work regarding consultation and participation undertaken by Groundwork at Bold Moss did help to bridge the gap between insider and outsider, expert and non-expert communities. However, to sustain this in the longer term representation for the local community needs to be firmly built into the management structure. Bold Moss provided the model for a national programme of reclamation projects, led by Groundwork and funded by the Millennium Commission and others, which is currently the subject of a detailed eco-cultural audit. An important preliminary finding is that where adequate resources are provided for promoting meaningful community involvement within a land reclamation programme, and where this begins early and is properly sustained, there can be major benefits to the reclamation outcome.

CONTAMINATED LAND—A SPECIAL CASE?

Contaminated land differs from derelict land in that it represents an actual or potential hazard to health or the environment as a result of some previous use. The land may also be physically damaged but land may become contaminated without visible damage, for example by atmospheric pollution or groundwater movement. The UK policy framework is set out in the 'Framework for Contaminated Land' (DOE, 1994g); in summary, it seeks to prevent or minimise future contamination and to control or treat existing contamination. In working to achieve these objectives a number of principles apply:

—the adoption of a 'suitable for use' approach in which the standard of remediation is dictated by after-use rather than the absolute standard associated with a multi-functional solution;
—prioritising action to deal with the most urgent and real problems having regard to economic constraints on the public and private sectors;
—clarifying the law on the clean-up of contaminated sites, thus enabling a proper land market to be created.

The perceived scale of the problem depends very much on the definition employed; the Royal Commission on Environmental Pollution quotes estimates ranging from fifty thousand to two hundred thousand hectares (RCEP, 1996). The 1995 Environment Act provides, for the first time in Britain, a statutory definition of contaminated land:

> any land which appears to the local authority in whose area it is situated to be in such a condition by reason of substances in, on, or under the land that:
> a) significant harm is being caused or there is a significant possibility of such harm being caused; or
> b) pollution of controlled waters is being or is likely to be caused.[5]

Government has taken 'harm' to include harm to the health of living organisms (including people), ecological systems and property. For 'harm' to exist, or potentially exist, there must be a pathway linking the contaminant source to a relevant target. The process of risk assessment on contaminated land therefore requires consideration of:

—the source of the harm—the contaminants;
—the target or receptor—the subject that can be harmed;
—the pathway—the route by which the target may come into contact with the contaminants.

[5] Now s.78A(2) of the Environmental Protection Act 1990.

The Environment Act 1995 introduced (as Part IIA into the Environmental Protection Act 1990) the new regime for contaminated land which covers:

—definition of contaminated land;
—which authority is responsible for regulation;
—serving of remediation notices;
—issuing of remediation declarations;
—definition of a responsible person;
—apportioning liability.

Local authorities are required[6] to inspect their area, from time to time, to identify contaminated land and, where necessary to issue remediation notices specifying what action should be taken by the 'appropriate person' i.e. the person deemed to have contaminated the land. If that person cannot be found, then the 'appropriate person' is the current owner or occupier. At the heart of the process is the identification of source/pathway/target relationships, if present, and evaluation of any associated hazard. The intention is to provide a science-based framework for the assessment and remediation of contaminated land which is complementary to the planning system.

The Interdepartmental Committee on the Redevelopment of Contaminated Land (ICRCL) has devised a 'guidelines'- and 'standards'-based approach supported by a series of guidance notes that defined tentative trigger concentrations for various soil contaminants for planned after-uses of differing sensitivity, for example car parks versus private gardens. Two trigger levels are defined for a selection of common soil contaminants and a range of proposed uses:

1. the lower **threshold trigger value** below which the site can be **regarded as uncontaminated.** Above this concentration, it may be necessary to carry out an additional investigation and/or take some form of remedial action; and
2. the upper **action trigger** value indicates a value at or above which then the site can be **regarded as contaminated.** Above this concentration it is likely that some form of remedial action will be required or the type of use must be changed (ICRCL, 1987).

This approach was criticised by, among others, the Royal Commission on Environmental Pollution (RCEP, 1996) and is to be superseded by new, more definitive guidance through the Contaminated Land Exposure Assessment Model (CLEA). These new guidelines have proved difficult to finalise and the Contaminated Land Regime was enacted[7] on 1 April 2000 in advance of their publication (DETR, 2000d).

The risk assessment process is focused on one particular outcome and, as we have seen, derelict and despoiled land may take on a variety of other attributes

[6] *Ibid.*, s.78B.
[7] Contaminated Land (England) Regulations 2000 (SI 2000, No. 227).

or values. In developing and implementing contaminated land strategies, local authorities should take account of other factors such as landscape quality, wildlife interest and recreational amenity. One alternative approach, piloted successfully on contaminated land sites from the alkali industry in St Helens (Wigley, 2000), uses the attribute-based approach to environmental capital developed for the Countryside Commission and sister agencies by Land Use Consultants and CAG Consultants (LUC and CAG Consultants, 1997). This 'New Approach' to environmental capital recommends public consultation during the evaluation process; the 'participative' dimension will be a major challenge during implementation of Part II A of the Contaminated Land Regime. Helpful guidance on communicating understanding of contaminated land risks has been provided by the Scotland and Northern Ireland Forum for Environmental Research (SNIFFER, 1999).

A recent survey for the Royal Institute of Chartered Surveyors revealed that the process of remediating contaminated sites was the most significant adverse factor for developers in making investment decisions on brown field locations (University of Ulster, 1998). This was a matter of real concern to the Urban Task Force. It considered that, with the obvious exception of nuclear waste, the problem of dealing with contamination was not so much technical as a problem of finance and/or perceived legal risk (Urban Task Force, 1999). It concluded that:

—most contaminated land is capable of safe remediation using modern technology at reasonable cost;
—the present barriers to redevelopment are largely to do with the perception of risk;
—we have to simplify and consolidate the regulatory systems which seek to protect the environment from the consequences of contamination; and
—we should promote greater standardisation in the way we manage the risks involved in redeveloping contaminated sites, and thereby promote a better and consistent understanding of the situation.

Regrettably the delays in implementing Part II A of the Contaminated Land Regime and the lack of published guidance on CLEA at the time of enactment have added to the climate of uncertainty. Moreover, the Environmental Health Departments of local authorities may not be best equipped to deal with the issues of public confidence which will be generated by the surveys of contaminated land (Parkinson et al., 2000). This can only deter land recycling for hard end-use, especially for residential use and 'green' alternatives such as nature conservation and forestry may have an important part to play. (Perry and Handley, 2000, 53). Meanwhile, as acknowledged by the Urban Task Force (1999), our ability to achieve the target of bringing all contaminated land back into beneficial use by 2030 'clearly depends on our ability to prevent new stocks of contaminated land coming on stream in the years ahead'. Here, by contrast with derelict land, we can be more optimistic because thresholds for triggering action can be identified and the new regulatory systems should in principle capture those sites which, though still in use, have potential to cause significant harm in future.

TOWARDS A STRATEGIC APPROACH

The Civic Trust Report (1964) identified derelict and despoiled land as a problem of similar magnitude to urban air pollution (specifically smoke and sulphur dioxide) and gross pollution of streams and rivers. Whereas substantial progress was subsequently made in tackling urban air pollution and in cleaning up the rivers, the twentieth century closed with a significant backlog of dereliction remaining, more in the pipeline and an unquantified but severe problem of land contamination. As Kivell (1987) observed 'after twenty years of reclamation, the problem of derelict land remains as large and intractable as ever'. The framework for a more strategic approach involves the integration of policies, plans and programmes (see Box 6.17). The project appraisal process ensures that policy considerations are taken on board in developing individual projects and that these projects are seen to form part of a wider programme (DOE, 1992d). The process is cyclical, rather than linear, with each round of the programme cycle being influenced, to some degree, by an evaluation of previous outcomes.

One important advantage of the 'strategic approach' is that it can better accommodate the new policy agenda for sustainable development. The UK Strategy (HMG, 1999) sets out four inter-linked objectives:

—social progress which recognises the needs of everyone;
—effective protection of the environment;
—prudent use of natural resources; and
—maintenance of high and stable levels of economic growth and employment.

The creation of English Partnerships was a deliberate attempt to transform the old Derelict Land Grant system which it inherited from being a passive vehicle for funding local authority land reclamation programmes to being a catalyst for supporting strategic regeneration (PA Consulting Group, 1999). This approach has not always been fully embraced by the local authority partners as made clear in the first stage of the Interim Evaluation:

> In some regions applications to English Partnerships' Land Reclamation Programme are running at a fairly low level, and this is perceived to be linked to EP's requirement to place reclamation work in the context of a strategy. Some LAs have stopped coming forward with poor projects but have not replaced them with well thought-out plans. Other authorities continue to make poor proposals which are declined funding. In part this has been put down to the 'deeply entrenched culture' of tackling land reclamation on a one-off basis which was fostered by DLG [P.A. Consulting, 1998].

Good practice guidance is now emerging on how the principles of sustainable development can be built into policies, plans and programmes (DETR, 1998f;

BOX 6.17: The strategic framework for reclamation of derelict and despoiled land

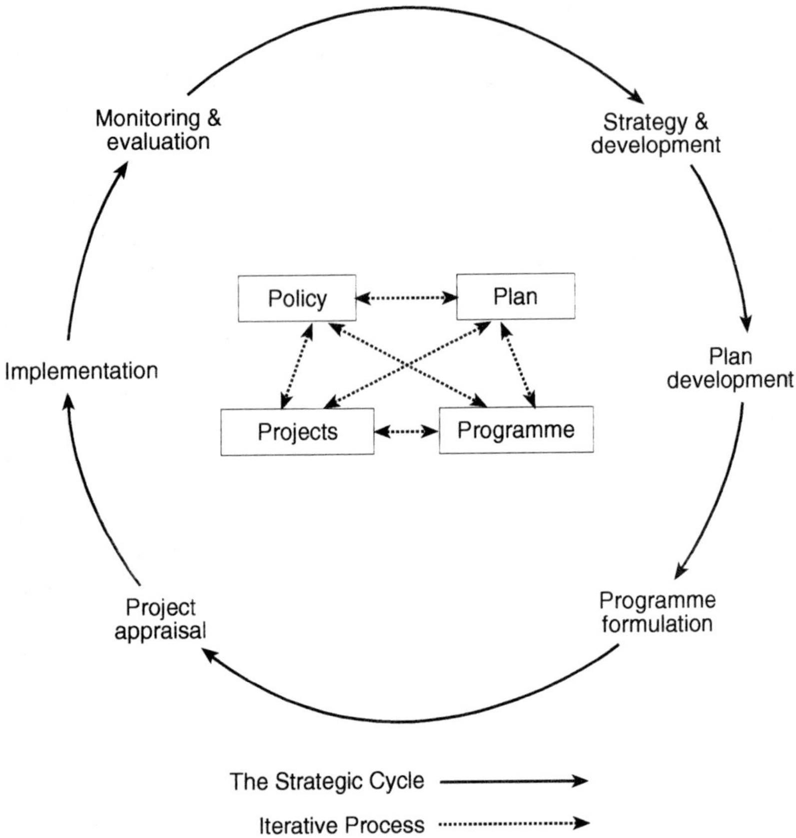

Source: Reisen, 1998, adapted from DOE, 1992d.

Urban Task Force, 1999; Llewelyn-Davies, 2000). The 1999 report on English Partnerships suggests that there is some way to go in moving from an economically driven model to a more balanced approach in which community involvement and environmental quality are given full weight (PA Consulting, 1999). This may in part be due to the difficulty of deriving satisfactory output measures for the more holistic approach; it is the output measures specified by DETR which all too often drive these programmes. It also reflects the financial strictures on English Partnerships which prevented them from contributing revenue funding. If projects are to be developed with proper community participation and sustained effectively in the aftercare period, ways need to be found to provide appropriate income streams.

The problem of long-term management of land at the end of its normal economic life is especially daunting; even contaminated land once made safe requires effective management if it is not recycled. Handley (1996) proposed the creation of a UK Trust for Derelict Land modelled to some extent on the National Trust. The concept has been well received by industry, and latterly by the DETR, and is now the subject of a feasibility study by Groundwork UK and English Partnerships. In April 1999, the new Regional Development Agencies (RDAs) took over the regional functions of EP (except in London) and the Rural Development Commission (RDC), as well as the administration of the SRB Challenge Funds. A prime task of the RDAs will be to develop and implement a regional economic strategy in order to boost regional competitiveness and employment. This could inhibit the moves which EP had set in train towards a more holistic approach to regeneration, and certainly there will be a greater diversity of approach. However, there are also advantages, for the regional scale provides distinct benefits in planning for sustainability (Forman, 1995) and the RDAs will have the lead role in creating a strategic focus for regional development. In particular, RDAs, unlike EP, will be able to provide both revenue and capital funding which should encourage greater community involvement in regeneration (PA Consulting, 1999). Already one of the RDAs in North West England has produced a more rounded regional strategy and instigated a fundamental review of land reclamation policy and programmes within its area (NWDA, 1999).

The incorporation of contaminated land within this framework presents a particular challenge. The principal responsibilities under Part IIA of EPA 1990 are divided between the local authorities and the Environment Agency (see Box 6.18).

Building effective links between the Contaminated Land Regime and land regeneration programmes will be especially difficult and Reisen (1998) has identified the need for better co-operation and communication between the various parties involved in the redevelopment process on contaminated land. This will require an operational framework which brings together the work of the regulators (Environmental Health Departments and Environment Agency) and the development community, in which Local Planning Authorities have a key role to play.

CONCLUSION

This chapter has explored the problem of derelict and despoiled land, an issue which is now firmly embedded in the regional development agenda. For all the achievements within land reclamation projects and programmes in the latter part of the twentieth century, there is still a major task ahead. Excellent progress has been made in providing technical solutions so that land can, in principle, be recycled for a wide range of uses. The former distinction between 'hard' and

BOX 6.18: Key responsibilities under Part IIA of the Environmental Protection Act, 1990

Local Authorities	**Environment Agency**
Duties:	Duties:
Prepare and publish an inspection strategy	Provide information to local authorities on land contamination
Inspect their areas to identify contaminated land	Ensure remediation of Special Sites
Consult the Agency on pollution of controlled waters	Maintain Public Register of Regulatory Action for Special Sites
Ensure remediation of land identified as contaminated land	Prepare a national report on the state of contaminated land
Transfer Special Sites to the Agency	
Maintain Public Register of Regulatory Action	
	Powers:
	Provide advice to local authorities on identifying and dealing with pollution of controlled waters
	Provide advice to local authorities on the remediation of contaminated land (non Special Sites)

Source: personal communications with Environment Agency.

'soft' end-use has been superseded within current funding regimes where the two approaches are seen to be mutually compatible within an integrated regeneration programme. The strategic approach to land reclamation will encourage a more holistic approach in which community benefit and environmental quality are given more equal weight within economic development. New legislative instruments are to hand, new administrative frameworks are in place. It remains to be seen whether this will provide the climate for action called for by Kivell (1987) under which inner city and other derelict areas would be speedily treated and recycled, 'not simply as a once and for all solution, but as part of a long term strategy for the management of urban change'.

7

Environmental Assessment

CHRISTOPHER WOOD

Yes, Minister (with the green portfolio)

MINISTER:	Do we really need environmental assessment—isn't it just pandering to the green lobby?
EA ADVISOR:	Yes, Minister, we really do need EA.
	EA works. The environment has often been protected from degradation because projects have been refused (for example, the Mersey Barrage) or adverse effects mitigated (for example, noise from Manchester's second runway) as a result of EA.
	As HM Government's policies deliver a more prosperous country, as they surely will, the electorate will inevitably demand higher environmental standards. Your own constituents believe the environment is worth protecting; you told them that when you were campaigning.
MINISTER:	But isn't EA just another example of European over-regulation?
EA ADVISOR:	Minister! The Directive on EA applies right across the European Union—to which the Government has said it is firmly committed!
	That means that the rest of the EU will have to come up to our high EA standards. Implementing EA effectively will help to remove the unjust slur that Britain is 'the dirty man of Europe'. The Prime Minister would love to lose that!
MINISTER:	Doesn't EA cost too much and take too long?
EA ADVISOR:	No, Minister. EA is very cost-effective.

	The cost of EA is only a tiny proportion of the cost of the project. EA helps to generate employment in high-tech environmental consultancy, one of our growing export sectors.
	EA may add a bit of time prior to approval but it saves time and public expenditure on later amelioration measures. Think of what the country could have saved on, for example, contaminated land remediation if we had had EA, Minister.
MINISTER:	If EA is so good, can we get rid of some of the other environmental regulations?
EA ADVISOR:	That would be courageous, Minister!
	EA is a way of bringing all the relevant environmental information together, often with economic and social factors, so you can take a properly informed view before permission is granted.
	For example, if you give permission for that new toxic waste incinerator in the Leader of the Opposition's constituency, you'd want to know that there were strong ongoing rules about preventing water contamination, poisoning the air and stopping people losing sleep because of noise, wouldn't you? Wouldn't you, Minister?
MINISTER:	That's a really difficult decision; will EA make it for me?
EA ADVISOR:	Unfortunately not, Minister.
	Although EA has been described as 'the theft of political decision-making by technical experts', it merely informs decisions but doesn't take them for you. Ultimately you have to make your own mind up.
	Your predecessor sometimes ignored EA. Do you remember when all those green protestors tied themselves in trees, got themselves on TV and embarrassed him? You wouldn't want that to happen to you, would you, Minister?
MINISTER:	Hmm! So will the public accept my decision more readily if the EA has been taken into account?
EA ADVISOR:	Yes, Minister.
	Generally, most people will accept unpopular decisions if they feel that they've been consulted, their opinions have

been listened to, and their suggestions have been taken into account. EA does that. Not everyone, of course, but enough of the electors.

If you don't appear to have taken the EA into account, the green protestors will take you to court and, worse, say wounding things about you on TV. And if there's no EA at all, people could call you an environmental vandal, Minister.

MINISTER: I'm not prepared to read more than a page on any decision! Those long boring environmental statements can't possibly affect recommendations to politicians, can they?

EA ADVISOR: Yes, Minister, they can.

Those academic chaps at Manchester did some research into that. They found that few 'yes's' became 'no's' or vice versa as a result of EA.

However, they did find that projects were better designed initially, that planners felt much more certain about the wisdom of their recommendations, that better quality projects ensued and that conditions on operation were more effective.

That means, Minister, that you can be more confident when you make your announcement about the toxic waste incinerator and any conditions you put on it.

MINISTER: I see. But surely there won't have to be EA on that business park I promised my constituents?

EA ADVISOR: I'm afraid so, Minister, if it exceeds the screening thresholds.

Screening ensures that all projects with certain effects are examined. You wouldn't want people to say you were exempting your favourite project, would you Minister?

And the EA will result in a much greener business park. Think of your speech when you open it, Minister!

MINISTER: But won't some of those green protestors raise a new issue—like a rare bird seen on a dark night—to try to stop the park?

EA ADVISOR: Not if you scope the project, Minister.

Scoping makes sure that everyone gets the chance to say

their piece early on. If there is a rare bird, the business park design might need to be modified to preserve its habitat; if there isn't, the issue can be dismissed in good time.

Look at those electricity pylons in Northumberland—they put the cables underground when scoping revealed that overhead lines would have interfered with a migration route and would have killed many birds.

MINISTER: If the proponent writes the ES, isn't it bound to be biased?

EA ADVISOR: You might think that, Minister, but I beg to differ.

Proper review and public scrutiny are the essential safeguards. Gradually, poor consultants lose their reputation and wise proponents only hire good consultants.

By the way, Minister, with this toxic waste incinerator due for decision, could you kindly return those two EA staff that you transferred to your political office, to make sure the review of the environmental statement is full and fair?

MINISTER: Aren't the proponent's promises in the ES just so many fine words?

EA ADVISOR: Like those of some politicians, Minister?

The words in the ES are hostages with which you can hold the developer to ransom.

Look at the incredibly tight conditions that were put on the fish flow arrangements on the River Bollin at Manchester Airport. That's why I need those two staff back, Minister, so that the promises in the ES can be translated into a watertight environmental management plan.

MINISTER: Won't this new strategic environmental assessment make project EA redundant?

EA ADVISOR: No, Minister.

There will always be difficult project decisions to make, but they will be much easier, much better informed, if there's been an EA of the plan or policy first.

In the toxic waste incinerator case, a strategic EA of either the land use plan or the waste disposal strategy would make your decision less difficult, Minister.

MINISTER: If I say 'no', the waste disposal industry will say I'm shirking my responsibilities but, if I say 'yes', the Leader of the

	Opposition will accuse me of vindictiveness and abuse of power, won't he?
EA ADVISOR:	You may very well think that, Minister, but I couldn't possibly comment. If I might make so bold, Minister, have you considered setting up a special expert review commission to examine the strategic environmental aspects of this toxic waste incinerator? I'd need a budget for the secretariat, please Minister. Also, I'm afraid that you'll need to find an appropriate expert to head the commission—perhaps an old chum from the Bar, Minister? By the time the commission has reported, the Prime Minister, in his wisdom, might have promoted you, and someone else would have to make this ticklish decision, Minister.

INTRODUCTION

This imaginary exchange between a new Minister and his Civil Service advisor illustrates many of the popular misconceptions about environmental assessment, which this chapter seeks to clarify. Environmental assessment (EA) is the evaluation of the effects likely to arise from a project (or other action) significantly affecting the natural and man-made environment. The EA of projects is generally referred to as environmental impact assessment (EIA) and the EA of programmes, plans and policies as strategic environmental assessment (SEA) or, in the UK, environmental appraisal. Consultation and participation are integral to this evaluation. EA is a systematic and integrative process, first developed in the United States in 1970, for considering possible impacts, and reporting them, prior to a decision being taken on whether or not a proposal should be given approval to proceed.

This chapter begins with an overview of the British EIA system. There follows an evaluation of its strengths and weaknesses. The various stages and aspects of the EA system are analysed against a set of fourteen evaluation criteria in the main part of the chapter. Finally, conclusions are drawn.

EA IN BRITAIN: AN OVERVIEW

In response to the growing interest in EIA world-wide, the UK Government guardedly announced that it favoured the limited use of EIA in 1978. There was no hint, however, of implementing any legislative changes to encourage its use. As the various drafts of the European Commission's original directive on EIA began to appear in the late 1970's, the Government, while rejecting the idea of any mandatory EIA system, continued to endorse the principle that EIA was a useful element in the planning process for considering large and significant proposals. Meanwhile, considerable experience of the use of non-mandatory EIA was being gained in Britain (Wood, 1995).

As a result of intensive negotiation in Brussels, major concessions limiting both the coverage of an EIA report and the range of projects to be subject to mandatory EIA were felt to reduce the ramifications of EIA to the point where the British environment minister could accept the Directive (Sheate, 1996; Wood, 1995; Bond, 1997). The Directive,[1] adopted in 1985, came into effect in July 1988. The Planning Regulations[2] and a circular implementing the Directive were published on 15 July 1988. It is significant that the Department of the Environment (DOE) adopted the term 'environmental assessment' rather than the US 'environmental impact assessment', given its earlier opposition to a formal EIA system. Whether it took the term from the name of the US preliminary (screening) document or from the Canadian name for EIA is a matter of conjecture. Further regulations[3] relating to projects authorised under consent systems other than the town and country planning legislation were promulgated subsequently. Various minor amendments to the Planning Regulations were later made to extend the range of projects subject to EIA and to rectify anomalies in the implementation of the original Directive.

Once it became apparent that an amended version[4] of the Directive was going to be adopted (as it was in 1997) the renamed Department of the Environment, Transport and the Regions (DETR) commissioned research on alternative approaches to meeting the anticipated screening requirements and issued a consultation paper. This paper contained the most unequivocal endorsement of EIA to date:

> The Government wholly endorses the use of the EA process to ensure that the likely significant effects of development projects are fully assessed and taken into account in deciding whether the projects may proceed [DETR, 1997d, para. 18].

[1] Directive 85/337/EEC [1985] OJ L175/40.

[2] Town and Country Planning (Assessment of Environmental Effects) Regulations 1988 (SI 1988, No.1199).

[3] E.g., Environmental Assessment (Afforestation) Regulations 1988 (SI 1988, No. 1207).

[4] Directive 97/11/EC [1997] OJ L73/5.

Following further consultation, the Planning Regulations[5] implementing the amended Directive came into force on 12 March 1999, accompanied by a circular (DETR, 1999a). Interestingly, the new Planning Regulations and Circular refer throughout to EIA, rather than to environmental assessment, bringing British usage closer to European and accepted international terminology. The 1999 Regulations relate to projects requiring planning permission and implement the provisions of the amended European Directive almost to the letter. Like their predecessors, the 1999 Regulations apply to two separate lists of projects, based on Annexes I and II to the (amended) Directive. But these lists now cover a wider range of projects than the previous regulations. In particular, Schedule 2 contains screening thresholds and criteria not specified in the Directive for each category of development. The Planning and Compensation Act 1991 enables[6] the Secretary of State to require the EIA of planning projects other than those listed in the European Directive. This power was used in the 1999 Regulations to include motorway service stations, sports stadia, leisure centres and golf courses, which are not listed in Annex II to the amended Directive.

The 1999 Regulations contain provisions for local planning authorities (LPAs) to give a formal 'screening opinion' that EIA is required where they are requested to do so by developers. They must also notify developers that EIA is required where a planning application is submitted without an 'environmental statement' (ES). In either event, the Regulations permit the developer to appeal to the Secretary of State for a 'screening direction' that EIA is or is not required. As a result of the amendments to the original Directive, a developer may request a formal 'scoping opinion' from the LPA or, where the LPA fails to provide one, a 'scoping direction' from the Secretary of State, regarding the information to be included in an ES. Another important requirement introduced to implement the amended Directive relates to the treatment of alternatives in the ES.

Certain statutory consultees (including the Environment Agency) are required to provide the developer with information should it be requested. The Regulations also set down the nature of prescribed consultation and publication arrangements and extend the amount of time available to LPAs to reach a decision on planning applications involving EIA.

Part II of Schedule 4 contains a list of the mandatory information required by Article 5 of the amended Directive and Part I replicates Annex IV of the amended Directive. An environmental statement is defined by reference to Schedule 4. It must include the information referred to in Part II and:

> such of the information referred to in Part I. . . as is reasonably required to assess the environmental effects of the development and which the applicant can, having regard

[5] Town and Country Planning (Environmental Impact Assessment) (England and Wales) Regulations 1999 (SI 1999, No. 293).

[6] S.15, which inserted s.71A into the Town and Country Planning Act 1990.

> in particular to current knowledge and methods of assessment, reasonably be required to compile. . .[7]

This is a formulation which follows the wording of the amended Directive closely and which should avoid many disagreements about whether the content requirements for ESs accurately reflect those of the Directive.

The 'environmental information' which must be considered in reaching a decision consists of the ES, together with any further information and the representations of consultees and members of the public about the impacts of the development. A further new requirement of the 1999 Planning Regulations is that the reasons for the decisions to grant or to refuse planning permission in cases involving EIA must be stated. An outline of the main steps in the EIA process for planning decisions is shown in Box 7.1.

Advice on procedures and on the implementation of the EIA Planning Regulations in England and Wales is presented in Circular 2/99 (DETR, 1999a) and in a comprehensive guide to EIA procedures (DETR, 2000h) which updated earlier guidance (DOE, 1989). The circular provides clear guidance on the operation of the procedures as well as the detailed indicative criteria and thresholds to be used by LPAs in reaching a judgement about whether EIA is to be required for Schedule 2 (Annex II) projects. The criteria and thresholds (and the other advice contained in the Circular) can therefore be changed easily and, in any event, do not have regulatory force. However, the Regulations provide a right of appeal against an LPA determination that EIA is required. Normal town planning appeal provisions against negative planning decisions also apply and the Secretary of State can call applications in for determination by central government. There is therefore relatively little discretion left to LPAs in determining whether or not the Regulations apply to particular applications.

Certain types of projects listed in Annex I and Annex II to the European Directive are authorised outside the British planning system. Accordingly, it was necessary to adopt additional regulations. The arrangements relating to these other regulations are broadly similar. Those[8] relating to highways, for example, require the Secretary of State for the Environment, Transport and the Regions to publish an ES for the preferred route at the time when draft orders are published. Others[9] require the EIA of afforestation projects in any case where, in the opinion of the Forestry Commission, the project is likely to have significant environmental effects. Various regulations relating to land drainage works, ports and harbours, offshore salmon farming, decommissioning of nuclear reactors, power stations, pipelines and new railways had either come into force in mid-2000 or were expected shortly to do so. Arrangements for the provision of

[7] Above n.5, Art. 2(1).

[8] Highways (Assessment of Environmental Effects) Regulations 1999 (SI 1999, No. 369).

[9] Environmental Impact Assessment (Forestry) (England and Wales) Regulations 1999 (SI 1999, No. 2228).

BOX 7.1: Main steps in the EIA process for UK planning decisions

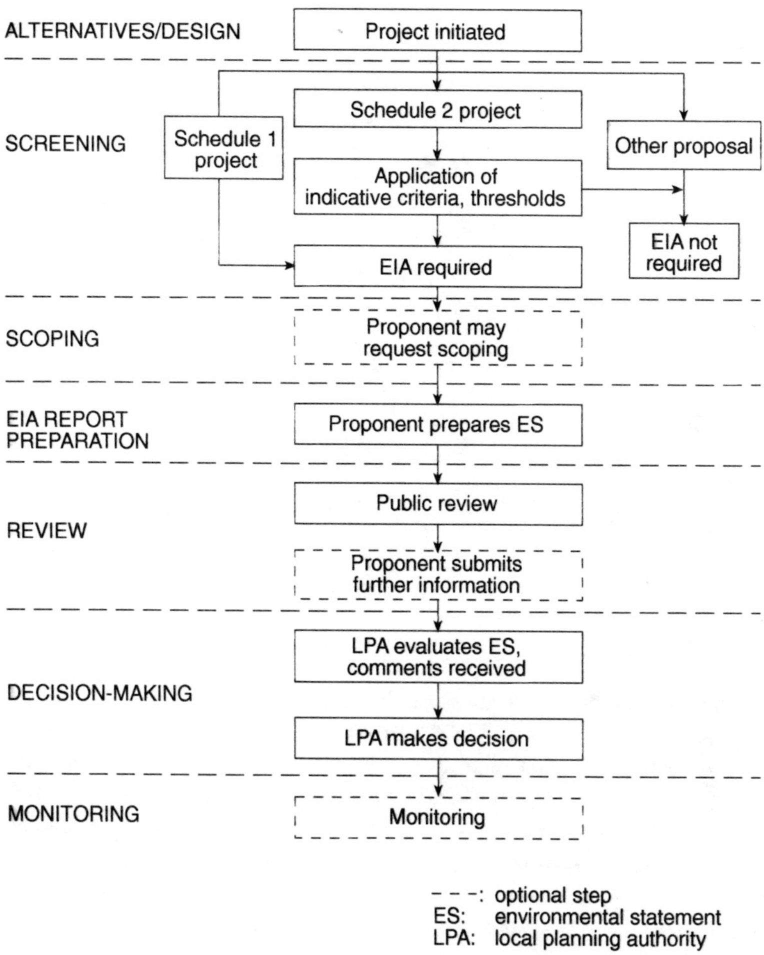

ESs with private and hybrid Parliamentary bills have also been made in the United Kingdom (Glasson et al., 1999).

Of about three thousand ESs prepared between 1988 and April 1998 in the UK, over two and a half thousand were produced under the various planning regulations (Wood and Bellanger, 1998). Less than 10 per cent of ESs related to projects falling within Annex I to the European Directive. Most ESs related to Annex II infrastructure, waste disposal, energy and extractive industry projects (Box 7.2). Most LPAs have received at least one ES but the county councils (in England) have received many more ESs than the districts and unitary authorities.

BOX 7.2: UK environmental statements July 1988–April 1998

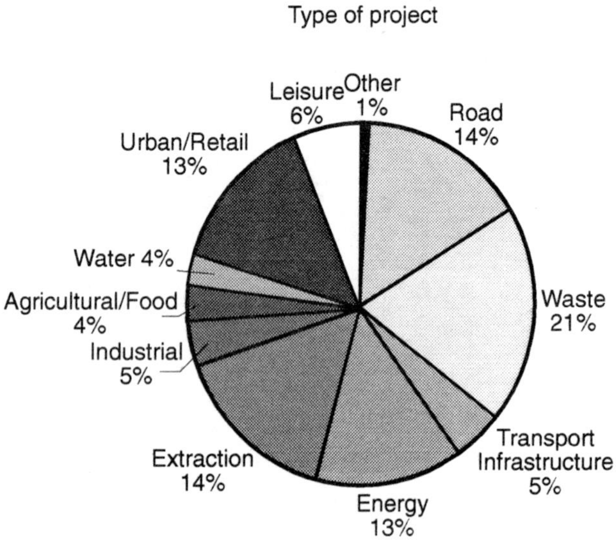

Source: Wood and Bellanger. 1998.

DETR has published advice both on the preparation of ESs (DOE, 1995c) and on reviewing and dealing with ESs (DOE, 1994h). Other guidance has been published by various national bodies, and by Essex County Council (2000). Commentaries have been published by Sheate (1996) and Glasson et al. (1999). Numerous EIA training activities have also been arranged by professional bodies and by universities, several of which have been supported by speakers from DETR. The UK has several successful established masters programmes in EA.

There has been considerable research interest in the implementation of EIA in the UK. Apart from work funded by research councils and undertaken by university researchers, DOE commissioned an early monitoring study on the operation of the EIA system (DOE, 1991e), work on the evaluation of ESs (DOE, 1994i), on the preparation of ESs (DOE, 1995c), on the quality of ESs (DOE, 1996f) and on the role of mitigation in EIA (DETR, 1997f). In addition, the European Commission has funded research into the British EIA system as part of larger studies.

There is no formal requirement for the strategic environmental assessment of policies, plans and programmes in the UK. In accordance with the Government's avowed intention to put 'sustainable development at the heart of every Government Department's work' (HMG, 1999) a brief guide to the incorporation of environmental considerations into policy appraisal (environmental appraisal) was published in 1998 (DETR, 1998g). In addition the Government has commissioned research into methods of environmental appraisal (DETR, 1998h). Therivel (1998) reported that, notwithstanding the absence of regulatory requirement, numerous environmental appraisals of development plans and a number of SEAs of European Structural Fund applications, and of water and other sectoral programmes, had been undertaken.

EVALUATION OF THE EIA SYSTEM

Many sets of principles, objectives and criteria have been advanced in the past to establish what constitutes effective EIA. The evaluation criteria used here to assess the extent to which the EIA system accords with recognised international good practice are those put forward by Wood (1995). These are derived from an analysis of the stages of the EIA process, including consideration of alternatives in project design, screening, scoping, report preparation, review, decision-making, monitoring of project impacts, mitigation of impacts and consultation and participation. There are additional criteria relating to the legal basis of the EIA system, its coverage, EIA system monitoring, the costs and benefits of EIA and SEA (Box 7.1). The performance of the EIA system is now judged against each criterion in turn.

1. Legal basis

The Planning Regulations[10] provide the legal basis for each of the steps shown in Box 7.1, including scoping should the developer request it. Not only are all the main steps covered by the Regulations but time limits are specified for each of them. However, no mention is made in the Regulations of monitoring.

Although EIA in the United Kingdom is largely integrated into the town and country planning system, the requirements are clearly distinct from those for normal planning applications, for example, in relation to timescales. The degree of discretion provided by the Regulations (which mirrors that in the existing land use planning system) appears to be broadly acceptable to most of the main participants. While there is no third party right of administrative appeal in the British planning system, access to the courts is possible where the EIA requirements have not been properly discharged. In practice, there have been only two or three such cases each year. Several of these have been influential: it is now possible to cite a number of cases in which LPAs have been adjudged to be at fault in not requiring EIA or in accepting inadequate ESs (see Chapter One above).

Circular 2/99 (DETR, 1999a) and government guidance (DOE, 1994h, 1995c; DETR, 2000h) together provide detailed guidance on the operation of

[10] Above n.5.

the procedures. The Regulations contain descriptions of developments and both indicative criteria and *de minimis* (or exclusion) thresholds to be used by LPAs in reaching a judgement about whether EIA is or could be required for Schedule 2 projects. Further explanation, together with advisory criteria and thresholds for Schedule 2 projects, is contained in the advisory Circular. It is apparent that the Regulations and accompanying guidance contain provisions which clearly and specifically define the basis of the EIA system integrated into British planning procedures.

2. Coverage

EIA applies to the various projects listed in the amended European Directive on EIA, subject to the use of screening criteria, no matter under which legislation they fall. This list is lengthy and more comprehensive than that in the original Directive. The EIA system, then, is not confined to projects approved under the town and country planning procedures. The 1999 Planning Regulations, together with the other project approval systems into which EIA requirements have been integrated, consolidated all the previous regulations and provide for the assessment of most types of project.

Nearly all types of public and private project are thus subject to assessment. However, whether a particular project is assessed depends upon the screening criteria and thresholds which apply to the project type. It also depends on the application of those criteria by LPAs and by other competent authorities. Practice is varied.

As in the Directive, the Regulations refer to aspects of the physical environment: 'population, fauna, flora, soil, water, air, climatic factors, material assets, including the architectural and archaeological heritage, landscape, and the inter-relationship between [these] factors'.[11] Social and economic impacts are not explicitly included in these factors. It is, however, open to LPAs to consider these matters in reaching a planning decision if they choose to do so. The definition of effects adopted in Britain should include 'direct effects and any indirect, secondary, cumulative, short, medium, and long-term, permanent and temporary, positive and negative effects' where this can be 'reasonably required'.[12] The coverage of environmentally significant types of projects requiring planning permission is thus, in principle, comprehensive, and, under the new Regulations, considerably improved, but some discretion relating to the coverage of certain types of environmental impacts remains.

[11] Above n.5, Sched. 4, Part I, para. 3.
[12] Above n.5, Sched. 4, Part I, para. 4.

3. Alternatives

While the consideration of alternatives is still not a mandatory requirement, the amended Regulations state that an ES must include 'an outline of the main alternatives studied by the applicant or appellant and an indication of the main reasons for his choice, taking into account the environmental effects'.[13]

The Circular makes it clear that, while the Directive and the Regulations do not expressly require the developer to study alternatives, the ES must record any alternatives which are considered. Proponents have been urged to consider strategic alternatives (for example, alternative processes and locations) early enough for them to be considered as feasible options (DETR, 1997f, 49).

The lack of regulatory weight given to the treatment of the environmental impacts of alternatives has been reflected in practice. A review of 100 ESs found that in 20 cases, no alternative sites, routes or processes were presented, and that in a further 13 cases, alternatives were considered, but without any environmental criteria being applied (DETR, 1997f). Encouragingly, in thirty-four per cent of the ESs 'it was evident that environmental criteria had had some influence in the selection of the site, route or process' (DETR, 1997f, para. 3.30). The introduction of the requirement to report the alternatives considered in the ES should lead to further improvements in practice.

4. Screening

For Schedule 1 projects (for example, oil refineries and waste water treatment plants), for which environmental impact assessment is mandatory, it is normally clear from the thresholds whether a particular project requires EIA. For the longer list of Schedule 2 projects (such as quarries, urban developments and golf courses), whether a project will require EIA depends on the likely significance of its environmental effects. These, in turn, will depend on the characteristics of the development, the environmental sensitivity of the location, and the characteristics of the potential impact (DETR, 1999a).

In essence, if the Schedule 2 development is a major development of more than local importance, which exceeds an exclusive threshold, it is considered to be a potential 'EIA development', i.e. one for which EIA may be required. If the development does not meet the indicative criteria and thresholds listed in Annex A of the Circular (DETR, 1999a), EIA is unlikely to be required. All developments in sensitive areas (national parks, national nature reserves, etc.—see DETR, 1999a, Annex B) are potentially subject to EIA and must be screened. Finally, a limited number of developments (usually involving emissions which are potentially hazardous or damaging) may be subject to EIA because of the nature of their impacts (DETR, 1999a, para. 41).

[13] Above n.5, Sched. 4, Part II, para. 4.

The EIA system is binary: either a project is subject to EIA or it is not. There is no provision for 'simplified' EIA, though, inevitably, the ESs for certain projects (especially those with potentially complex impacts such as toxic waste incinerators) tend to present a much fuller treatment than those for others (for example, afforestation projects). The vast majority of developments which fall to be approved by LPAs within the town and country planning system are minor and therefore not subject to EIA.

LPAs are generally responsible for screening decisions in the first instance, following the approach set down in the Circular and are required to reach, and record, a formal 'screening opinion' for all Schedule 2 developments unaccompanied by an ES. A formal opinion of this kind may be requested by the proponent, in which case the LPA may, 'exceptionally' (DETR, 1999a), refer to the statutory consultees for advice. If the LPA, on receipt of this information, or of a planning application unaccompanied by an ES, determines that an ES is required, there is provision for the developer to appeal to the Secretary of State for the Environment against this screening decision.

It appears that planning officers with greater experience of EIA are more likely to request an ES than less experienced planners—a small minority of whom may try to avoid EIA altogether (Weston, 2000). About fifty-five per cent of developers asked LPAs if an ES would be required, nineteen per cent submitted an ES without prior consultation and twenty-three per cent only provided an ES later, when requested to do so. The most important screening criteria in deciding whether to request an ES were the nature of the project and its proximity to a sensitive environmental receptor. The Secretary of State has been issuing about twelve directions a year, just under half requiring EIA with a small majority ruling that no EIA was necessary (Weston, 2000).

Screening practice has not always been effective but has improved over the years (Wood, 1995). The 1999 Regulations and Circular provide clearer criteria and thresholds, which should improve practice further.

5. Scoping

There is no requirement in the United Kingdom for the proponent to consult the LPA prior to submission of the ES, or to undertake any form of scoping. However, the 1999 Regulations allow a developer to request a formal pre-application 'scoping opinion' from the LPA. The LPA is under a statutory requirement to consult the various EIA statutory consultees and to provide an opinion within five weeks; where it fails to do so, the developer may apply to the Secretary of State for a 'scoping direction' instead. These provisions codify previous Government advice, since DETR has consistently advised developers to consult LPAs about the coverage of ESs (DOE, 1995c; DETR, 2000h). Consultation of statutory consultees and, in some instances, of the public during scoping has also been recommended (DETR, 2000h, para 39).

The statutory minimum content of an ES consists of a description of the development, a description of mitigation measures, the data necessary to identify and assess the main effects, an outline of the main alternatives considered and a non-technical summary. Further information, describing the environment and the likely significant effects, is to be included to the extent that is reasonably required for the effects to be assessed.[14] The Circular (DETR, 1999a) recommends these topics, together with other information in the Circular, as a starting point (see also DOE, 1989, Appendix 4; DOE, 1995c).

Weston (2000) found that two thirds of LPAs reported that developers consulted them in all the EIA cases they dealt with and that another quarter of LPAs were consulted in seventy-five per cent of the EIA cases they dealt with. The scoping methods used by a sample of thirty-three consultancies centred on consultation with the LPA and other consultees, on previous experience and on professional judgement. Jones et al. (1998) found that the public (mainly in the form of major public interest and local action groups) was involved in scoping in about forty per cent of cases but influenced the ES content in only a proportion of these.

It is clear that informal scoping arrangements between the developer/consultant and the LPA and, to a lesser extent, with consultees are working reasonably well and that the amended Regulations should codify existing practice. However, it is also clear that public involvement in scoping is less satisfactory.

6. ES preparation

While the developer is responsible for the content of the ES finally submitted and for the assessment methods employed, the Regulations enable the developer to collect relevant existing information from the statutory consultees (for example, English Nature) who are under a duty to provide it. Where a local planning authority is informed in writing that an ES is in preparation, it must notify the statutory consultees so that they can be ready to provide the developer with information if requested to do so.

Developers and their consultants approach the statutory consultees in the vast majority of cases. On the basis of forty case studies, Jones et al. (1998) reported that the consultations, which took place in over ninety per cent of cases, often consisted of requests for information concerning, for example, statutory designations. The proportion of EIAs in which information is sought appeared to have increased. In a study of a sample of forty submitted ESs, eighty-five per cent were prepared with assistance from outside consultants, an increase over earlier years (Jones et al., 1998). There is a discernible trend for certain clients to demand that their consultants utilise an independent panel to verify the quality of ESs before finalisation. While the guide to the preparation

[14] Above n.5, Sched. 4.

of ESs (DOE, 1995c) provides general guidance about the outline structure and content of any ES, there remains amongst developers and consultants a sense of inadequate guidance on ES structure, methods and techniques (Jones et al., 1998).

In summary, ESs have to meet limited content requirements but there are no formal checks to prevent the release of inadequate EIA reports. In practice, checks on content and adequacy are made at the review stage.

7. ES review

There is a requirement for the ES to be made available for consultative and public review. The LPA review of the EIA report is normally in two stages. The first stage is an early evaluation of the ES to see whether more information should be requested and the second is a fuller review once the results of consultation and participation have been received. The responses from consultees and public participants, together with the LPA's own review, are usually open to public inspection. Government guidance on the review of ESs has been published, providing a framework for reviewing the content of an ES and advice on evaluating the treatment of individual environmental effects (DOE, 1994h). A planning application accompanied by an ES must be advertised and copies of the ES must be made available to the public for inspection and to a set of statutory consultees.

Notwithstanding the availability of review guidance, LPAs review ESs without the benefit of formal review criteria beyond Schedule 4 to the Planning Regulations or of any specialised review body. Where they undertook their own reviews, the LPAs studied by Jones et al. (1998) relied on the Regulations in a quarter of cases, on consultations in two fifths of cases and on combinations of consultation and the use of guidance documentation in a quarter of cases. Kreuser and Hammersley (1999) confirmed that LPAs are very dependent on consultees for comment on ESs. The LPA may commission consultants or the independent Institute of Environmental Management and Assessment to review the ES. A study of forty ESs showed that nearly a quarter had been reviewed by external consultancies (Jones et al., 1998; see also Glasson et al., 1999, 233). As a result of its own review and the responses from statutory consultees and the public, LPAs may request further information (for example, on how certain objections are to be overcome). However, DETR (1999a, para. 111) has indicated that this power should be used sparingly. In practice, LPAs appear to request additional information in about two thirds of EIA cases (Glasson et al., 1999, 233).

The quality of ESs has improved over the years. DOE (1996f) reported that sixty per cent of post-1991 ESs were satisfactory, compared with thirty-six per cent of pre-1991 ESs (Box 7.3). DOE (1996f) reported that statutory consultees felt that the quality of ESs was improving, though was still wanting. Although

BOX 7.3: Quality of pre-1991 and post-1991 UK environmental statements

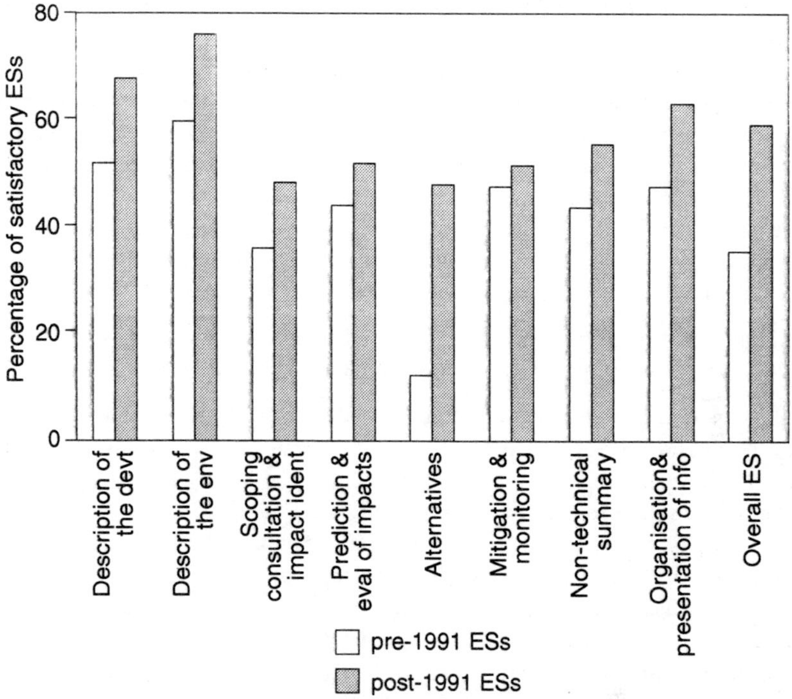

Source: data derived from DOE, 1996f, p. 29

these findings suggest progress, there remains considerable scope for improvements in ES quality (Jones et al., 1998).

8. Decision-making

LPAs are required to have regard to the 'environmental information' (the ES and the various submissions by statutory consultees and the public) before making their decisions. It is mandatory[15] that the LPA state in writing that the environmental information has been taken into account in reaching the decision. The planning decision must be publicised in a local newspaper. In addition, the decision, the conditions attached to it, and the reasons for the decision, whether the application is refused or approved, must be published in the planning register that every LPA is required to maintain. Where permission is granted, the main mitigation measures must be listed.

[15] Above n.5, reg. 3(2).

Guidance on decision-making involving EIA has been issued to LPAs in the United Kingdom (DOE, 1994h). LPAs must first balance the relative merits of different environmental topics. Secondly, LPAs must draw together environmental, economic and social factors in reaching their decisions (DOE, 1994h, para. 7.10). In a study of forty cases where an ES had been submitted, nearly two-thirds of the planning officers involved had found the ES (and especially the consultations on it) to be useful in helping them to reach the recommendations in their reports to planning committees, which were nearly always accepted by the planning committees. Planning committees were believed to give considerable weight to the contents of the ES in reaching their decisions in about one third of cases. However, the EIA was thought to have led to a reversal of the final decision in only one case. As Read (1997, 991) has stated:

> So often the fate of EIA cases depends on judgements that do not have a technical basis. It is the political process that has to complete a planning authority's review.

Environmental conditions were imposed by LPAs in all the cases where planning permission was granted and many of these arose from the EIA process (Wood and Jones, 1997).

These results are reflected in the outcome of a study (Jones and Wood, 1995) of ten public inquiries which involving EIA, in which it was found that the importance of the ES to Inspectors in evaluating the information about a case varied, but was generally less than the additional evidence presented and examined at the inquiry. Weston (1997, 124) confirmed this finding in a study of 54 public inquiry decision letters.

It appears that EIA has had a gradual, rather than a revolutionary, effect on planning decisions, enhancing the provision of environmental information to decision-makers and, to a lesser extent, providing assistance in setting conditions. It must be concluded that, while the environmental information is an increasingly important material consideration in planning decisions, it is not yet a central determinant in many of them.

9. Monitoring

Like the European Directive on EIA, the Planning Regulations are silent on the question of monitoring. The official guidance on EIA in the United Kingdom makes no reference to the monitoring of implemented project impacts. This is not to say that monitoring does not take place. It is customary for LPAs to impose planning conditions on permissions and for compliance with these to be checked as the need arises (generally when complaints are received).

The requirements relating to the making public of monitoring results vary. However, EIA does not provide any regulatory mechanism for bringing together the monitoring results arising from different legislative requirements. Where the proponent is shown to be in breach of the conditions on the planning approval or a pollution control permit, enforcement action can be taken. However, the enforcement of both planning and pollution control conditions has left much to be desired in the past.

In a study by Wood et al. (2000) of twenty-eight projects granted planning permission, it was confirmed that very little monitoring of environmental impacts actually occurs. Just over half the 865 predictions in the relevant ESs were found to be auditable; the others lacked data or were too vague or ambiguous for auditing to take place. There were only six unpredicted impacts. Eighty per cent of auditable predictions were deemed to be reasonably accurate and there was no evidence of systematic bias or under-prediction of impacts (Box 7.4; see also Frost, 1997). It is, nevertheless, apparent that there is still ample scope for improvement in monitoring and auditing practice.

BOX 7.4: Bias in ES forecasts by project type

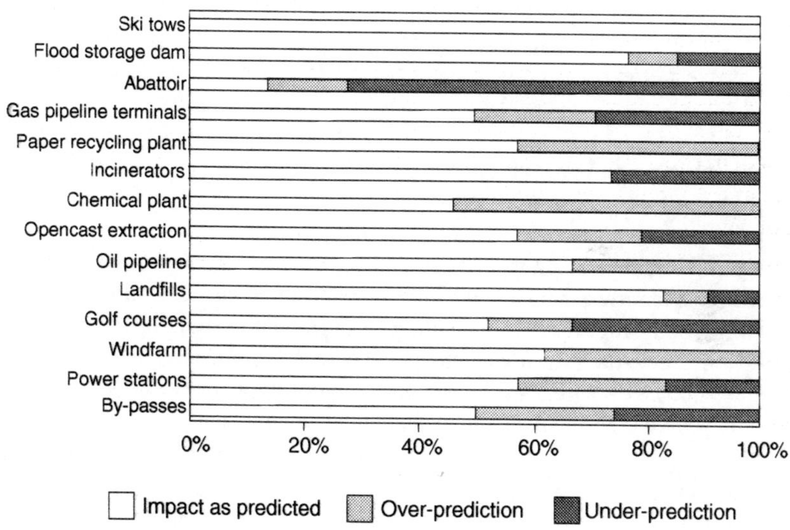

Source: derived from data selectively utilised by Wood et al., 2000.

10. Mitigation of impacts

The Planning Regulations require that the ES contains 'a description of the measures envisaged in order to avoid, reduce and, if possible, remedy significant adverse effects'.[16] The Circular makes it clear that local planning authorities are

[16] Above n.5, Sched. 4, Part II.

expected to impose conditions designed to mitigate impacts, or to require a legal planning agreement for this purpose, when granting planning permission (DETR, 1999a, 26). In addition to the Circular (DETR, 1999a) there is other published guidance on mitigation and modification, most of which focuses on avoidance, reduction and remedy (DOE, 1995c; DETR, 1997f, 2000h).

There have been several studies of practice relating to modifications and mitigation. In a sample of forty projects, seventy per cent were modified as a result of EIA. Modifications took place prior to ES submission in fifty per cent of cases, both before and after submission in thirty per cent of cases, and following the ES in twenty per cent of cases. Most modifications arose as a result of formal consultations. These results tended to confirm earlier studies (Jones et al., 1998). Barker and Wood (1999) found that EIA resulted in modifications in all the cases they examined and that seventy-five per cent of these were regarded as being of major significance. Most developers incorporated measures to mitigate adverse impacts into project design. This finding was confirmed in a study of the treatment of mitigation in the EIA process (DETR, 1997f).

It is apparent that while there is scope for further improvement in the mitigation of project impacts throughout the EIA process, practice (particularly in the treatment of mitigation in ESs) has developed as experience has been gained.

11. Consultation and participation

The use of consultation and participation is officially encouraged at the screening, scoping and ES preparation stages of the EIA process However, it is only once the ES has been submitted that the LPA must consult the public. The LPA is required to forward, or arrange for the forwarding of, copies of the ES to the statutory consultees and to take their comments, together with those of the public, into account before reaching a decision. Advertisements and site notices must be placed where EIA is required. The environmental statement must not only be made readily accessible to the public, but available for purchase at a 'reasonable' charge. On the whole, the purchase prices of ESs in the United Kingdom are indeed reasonable (many being free of charge) but a minority are expensive and some have been priced in excess of £100. Issues of confidentiality and secrecy have seldom arisen in relation to the EIA process in the United Kingdom.

There is some published guidance on consultation and participation (DOE, 1994h, 1995c; DETR, 1999a, 2000h) but no requirements as to consultation and participation methods are laid down. Apart from the usual statutory consultees for planning applications, the Countryside Agency, English Nature and, for certain developments, the Environment Agency must be consulted where an ES is received in England. Consultation of neighbouring local authorities is at the discretion of the LPA. As required by the Directive, adjoining Member States must be notified whenever a project is likely to have significant effects on their environment. HM Government has rarely been required to meet this requirement.

In a sample of forty ESs, consultation with statutory EIA consultees, major public interest and local action groups took place in ninety-five to ninety-eight per cent of cases. The ES was supplied to statutory consultees in about 90 per cent of cases but to public interest and local action groups in only half the cases (Jones et al., 1998). Practice in consultation and public participation appears to be improving, but there is clearly scope for an increase in effectiveness, especially in relation to the largely marginal role played by the general public in the EIA process (Glasson et al., 1999, 170).

12. Monitoring of EIA system

There is, at present, no single official comprehensive listing of all the environmental statements which have been published in the United Kingdom. Unofficial lists of ESs have been prepared (see, for example, Wood and Bellanger, 1998). Equally, there is no single repository of ESs though several collections exist (for example, at the Institute of Environmental Management and Assessment: see Glasson et al., 1999, 223). There is no monitoring of LPA EIA decisions or of decisions on planning appeals or call-in cases involving EIA.

Inevitably, as experience has been gained with EIA, practice has improved (see, for example, DOE, 1996f; Leu et al., 1996; Jones et al., 1998) and modifications have been made to the operation of the EIA system. DOE commissioned a series of studies on the EIA system (DOE, 1991e, 1994h, 1994i, 1995c, 1996f; DETR, 1997f). The 1999 Regulations, necessitated by the requirements of the amended Directive, also reflected the findings of the various commissioned studies, of other research, and of experience gained. Proposed changes to EIA procedures are circulated to consultees by DOE/DETR, made available to the public, posted on DETR's web-site, and frequently modified as a result of comments received, in much the same way as a proposed project subject to EIA (see, for example, DETR, 1997d, 1997e).

13. Costs and benefits of EIA

Under the Planning Regulations, most of the cost of EIA is borne by the developer and by LPAs. DETR devotes six staff to EIA policy work but no estimates of personnel involved in EIA more generally (for example, in consultancies and LPAs) exist. Jones et al. (1998) found that consultants frequently charged fees in the range £10,000–£100,000 for their services (see also DOE, 1991e, 1996f; Glasson et al., 1999). DETR suggested that an appropriate median figure for the cost of undertaking EIAs under the new Regulations might be £35,000 (DETR, 1997d). These figures equate to one tenth to one per cent of project costs in most cases (CEC, 1996; DETR, 1997e).

While consultants would often have been employed in the absence of EIA, there has undoubtedly been an increase in consultancy activity as a result of its introduction. Many developers feel that EIA has caused a slight increase in the cost of obtaining planning permission (Glasson et al., 1999). The cost of consultants used by LPAs to evaluate ESs ranged from less than £1,000 to over £20,000 in addition to LPA staff time (Glasson et al., 1999) with over half expending less than £5,000. Consultees also incur considerable staff costs in dealing with EIA (DOE, 1996f).

The mean ES preparation time for a sample of 40 ESs was about thirty weeks, within a range of three to one hundred weeks (Jones et al., 1998). The Regulations extend the time allowed to the LPA to reach a decision from eight weeks to sixteen weeks. Various studies have indicated that the mean time to determine applications involving EIA is about forty weeks, considerably more than for those unaccompanied by an ES (DOE, 1991e, 1996f). There is some evidence that the time taken by LPAs to reach a decision is inversely proportional to the quality of the ES (Lee and Brown, 1992; CEC, 1996).

There is little evidence, to date, that EIA has led to a reversal of the outcome of decisions. However, modifications appear to be made to two thirds of the projects as a result of EIA. In general, it is believed that the benefits of EIA in the United Kingdom outweigh its costs:

> the developers, competent authorities and statutory consultees all agreed that the benefits of the individual EIA had outweighed the costs. . . . the key environmental benefits include the avoidance of environmentally sensitive areas, improvements in project design to reduce potential environmental damage at source, higher standards of mitigation, and the provision of a better framework for environmental monitoring [CEC, 1996, 96].

14. Strategic environmental assessment

It is a statutory requirement[17] that LPAs take environmental (together with economic and social) considerations into account in preparing their land use plans. It has been expected (but not legally required) that LPAs should appraise the environmental implications of policies and proposals in land use plans since 1992. In 1999 DETR asked LPAs to include, in their plan documentation, an explanation of how the outcomes of the iterative environmental appraisal process, which was to be applied at every stage of the development plan process, had informed the policies and proposals in the plan. LPAs were also asked to develop appraisal methodologies to encompass environmental, economic and social (i.e. sustainability) issues (DETR, 1999b).

In 1993 a good practice guide to the environmental appraisal of development plans was published (DOE, 1993c). Further guidance for local authorities,

[17] Town and Country Planning (Development Plan) (England) Regulations 1999 (SI 1999, No 3280).

resulting from direct experience of carrying out environmental appraisal, was published in 1996 (Bedfordshire County Council and Royal Society for the Protection of Birds, 1996).

Therivel (1998) reported that about three quarters of LPAs had begun to carry out an environmental appraisal. Most LPAs followed the 1993 guide to environmental appraisal, with little adaptation of methodologies or approach to local circumstances (Curran et al., 1998). It is clear that practice has developed very rapidly over the last decade:

> The SEAs have generally raised awareness of environmental issues and are increasingly resulting in changes to the relevant policy, plan, or program. What was 'best practice' a few years ago is now normal practice, . . .SEA is becoming a mainstream activity with considerable benefits in Britain. . . [Therivel, 1998, 56].

CONCLUSIONS

The British EIA system fully meets six and partially meets another four of the 14 evaluation criteria employed in this analysis (see Box 7.5). The new Regulations have led to marked improvements but Britain's is still a fairly weak EIA system. Provisions relating to alternatives, screening, partial scoping, ES publication and public participation are well integrated into existing town and country planning decision-making processes. But the same cannot be said of provisions enabling early participation, third party appeal, monitoring, or those which ensure that EIA is truly central to the final decision.

Obviously, experience of EIA has been gained by LPAs, developers and consultants as the diffusion of practice has taken place, and the quality of EIA practice has improved (Lee and Brown, 1992; Jones et al., 1998; Glasson et al., 1999). However, while the range of experience within consultancies is growing, local authority experience of EIA is still surprisingly limited in many cases.

The shortcomings of the EIA system relate to mandatory scoping, to the use made of EIA in decision-making, to project monitoring, to consultation and participation, to formal system monitoring and to strategic environmental assessment (see also Sheate, 1996; Glasson et al., 1999). They are a reflection of British implementation almost to the letter of the compromise requirements of the amended European Directive. In these and other aspects of the EIA process practice varies considerably (DOE, 1991e, 1994i, 1996f; Leu et al., 1996, DETR, 1997f), from the exemplary to the unprofessional.

These shortcomings mean that the aims of EIA, better quality project planning and better quality decision-making, are still not being universally achieved. If weaknesses continue to be evident as practice under the 1999 Regulations evolves, then more radical changes than those made to implement the amended directive will be necessary. As a first step, measures relating to:

—better diffusion of EIA information and, in particular, of ESs;

BOX 7.5 Performance of the UK EIA System

Criterion	Criterion met	Comments
1. Is the EIA system based on clear and specific legal provisions?	Yes	Regulations specifically implement amended European Directive on EIA. EIA mainly integrated within town and country planning system, administered by local planning authorities (LPAs).
2. Must the relevant environmental impacts of all significant actions be assessed?	Yes	Comprehensive coverage of projects approved under town and country planning process. Marginal discretion in impact coverage.
3. Must evidence of the consideration, by the proponent, of the environmental impacts of reasonable alternative actions be demonstrated in the EIA process?	Yes	Regulations now require discussion of alternatives (where studied) and guidance has long advised it. Practice improving.
4. Must screening of actions for environmental significance take place?	Yes	Use of lists of projects, indicative criteria and thresholds in screening by LPAs varies.
5. Must scoping of the environmental impacts of actions take place and specific guidelines be produced?	Partially	Regulations require participation by LPAs and statutory consultees if developer opts for scoping. Guidance strongly advises. Frequently occurs.
6. Must EIA reports meet prescribed content require ments and do checks to prevent the release of inadequate EIA reports exist?	Content: Yes Checks: No	Regulations prescribe content but no formal requirement for proponent to consult or for checks on environmental (ES) statement prior to release.
7. Must EIA reports be publicly reviewed and the proponent respond to the points raised?	Yes	LPA may request further information and, though not mandatory, proponents usually provide it.

8. Must the findings of the EIA report and the review be a central determinant of the decision on the action?	No	Environmental information is a material consideration but not necessarily a central determinant. Practice varies.
9. Must monitoring of action impacts be undertaken and is it linked to the earlier stages of the EIA process?	No	No provision for monitoring. Uncoordinated implementation monitoring takes place under planning and other legislation unrelated to earlier stages in EIA process.
10. Must the mitigation of action impacts be considered at the various stages of the EIA process?	Yes	ES must cover mitigation and LPAs impose conditions upon permissions to mitigate impacts. Practice improving at various stages in EIA process.
11. Must consultation and participation take place prior to, and following, EIA report publication?	Partially	Some consultation and participation takes place prior to ES if scoping undertaken and must be undertaken following ES release.
12. Must the EIA system be monitored and, if necessary, be amended to incorporate feedback from experience?	No	No formal general requirement to monitor but some records have been published. EIA system reviews undertaken, and changes made to improve operation.
13. Are the financial costs and time requirements of the EIA system acceptable to those involved and are they believed to be outweighed by discernible environmental benefits?	Yes	Consensus (but not unanimity) as to increasing utility of EIA in improving project design and mitigation measures.
14. Does the EIA system apply to significant programmes, plans and policies, as well as to projects?	No	No formal requirement for SEA but SEA of local land use plans 'expected'. Guidance on environmental appraisal at central government and local government levels exists. Substantial LPA SEA practice.

—provision of project-specific guidance;
—provision of guidance on methods of public participation;
—further 'on the job' training provision;
—improvement of LPA procedures for coping with EIA;
—improved incorporation of ES mitigation measures into planning conditions;
—better provision of information to the public;
—briefing of planning inspectors on the acceptability of ESs;
—research into the operation of the various stages of the EIA process could be taken (Jones et al., 1998).

If practice subsequently failed to improve sufficiently then the EIA system itself would need to be strengthened further, as has happened over the years in many mature EIA systems (for example, the United States, The Netherlands, Canada, New Zealand, Commonwealth of Australia) which now satisfy more criteria than does the British (Wood, 1995). As Leu et al. (1996, 11) have stated 'the proactive imposition by central government of strong legislative and procedural control is required if the highest standards of EIA practice are to be universally applied'. Changes to the EIA system (and in particular to mandatory scoping, to formal ES review, to the centrality of EIA to decision-making, to project monitoring and to formal provision for SEA) should be designed to ensure that the imaginary briefing session—between a Civil Service EA advisor and his new Minister—would conclude thus:

MINISTER:	Maybe getting rid of EA isn't such a good idea, after all?
EA ADVISOR:	Precisely, Minister!

8

Planning for Sustainable Waste Management

JUDITH PETTS

INTRODUCTION

THE SUSTAINABLE MANAGEMENT of wastes represents one of the most basic and pervasive societal requirements. An integrated, holistic approach is necessary that not only seeks to reduce waste production, but optimises its reuse and recovery. Provision for residual waste treatment and disposal at suitable facilities requires appropriate siting and control to minimise environmental impacts and to maximise the use of energy and heat generated.

Within this integrated system the role of planning is fundamental and essential, not least because of its primary ability to prevent potential harm to the environment. But sustainable waste management also requires control over waste production as well as the effective operation of waste facilities. Waste management planning has been institutionally fragmented, and challenged by the technical, environmental and economic complexity of decisions with long-term (potentially hundreds of years) implications. Among local planning's greatest assets is its direct public accountability. The need for the public to be engaged in the choice of options and the implementation of solutions which will provide for sustainable waste management places considerable emphasis upon its participatory mechanisms.

This chapter considers the role of planning in a sustainable waste management policy framework. It discusses the limits and barriers to that role, in relation to both strategic planning and development control, including consideration of the tools available to assist decisions. Finally, it considers the need and potential for extended public involvement in sustainable waste management decisions. It is necessary to begin with a brief review of environmental and other pressures on waste management.

ENVIRONMENTAL IMPACTS AND PRESSURES

While the management of radioactive waste can provoke vociferous debates and objections in principle to the source activity, non-radioactive wastes arising from industry, commercial activities and households (the focus of this chapter) tend to generate the contempt which familiarity breeds. However, because the production of these wastes cannot be divorced from fundamental needs and basic human activities, it is possible to generate public support for effective management, not least when considering the full environmental impacts which may arise from a failure of management.

Box 8.1 summarises the key environmental impacts from waste management. These include both physical impacts on the natural and human environment and social and economic impacts. Importantly from a sustainability perspective, both intragenerational and intergenerational impacts are evident (Petts, 2000a). Intragenerational concerns tend to dominate local planning disputes about waste strategies and also siting decisions—particularly disamenity impacts and potential health impacts. The intergenerational impacts—for example, methane emissions' impact on global warming, potential groundwater pollution from landfills over thirty to more than a hundred years timescales, chronic health impacts from substances such as heavy metals, dioxins, polychlorinated biphenyls (PCBs)—place demands upon the planning assessment regime and also present significant predictive uncertainties. The uncertainties surrounding the prediction of the intergenerational risks makes them 'fair game' for the public to feed upon to promote their case against a particular waste management option (Petts, 2000b).

Members of the public might argue (on the basis of past experience) that institutional control is going to be lost or weakened over the normal ten to fifteen years relevant to strategic planning, let alone the ten to one hundred year timeframes of environmental impact. The planning system, therefore, is often required to question the potential for other environmental regulation regimes to minimise impacts (discussed below) and the potential for new technology not only to limit impacts but also to reduce fundamentally the need for certain potentially polluting facilities. Waste planning becomes a battleground between the authorities' need to ensure adequate provision of waste management facilities over the long term and public pressures to minimise the need for new facilities to be built. Furthermore, decisions have often been taken in a policy vacuum, which has resulted in facility siting being decided by reference to immediate priorities at the expense of a longer-term perspective.

NATIONAL SUSTAINABLE WASTE MANAGEMENT POLICY

Waste management in Britain from the 1960s until the mid-1980s was dominated by a philosophy of 'hole filling', a significant change from the practice of

BOX 8.1: Environmental Risks from Waste Management

Potential Impact/Effect	Source	Timescale
Resource depletion	Waste Production	S + L*
Human health risks	Fly-tipping All treatment and disposal options**, particularly landfill and incineration Transport	S + L
Noise	Collection Transport All treatment and disposal options	S
Litter	Collection Recycling Landfill	S
Visual impact	All treatment and disposal options	S
Dust	All options except composting	S
Vermin	Landfill and composting in particular	S
Odour	All treatment and disposal options	S
Air pollution	Transport of waste and recyclate Incineration Landfills	S + L
Global warming impact	Transport of waste Landfills Incineration	L
Water pollution	All options, Landfills & Composting in particular	S + L
Ecological impacts	All treatment and disposal options, Landfill in particular	S + L
Explosion/fire	Landfills	S
Land degradation and instability	Landfills	S + L
Planning blight	All treatment and disposal options	S + L
Stress and fear	Landfills and incineration in particular	S
Loss of local amenity	All treatment and disposal options	S

* S = short term, i.e. immediate effect or over a few years; L = long-term, i.e.10s -100s of years

** All treatment and disposal options—including materials recycling centres; composting; anaerobic digestion; landfill, incineration

burning waste which had been so important from the beginning of the century: Britain had some three hundred incinerators in 1912, seventy-six of them generating power from waste (Santen, 1993). The change to landfill dominance was encouraged and supported by a mixture of political, institutional, economic and geographical pressures and advantages, namely:

(i) an active minerals extraction industry;
(ii) a clay (relatively impermeable) geology in many areas;
(iii) a relatively low dependence on groundwater for drinking water supply (only about thirty per cent nationally but with significant regional variations);
(iv) until implementation (1986) of the EC Groundwater Directive,[1] low awareness of the need for, and means of, groundwater protection;
(v) the failure of local authority financial arrangements to invest in technology, particularly to reinvest in incinerators when plant came to the end of their life;
(vi) economic slowdown not least with the oil crisis in the 1970s, with immediate impacts on recycling in the light of high kerbside separation and collection costs; and
(vii) the intensification of private sector financing of waste disposal particularly in the 1980s, which in introducing market mechanisms saw a focus on economic efficiency rather than environmental efficacy.

When a tonne of household waste could be disposed to landfill for £2 in some areas of the country the dominance of disposal (for eighty-eight per cent of municipal waste) was, albeit lamentable, hardly surprising. Waste management policy lacked any national support and developed in the local authorities against a weak discourse on recycling (Gandy, 1994; Davoudi, 2000). Landfill had become the 'most adaptive and least expensive' option (DOE, 1995d).

The concept of sustainable waste management was a product of the 1990s, which is only now acquiring some clarity of definition and policy response. The European Community encompassed the concept of sustainable waste management in its 1989 waste strategy (CEC, 1989) which, with its revised Framework Directive on Waste,[2] was intended to respond to the increasing volumes of waste in Europe and predominance of disposal over waste reduction and recycling activities.

Britain did begin to respond to the concept, but it has taken nearly a decade to incorporate a working definition into national policies (SEPA, 1999; DETR, 2000e). Compared with its northern European neighbours and primary economic partners—Germany, Austria, France, the Netherlands, Denmark—Britain is significantly out-of-step both in terms of its low rate of recycling (less than ten per cent) and its high reliance on landfill (more than eighty per cent of

[1] Directive 80/68/EEC [1980] OJ L20/43.
[2] Directive 91/156/EC [1991] OJ L78/32.

household waste). Indeed, Britain performs more like one of the less developed economies of Europe—Greece, Spain, Portugal, Ireland. The White Paper 'Making Waste Work' (DOE, 1995d) provided the first explicit national policy statement supporting the European waste hierarchy (Box 8.2). Earlier regional initiatives had provided some guidance on strategic waste management planning, for example, SERPLAN (1992) contained seven objectives which mirrored the hierarchy. Waste Management Paper no 1. (DOE, 1992e) had encouraged the selection of preferred waste management options on the basis of the EC Strategy.

BOX 8.2: The waste hierarchy

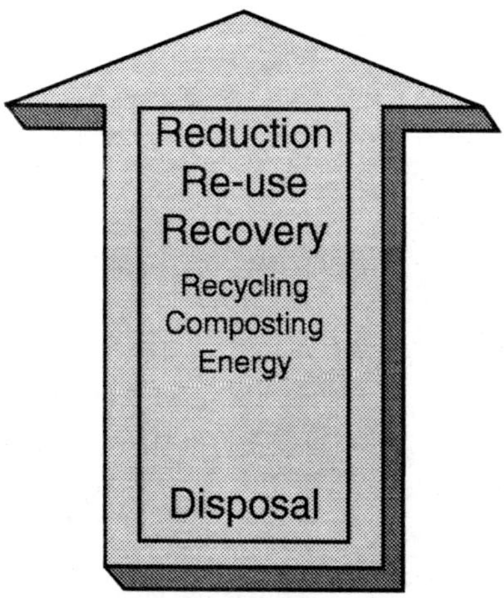

The waste hierarchy provides a conceptual framework for ensuring that consideration of the potential to reduce, reuse and recover (by recycling, composting and energy recovery) waste takes priority for any waste stream before decisions to dispose. The waste strategy adopted for England and Wales stresses that:

> We cannot continue to rely on landfill as we have done in the past. Landfilling wastes can be a wasted opportunity. If we are to deliver a more sustainable economy we must do more with less, and make better use of resources—and that means putting these materials to good use [DETR, 2000e, para. 1.5].

The need to reduce landfill usage has been given added impetus and urgency by the Landfill Directive,[3] which has to be implemented by July 2001. This requires member states to reduce the amount of biodegradable municipal waste

[3] Directive 99/31/EEC [1999] OJ L182/1.

sent to landfill—the UK target is set at thirty-five per cent of the 1995 level by 2020.

The 'decision' process implied by consideration of the waste hierarchy is supported by an analysis of alternatives, i.e. consideration of the Best Practicable Environmental Option (RCEP, 1988). Selecting the waste management option(s) which, for a given set of objectives, provides the most benefit or least damage to the environment as a whole, at acceptable cost, requires a structured decision process (see Box 8.3).

The BPEO determination encompasses not only consideration of the waste hierarchy, but also two further European waste policy principles:

(i) the *proximity principle,* which requires waste to be disposed as close as possible to the point of production or arising so avoiding passing the environmental costs of waste management to other communities; and

BOX 8.3: Summary of steps in selecting a BPEO (adapted from the RCEP's Twelfth Report, 1988)

Steps in a BPEO Assessment	**Outline Description of Steps**
Step 1: Define the objective	State the objectives in terms which do not prejudge the outcome.
Step 2: Generate options	Identify all feasible (practicable and environmentally acceptable) options for achieving the objective.
Step 3: Evaluate the options	Analyse options to expose advantages and disadvantages. Both quantitative and qualitative methods can be used.
Step 4: Summarise and present the evaluation	Present the results of the evaluation concisely and objectively.
Step 5: Select the preferred option	Select the BPEO from the feasible options. The choice will depend on the weight given to the environmental impacts and associated risks, and to the costs involved.
Step 6: Review the preferred option	Scrutinise the proposed detailed design and operating procedures to ensure that no pollution risks or hazards have been overlooked.
Step 7: Implement and monitor	Monitor the achieved performance against the desired targets, especially those for environmental quality.

Notes:

(1) Some steps may proceed in parallel.

(2) Throughout Steps 1–7, an audit trail should be maintained. Record the basis for any choices or decisions throughout all these stages.

(ii) *self-sufficiency*, in both national and regional terms, which will reduce the need for 'export'.

It is immediately evident that the BPEO will vary not only by waste stream but by area of the country. For example, the BPEO for a particular waste stream in London may differ considerably from that for Cornwall, reflecting different volumes, transport costs, availability of void capacity, access to materials processors, socio-demographic characteristics, social preferences, etc.

There is a need to change the fundamental use of resources at the top of the hierarchy; to develop markets for recycled materials; to assess the need for particular waste management facilities in local areas; to identify sites for required facilities; to assess the environmental impacts of proposed activities, as well as to control and audit facilities to minimise their environmental, social and economic impact. All of this has to take place in a market-dominated economy with waste management service provision largely within the private sector and at a time of changing institutional arrangements (Davoudi, 2000). Key questions are raised about both the role of land use planning and its ability to contribute to sustainable waste management in a complex multi-functional, multi-institutional and multi-stakeholder regime.

WHAT ROLE FOR LAND-USE PLANNING?

It is argued that the land use planning system should play a key role in achieving, or at least promoting, sustainable development (for example, DOE, 1992f; Healey and Shaw 1994; HMG, 1999). However, despite its acknowledged importance for sustainable waste management (DOE, 1995d; DETR, 2000e), land use planning faces pressures upon, and challenges to, its role, not least because 'planning', in the context of waste, encompasses more than land-use planning.

Britain has suffered from waste management policy neglect and fragmentation of responsibilities enhanced by discrete, unco-ordinated legislative developments in different policy arenas. Arguably, until the late 1980s, waste management was primarily focused on end-of-pipe control through the licensing and regulation of waste facilities. This function lay with the Waste Disposal Authorities (WDAs) within local authorities (counties and metropolitan districts in England and districts in Wales and Scotland). The WDAs also had responsibility for drawing up Waste Disposal/Management Plans which identified the need for new waste facilities. While planning authorities determined the location of the waste disposal sites (at the same tiers of local government as waste regulation) this took place in a national policy vacuum, and often with only an out-of-date plan to guide consideration of need.

The Environmental Protection Act 1990 created a four-part waste management system, all ostensibly within the local authorities, but of such a contrasting nature that the potential for cross-departmental integration, especially in a policy vacuum, was weak (see Box 8.4). Waste regulation, disposal, collection and planning now had defined functions. At the same time, the 1990 Act introduced the requirement for local authorities to set up arm's-length Local Authority Waste Disposal

BOX 8.4: Local Authority responsibilities for waste management 1990–6

Local Authorities	Responsibilities
Waste Collection Authorities (District and Unitary Authorities)	• Collection from households and commercial premises • Powers to recycle • Street cleaning • Litter control • Delivery of waste not to be recycled to sites specified by Waste Disposal Authorities • Preparation of Statutory Waste Recycling Plan • Discretion to make payment of net savings in collection to third parties who collect waste
Waste Disposal Authorities (County councils in England, district councils in Wales and Scotland and Unitary Authorities)	• Arrangement via waste contracts for dis posal of waste including setting up of Local Waste Disposal Companies • Arrangements for provision and operation of civic amenity sites where public can take own waste • Payment of disposal cost savings (credits) to Waste Collection Authorities • Own and maintain plant and equipment • May prepare non-statutory Waste strategies to assist with the above
Waste Regulation Authorities (County councils in England, district councils in Wales and Scotland and Unitary Authorities)	• Responsible for implementation of Part II of Environmental Protection Act 1990, particularly issuing of waste licences and enforcement of licence infringements and pollution of environment arising from waste • Prepare Waste Disposal/Management Plans
Waste Planning Authorities (County councils in England, district councils in Wales and Scotland and Unitary Authorities)	• Preparation of waste local plans identifying sites where waste facilities could be sited • Granting and enforcement of planning permission for new facilities

Companies (LAWDCs) which extended the privatisation process which had commenced with competitive tendering of waste collection services.

The Planning and Compensation Act 1991 made mandatory the preparation of development plans for waste management and also enhanced the status of plans in development control decisions. Discussion on waste was given a higher profile within planning (Davoudi, 1999). However, fundamental questions about the need for facilities (particularly in relation to municipal waste), which should include a consideration of the BPEO, were still also addressed outside the planning regime in the WCAs and WDAs. Pressures were beginning to mount on landfill void capacity, particularly in the South East of England, and the old planning ethos—of permitting the filling of holes linked to minerals extraction—was beginning to come under sustained attack.

Local planning authorities received little early encouragement to apply BPEO in strategic planning. Planning Policy Guidance No. (PPG) 12, for example, made no specific mention of BPEO or of equivalent integrated environmental considerations to be taken into account in waste management planning. PPG 23 (DOE, 1994b) included a tacit statement of the BPEO concept—'planning policies should encourage methods of waste management that have the least overall impact, taking into account the potential for energy and materials recovery'—but provided no further guidance on how to do this. It was only in 1999 (DETR, 1999c) that an explicit reference to the role of BPEO assessment was made. Some authorities—such as Lancashire (Davoudi, 2000) and Hampshire (Petts, 1995)—did attempt to use the planning process to respond to the developing sustainable waste management discourse. However, they were in a minority.

The creation[4] of the Environment Agency (for England and Wales) and the Scottish Environment Protection Agency in 1996 served to throw more 'spanners in the works'. By removing waste regulation functions from local authorities, it provided for a separation of consideration of siting and pollution control and the break-up of regional waste regulation offices. Waste planning co-ordination (such as there was) collapsed, with established networks and arenas disrupted (Davoudi, 2000). A report to DETR (1999d) concluded that waste planning was not being given as high a priority as minerals planning.

At the same time as the removal of regulatory functions, the system of LAWDCs was crumbling fast, with seventy-five per cent of local authorities having sold their companies to the private sector by 1995, leaving questions about need and siting of facilities subject to strong market pressures. The waste industry became increasingly vociferous about the land use planning regime not responding to its needs (Adams, 1996), in particular concerned that significant delays and also outright refusal of planning permission were preventing the required development of facilities. However, this concern might be taken as evidence of the industry's misunderstanding of the role of planning rather than

[4] S.1 of the Environment Act 1995.

planning's failures *per se*. At the same time developing national policy (see above) was raising sustainable waste management issues.

Planning became a battleground for competing and conflicting interests with pressures to move to the high cost recycling and recovery options pitted against the economic priorities of the waste industry. At the same time the Environment Agency came under public scrutiny in terms of its capability to control facilities once built, and this issue became entangled in the land-use planning regime and consideration of potential environmental impacts (see below).

A final complication to the whole planning regime has been inflicted by the convening by the Regional Planning Bodies of officer-level Regional Technical Advisory Boards (RTABs). Introduced by PPG10 (DETR, 1999c). The focus is regional strategies for meeting waste management demands, with the RTABs collecting and analysing data on waste arisings, transport and facilities and considering implications for development over 15 to 20 years. The conclusions of the RTABs will be reflected in the Regional Planning Guidance. At the time of writing (July 2000), nine RTABs have been formed, but only three have an agreed work programme underway. It is therefore too early to comment on the impact of this latest tier of decision-making. The all-important surveys of municipal waste arisings which will determine the work of the RTABs are only just being completed by the Environment Agency. Therefore, waste planning has progressed in a regional information vacuum, while pressures upon many authorities to address long-term waste management needs and to let contracts for the municipal service provision demand immediate action.

Key questions have to be raised about the relevance of regional strategies to local authority self-sufficiency; about the likelihood of public acceptance of large-scale regional facilities; about how the environmental impacts of waste collection, movement and disposal on a regional scale would compare with those within a single local authority, and about the public acceptance of decisions based in a largely administrative, as opposed to directly accountable, body. Regionalisation increases the amount of waste considered with potential scale efficiencies. These in themselves, however, do not necessarily promote the BPEO. However, this is not to suggest that for certain waste streams, perhaps of particular hazardous wastes produced in small volumes in a local authority area, a regional perspective may be appropriate.

Land use planning must continue to consider what new facilities may be needed and provide a

> framework which enables adequate provision to be made for waste management facilities to meet the needs of society for the re-use, recovery and disposal of waste, taking account of the potential for waste minimisation and the particular needs of special [hazardous] waste [DETR, 1999c].

At the same time it must encourage 'sensitive waste management practices' so as to preserve the quality of the environment and avoid risks to human health, and minimise environmental impacts. To do this planning needs information from the Environment Agency, WCAs and WDAs and the RTABs. Co-ordination with the WDAs and WCAs to address joint municipal waste strategies is encouraged (DETR, 2000e), but lacks statutory support.

Today, land-use planning has a stronger basis in the development plan system, is receiving a clearer remit in relation to waste management planning and still retains the pre-eminent advantage in terms of sustainable waste management, *viz.* it alone is directly open to public involvement and influence upon decisions (discussed below). However, while a major cog in the machinery of waste management, planning is not the only control mechanism.

STRATEGIC PLANNING

1. Issues

Demands for sustainable waste management come at a time when municipal arisings are growing at three per cent per annum in Britain despite attempts to encourage reduction and reuse. Part of the increase is due to changing sociodemographic characteristics, particularly the increasing number of single-person households which produce more waste *per capita* than a multi-person household (approximately 11kg per week compared to 4kg). Strategic planning has to take place in the context of significant uncertainty about future arisings despite newly imposed statutory recycling performance targets for the local authorities (DETR, 2000e). Current DETR forecasts (of the volumes of waste to be diverted from landfill to meet the requirements of the Directive[5]) assume a worst-case scenario of a continued three percent *per annum* increase over the next twenty years (from twenty-eight million tonnes *per annum* to 33 million tonnes of municipal waste).

While land-use planning usually operates strategically over a time-frame of ten to fifteen years, local authorities need to plan over much longer periods (typically twenty-five to thirty years) when providing for the letting of contracts for waste collection, transport and disposal services. The capital investment required for a new energy-from-waste incinerator (typically from £35–£90 million), for example, usually requires a minimum payback period of fourteen to eighteen years. Thus, there can be tensions between the time-frames of planning by the WDAs and those of the planning authorities. The development of an appropriate waste strategy which will provide for more than twenty-five years of effective management involves complex environmental, technical, economic and social judgements. It is an area in which rapid development of both decision tools and deliberative processes (see below) has been taking place (Petts, 2000a).

There can be a tension between local BPEOs and national policy priorities (Owens, 1990), for example, to increase recycling rates. Indeed, in remote rural

[5] Above n.3.

areas with dispersed, small populations, the collection and transport of recyclate to processing centres presents potentially important environmental and cost disbenefits—it may be that direct landfill of waste with minimal recycling is the BPEO in such circumstances (Barrett & Lawlor, 1997). The potential for increased reuse and recycling of waste represents the most significant basis of questioning by environmental groups of most applications for waste facilities.

Sustainable development arguably requires a more holistic approach to planning. Such an approach would not only address the BPEO for a waste stream, but would also co-ordinate waste planning with transport planning to encourage bulk waste movements by rail. Housing and industrial planning could promote renewable energy production and heat generation from waste. Britain's low up-take of combined heat and power (CHP) schemes related to waste is partly attributable to a lack of integrated planning (although the impact of declining provision of public sector housing is an important influence). It is ironic that the first incinerator for municipal waste was commissioned in Nottingham in 1874 and provided district heating to the St Annes housing area (subsequent plant on the site have continued to do so). However, all of the most recent energy-from-waste incinerators built in the country are not currently operating as CHP systems. The fundamental problem is a lack of a holistic approach to sustainable waste management as part of sustainable environmental management. There is little scope to address the life-cycle of materials; but the life-cycle of waste once generated does fall within the ambit of planning.

2. Tools for strategic planning

Life-cycle assessment (LCA) is currently the popular expert tool for strategic waste planning (White et al., 1995). The Environment Agency in England and Wales has recently launched an LCA software package called 'WISARD' to assist local authorities in strategic planning. However, there is limited experience as yet of its practicability and relevance in the local context. It is important to note that most waste strategies drawn up by WDAs and most waste local plans drawn up by Waste Planning Authorities have not been subject to any formal and openly accessible assessment relative to the BPEO. It is not surprising that proposals for facilities are usually challenged on the question of need (Petts, 1994).

LCA is an analytical tool which can be used to evaluate the environmental effects of a product, process, service, or activity. It is not site specific. It does not predict individual environmental impacts in the manner of environmental impact assessment (EIA). LCA is a comparative tool which reduces data on environmental impacts of different waste management options to mass loadings or burdens on the environment. It can add independent effects (such as global warming potential, acidification, energy balance, etc.) into an overall hazard score on a system-wide basis. At the current stage of its development LCA cannot deal with those localised impacts which tend to become a public priority in siting (for example, health effects, landscape and amenity).

LCA is nearly always complex in its calculations and there is concern that attention needs to be paid to qualitative as well as quantitative information and that the assumptions need to be made explicit and subject to sensitivity analysis (Sadler & Verheem, 1996). LCA has been, and to a large extent still is, a technocentric tool. The monetisation of environmental impacts is a further step beyond the traditional LCA, which is being tested, although the multi-criteria evaluation of combining costs with environmental impacts must be seen as a means of structuring a problem rather than of finding a solution (Powell, 1994). LCA is a tool applied to attempts to organise disparate information about a diffuse system and to take an integrated view of a system.

If the LCA process and output are to be subject to greater public examination and testing it will require more robust data than are currently available (even related to fundamental issues such as the projected waste arisings over the long term). LCA output will face significant public questioning unless data and the uncertainties surrounding them are made transparent (Petts, 1999a). If too much expert emphasis is put on the output of LCA at the expense of consideration of other important (from the public perspective) decision criteria the credibility of the process will be at risk (Petts, 2000a).

Greater potential in strategic waste planning lies in the use of strategic environmental assessment (SEA), which is presented internationally as a means of providing for cross-cutting environmental and sustainability perspectives (for example, waste minimisation and social equity) to be built into policy goals and objectives (Thérivel & Brown, 1999). There has been much debate about whether SEA is something different—a new tool—or whether it merely takes project-specific tools and shifts them to upstream decisions. A consensus seems to be emerging that it is not the latter because these tools often cannot deal effectively with indirect, secondary and cumulative impacts. SEA focuses attention on the need to integrate different tools (LCA, risk assessment, cost-benefit analysis, etc.) into the decision process so as to optimise their benefits (Petts, 1999a).

The weak support given to a form of SEA in the UK (DOE, 1993c) has undoubtedly encouraged less than robust waste plan assessments. Perhaps the most apparent weak link has been in the assessment of alternative sites. Rarely has it been evident how sites identified in plans were assessed as to their relative environmental benefits (a deficiency not limited to waste planning). Even greater problems have been evident when plans have failed to identify sites or even to define robust criteria for site selection for waste facilities. PPG 10 stresses that local authorities should identify the combination of facilities and other waste management options that give the best balance between environmental, economic and social needs. However, it states that sites for waste management and disposal facilities should be identified only 'where possible'.

Other countries have long favoured the specification of national or state siting criteria for waste facilities (for example, Victoria Environmental Protection

Authority, 1990; Victoria Government, 1991; US Environmental Protection Agency, 1991). However, the UK approach has been more limited (for example, restricting landfill development to suitable hydrological settings). A few authorities have considered the value of defining separation distances or buffer zones between possible waste facilities and sensitive receptors such as schools, housing, and hospitals. Buffer zones have been applied to the separation of major chemical hazards from surrounding development to protect people in close proximity from the effects of major, acute and potentially catastrophic effects (see Chapter Four). However, separation distances are more difficult to apply to facilities such as incinerators which have continuous releases which occur at height and whose maximum impact (not necessarily a significant impact) occurs at some distance (often over 1km). Separation to these distances could have the effect of sterilising large areas of land. For some waste facilities, such as clinical incinerators or CHP plant proximity to users is essential. Environmental and risk assessments for new facilities have to be the primary means of identifying the spatial area over which unacceptable impacts would be evident. Generic buffer zones are likely to present an overly stringent control which a site-specific assessment would not support. While the flexibility offered by planning to define relevant and acceptable local criteria is a strength of the decentralised approach, problems result when authorities choose either to abdicate their responsibilities or to impose overly stringent restrictions on development (i.e. 'not in my local authority').

SITING WASTE FACILITIES

1. Pressures

The siting of waste facilities has often been presented as being very difficult, bedevilled by 'irrational' public opposition. However, the UK has not suffered particular difficulties in siting waste facilities, the literature over some twenty-five years having identified problems in most developed economies (for example, Hirschhorn, 1985; Ehrenfeld, 1989; Wolsink, 1990; Portney, 1991; Petts, 1992; Gray, 1995). The social, cultural and psychological construction of opposition to waste facilities reflects opposition to any decision perceived not to be in an individual's or community's interest. A review of opposition to locally unacceptable land uses shows that hostility can range across a wide spectrum: from a reluctance to have the facility in the neighbourhood regardless of a positive attitude to the proposed method of waste disposal; to a resistance created by a concern that the particular proposal is flawed although the technology itself is acceptable; to a rejection of a proposal because of a belief that there are better ways of managing waste (Wolsink, 1990; Petts, 1992).

Such different views can exist at the same time, within, as well as between, single communities and groups. The influence of such divergent views on information requirements and the responses of an authority or proponent demands careful, but frequently in practice misunderstood, attention. Of course, it is necessary to define 'siting difficulties' more specifically. Planning statistics suggest that the waste industry has faced no greater problems than other proponents of major infrastructure and industrial projects—for example, 1996 figures suggested that seventy-nine per cent of planning applications for waste facilities were successful (Biffa, 1997). Of the eleven energy-from-waste incinerators operating at the time of writing (both old plant subject to upgrades and extensions since 1996 and new plant), all have been granted permission without recourse to a public inquiry. Nevertheless, it is not denied that the siting of waste facilities is frequently contentious, raising significant local concerns. While proposals might be successful, decisions frequently take longer than the allocated planning decision time (16 weeks if an application requires an EIA, eight weeks if not).

Currently there is great debate about how many new energy-from-waste incinerators will be required to deal with the required diversion of waste from landfills over the next twenty years. Estimates ranging from 21 to 166 new plant have been presented (DETR, 2000e). While the top estimate is extremely unlikely, there is little doubt that new plant will be required over the next decade. Even 21 new plant will not proceed without some applications requiring recourse to public inquiry. This will particularly be the case if strategic planning continues in a largely 'announce and defend mode' so that polarised debates emerge 'end-of-pipe'—i.e. at the siting stage. There is already evidence of a strengthening of public debate around waste reduction, reuse and recycling, which the imposition of statutory recycling performance targets (DETR, 2000e) will serve to focus attention on. Not more than five years ago low recycling achievement and potential served to direct attention to what should be done with the large residual volume of waste. Current public debates increasingly focus on only having a small residual, albeit that suggested timeframes for achieving this are often unrealistic.

2. Tools

1. *Environmental impact assessment*

Under the latest European directive,[6] EIA applies to all development applications for waste disposal and treatment facilities which will handle hazardous waste (as defined by an earlier directive[7]) and to incinerators and chemical treatment plant for non-hazardous waste with a capacity exceeding one hundred tonnes per day. Other developments including incineration or any facility within 100 metres of controlled waters may be required to be subject to EIA as

[6] Directive 97/11/EC [1997] OJ L73/5.
[7] Directive 91/689/EC [1991] OJ L377/20.

'Schedule 2' development.[8] Experience in Britain of EIAs for waste planning applications is now relatively large, representing some twenty-five per cent of total EIAs submitted annually. However, it is evident that quality is still a problem (Petts, 1996).

The systematic application of EIA procedures to waste management projects was a relatively late development primarily because formative development in the US and Canada was focused on government infrastructure projects (Eduljee, 1999a). Waste management projects, being proposed mostly by private sector bodies, have suffered from their relative inexperience of EIA. A review, by the Institute of Environmental Assessment, of the quality of environmental statements (ES) submitted with planning applications (1990–6) suggested that some forty-four per cent of landfill-related ESs were unsatisfactory (Petts, 1996). Experience of incineration ESs is better, since they are smaller in number and their technical complexity often results in more experienced consultancies being engaged to undertake the work.

Considering Box 8.1, it is evident that many waste management facilities have potentially significant environmental impacts. Indeed, the relatively high number of impact assessments for waste facilities (approximately twenty-five per cent of the annual production of ESs) partly reflects voluntary EIAs by developers in recognition of the potential for questioning and concern about proposals.

This is not the place to discuss in detail good practice for waste management EIAs. However, it is appropriate to identify some of the problems which have arisen in practice. First, for planning authorities the potential impacts of major landfills and incinerators require significant technical understanding such that reliance on statutory consultees for advice is important but may not provide all of the answers. Secondly, as the consideration of alternatives was not required under the 1988 Regulations,[9] EIAs have often inadequately addressed both alternative sites and processes. Where companies own landfill void space, the extent to which they may consider alternative sites is evidently limited by commercial realities. Where waste plans have been deficient in consideration of sites there has been little support to companies to undertake site selection processes with any degree of robustness, except where regional or national facilities (such as for hazardous waste incinerators) have been involved. The lack of explicit consideration of alternatives has served to fuel public questioning of 'need'. Whether the requirement now to address alternatives and the obligation on planners for the first time to justify planning approval as well as refusal will result in 'need' becoming a more decisive consideration has still to be seen (Miller, 1999b).

Thirdly, baseline assessments have suffered from spatial and temporal deficiencies. A European study of twenty-eight EIAs for waste treatment and disposal facilities (Columbo et al., 1996) identified surveys which had a lack of

[8] Town and Country Planning (Environmental Impact Assessment) (England and Wales) Regulations 1999 (SI 1999, No.293).

[9] Town and Country Planning (Assessment of Environmental Effects) 1988 (SI 1988, No. 1199).

relevance to the prediction of effects. Where the potentially affected area can extend to one to five km beyond the site, and where odour or air quality surveys may require six to twelve months of monitoring (as was undertaken in Hampshire in relation to three potential energy-from-waste incinerators: Eduljee, 1999a) it is evident why cost and time savings may have an effect on the EIA process.

Fourthly, the spatial and temporal extent of impacts and the complex nature of indirect and cumulative impacts associated with some releases can present significant challenges to impact prediction and evaluation. Prediction of impacts upon human health is among the most controversial and difficult issues in waste management and has driven the development of risk assessment techniques.

Finally, there is an overlap of environmental assessment functions between planning authorities and the environment agencies' permitting responsibilities. A compelling case can be made for an integrated land use planning and licensing/permitting process, bringing together pre-project scrutiny and post-implementation regulation. However, this remains an unfulfilled goal. Article 6 of the IPPC Directive[10] allows material produced as part of an EIA to be included in an application for an authorisation, while Article 9 requires information obtained during an EIA to be taken into consideration in IPPC permitting. A single EIA is likely to satisfy both regulatory regimes and enhance public credibility of the decision process, although guidance has as yet avoided such logic (Eduljee, 1999a).

2. *Risk assessment*

It was in relation to consideration of the health risks from incineration that the UK first witnessed public demand for the use of risk assessment in planning decisions, despite neither a regulatory requirement nor official encouragement of its use. Planning guidance has suggested a rather limited view of risk assessment as being relevant only to accident hazards rather than the assessment of planned and continuous releases. The orthodox view is that the detailed assessment of releases to the environment should be the responsibility of the pollution control authorities (DOE, 1994b, 1995d). This attempt to compartmentalise responsibilities has been seen as bureaucratic fine-tuning by the public (see below).

The first quantified health risk assessment accompanied the planning application for the hazardous waste incinerator at Seal Sands (1989) (Petts & Eduljee, 1994). Since then risk assessments have become common to applications for incinerators, and have usually been a part of the EIA process (Petts & Eduljee, 1994; Petts, 1998; Eduljee, 1999b). Risk assessments have also started to be evident in applications for landfills, although it is interesting that the Environment Agency (still largely rooted in the water expertise and interests of the old National Rivers Authority) has taken a stronger role in this context developing

[10] Directive 96/61/EC [1996] OJ L256/26.

its own risk assessment model (LANDSIM—Landfill Simulation) for assessing risks to groundwater from proposed (and existing) sites. While the public may be content to leave consideration of this technical appraisal to the Agency, as a statutory consultee in the planning process, it has not been willing to let this happen in relation to the consideration of the health impacts of air emissions. The broad definition of impacts on human beings which underpins the EIA requirements has provided for a relevant positioning within the planning process.

Risk assessments within EIAs are not without their problems. For example, they have often ignored background or prevailing exposure and risks in an area. This is a source of significant public contention in local siting decisions, enhancing environmental justice concerns in areas of relatively poor health, for example in urban areas with elevated levels of bronchial illness. Concerns about existing poor air quality in an area around the site of a proposed large Thameside energy-from-waste power station in Bexley, south-east of London, resulted in a cumulative impact assessment being undertaken relating to the multiple combustion sources along the River Thames corridor. Cumulative risk assessments are still rare (particularly when regulatory support is missing) and there remain significant difficulties in fully characterising the cause and effect chain in relation to multiple, low-level chemical exposures (Ashford & Miller, 1998).

Risk assessment is demanded not because the public believes that actual risks can be predicted, but as a means of exposing expert assumptions, knowledge and claims to scrutiny (Petts, 1997). It is significant that risk assessments are demanded although plant will be operated to emission limits which take account of the precautionary principle as well as local conditions. This 'expert challenging' role demands that risk assessment application is open to public involvement and influence—for example, allowing for public input to the choice of exposure scenarios and to the definition of actual activity patterns in local populations, etc. (Petts, 2000a). However, it will also require public input to local decisions on the acceptability criteria to be used and the standards against which measurements should be compared. In the development of the application of risk assessment to both siting and pollution control decisions there is now recognition that an 'analytic-deliberative' process is required (Stern & Fineberg, 1996; ILGRA, 1998), i.e. a decision process that opens expert and technical consideration to direct public involvement.

PUBLIC INVOLVEMENT

1. Decision-making credibility

The complex reasons for public opposition to the siting of new facilities have been identified earlier. While questioning of need and of environmental impacts is most directly apparent, indirect questioning (or the underlying basis for concerns) often relates to issues of trust and confidence in the decision-making process and decision-makers. Public questioning of waste facility proposals often reveals a lack of trust in both the operator and the regulator to minimise impacts through effective controls (Petts, 1992; 1994; Petts et al., 1996). However, government has been adamant that:

> Lack of confidence in the effectiveness of controls imposed under pollution control legislation is not a legitimate ground for the refusal of planning permissions or for the imposition of conditions on a planning permission that merely duplicate such controls [DOE, 1994b, para. 3.23].

The English courts (see the discussion of *Gateshead*[11] and *Bolton*[12] in chapter 3) have conceded that perceived risk can be a material consideration, but so too is the existence of a regime of technical controls designed to minimise both risk and pollution. When the Court of Appeal allowed[13] a challenge by Newport Borough Council to the award of costs against it on the grounds that it had behaved unreasonably in refusing permission for a chemical waste treatment plant, it was establishing that public concern, even if objectively unfounded, is a material consideration.

The incorporation into UK law (October 2000) of the European Convention on Human Rights and decisions of the European Court of Human Rights by the Human Rights Act 1998 could give rise to a number of new influences on the way waste planning decisions are taken. Individuals will be able to pursue claims in the domestic courts (not just the European Court) for alleged infringement of the right 'to respect for private and family life' (Article 8 of the Convention), 'to the peaceful enjoyment of possessions' (First Protocol, Article 1) and entitlement to civil rights (Article 6). Objectors may claim infringement of their individual rights by industrial emissions and their impacts even if the latter may comply with an environmental licence. Whatever the merits of any such challenge, it seems that one way to minimise the opportunity for this to occur will be to ensure that all of the issues are addressed adequately and discussed publicly during the decision-making process (Stanley, 1998).

2. Deliberative processes

Strategic waste management planning in Europe has seen a significant increase in interest in extending public involvement from the required consultation to the use of more participatory and deliberative processes. This reflects the general growth in understanding of the need for the latter (for example, Healey & Shaw,

[11] *Gateshead MBC* v. *Secretary of State for the Environment* [1995] JPL 432.

[12] R. v. *Bolton MBC ex parte Kirkman* [1998] JPL 787.

[13] *Newport Borough Council* v. *Secretary of State for Wales and Browning Ferris Environmental Services Ltd* [1998] JPL 377.

1994; DETR, 1998i, 1998j; RCEP, 1998). It also stems from a recognition of the complex nature of waste management decisions, combined with a decline in public trust in the decision process, and of the need to encourage public engagement with the implemented solutions (Petts, 1994; 1997). Unfortunately, practice is not widespread and public involvement in the actual siting process, including EIA, still suffers from relatively passive consultation on already submitted proposals (Petts, 1999b).

The new approaches being used have thus far favoured either forms of citizens' juries, community advisory committees (CACs) or planning cells. Box 8.5 summarises experience in Switzerland in the site selection process for a landfill. Box 8.6 summarises the Hampshire experience in using CACs to develop an integrated waste management strategy. Box 8.7 summarises the programme of the five-day citizens' jury used by Lancashire County Council. CACs have been used by Hampshire, Essex and West Sussex WDAs. These have been in addition to more traditional public consultation methods as part of planning processes. CACs and planning cells provide the better opportunities for the key elements of public involvement which will ensure the robust consideration of long-term waste management strategies (Schneider et al., 1998; Petts, 2000a, 2000b), i.e.

- (i) education of the decision authorities with regard to public concerns;
- (ii) encouragement of strategic thinking;
- (iii) promotion of a degree of public ownership and identity with the chosen management options and agreed sustainability goals;
- (iv) explicit linking of technical expertise and public values and preferences and exposure of hidden agendas;
- (v) exposure of technical uncertainty to debate and formal checking of the validity of assessments;
- (vi) provision of a communication link to the wider public—the 'silent majority';
- (vii) building of decision-maker confidence to take decisions;
- (viii) attempting to find a fair solution whenever conflicting values or preferences occur, including compensation or other forms of benefit exchange, and
- (ix) consensus as to what the decision should be.

Unlike citizens' juries (currently attracting considerable UK government interest for policy discussion), CACs and planning cells provide the mechanisms to achieve the above, because they provide time for discourse and promote critical enquiry into factual issues (Petts, 2000b). They provide for multi-way communication and revisiting of issues as time progresses, and opportunities for direct interaction between participants and decision-makers. Key questions always arise about the extent to which the people who take part in such processes are representative of the public in general. Structuring of the processes can optimise representativeness and if the process is integrated with other methods this provides the best opportunity to ensure that as many voices as

BOX 8.5: Landfill Siting in Switzerland

Decision Context	Need to site one of several landfills in canton of Aargau. The landfill would meet local needs for a period of approximately 40 years. The authority had identified potentially 13 sites
Process	Planning cells formed in each area of the identified sites, to develop criteria for comparing the sites, eliminate unsuitable sites and prioritise remaining sites Four citizens' panels consisted of 2 representatives of local communities round the sites—104 citizens took part. People were chosen by an oversight committee—random selection not appropriate within the Swiss culture. Panels met 7–9 times over 6 months.
Decision	Each panel reached an unanimous decision and the first ranked site was the same in each panel, but had not been the authority's choice which had reflected geology more than the social and aesthetic issues stressed by the panels. Panel selected site was agreed by the canton.

Source: Renn et al., 1995.

possible are heard. Where people do not wish to comment, at least they are given information.

UK application of more deliberative processes in the waste management context has to date been largely 'by the book', which is entirely understandable as progress will be dependent on decision-makers and experts gaining confidence that such processes have value. There is a need in the UK to combine the confrontational style of citizens' juries with the learning style of CACs, the construction of processes using multiple public participation methods, and structuring of methods of integrating more effectively with the analytical assessment processes (Petts, 2000b).

The 'co-operative discourse model' of public involvement applied to waste disposal issues in West Germany and Switzerland (Webler et al., 1995; Schneider et al., 1998) has most directly allowed for the identification of public concerns and evaluative criteria and the measurement of impacts and consequences related to different options. Such approaches incorporate multi-criteria analysis and are more consistent with the objectives of resolving problems as they force values and problem framing to be made transparent. The purpose is to seek implementable and publicly-supported solutions that are based on some informed understanding of the pros and cons of alternatives. Participation based in traditional consultative approaches which require the expert to draft the solution in advance of public involvement is less likely to achieve this.

BOX 8.6: Hampshire's Community Advisory Committee process

Decision Context	Failure of an application for an energy-from-waste incinerator in Portsmouth in 1991. Recognition that traditional consultation process had failed and need for public consensus on waste strategy
Method	3 Community Advisory Groups, 16–18 people per group recruited to be representative of interests in the broad community but not to represent specific interests. One group for each of the waste management areas. Regular meetings once a month over 6 months (1994), including discussion, seminars, site visits, expert seminar. Participants provided with any information they requested. Meetings facilitated by independent company. Meetings open to public to observe but not to participate. Objectives of CACs to act as a sounding-board for development of an integrated waste management strategy, to identify issues of concern and provide feedback to county and districts. Consensus recommendations on the strategy produced. At end of process a single core forum formed from the 3 CACs to extend over a period during which waste management contract was to be tendered (1995). Further seminars and meetings including with the shortlisted waste companies tendering for the contract. End of process, a series of focus groups run with members of the public to canvas wider views together with a questionnaire survey. Parallel to whole process a full public consultation process using traditional methods—exhibition, leaflets, TV & radio etc.
Outcome	Consensus on need for integrated waste strategy. Energy-from-waste accepted but agreement that 3 plant should each be less than 200K tonnes per annum capacity. Views of public taken into account in the waste strategy adopted and contract let.

Source: Petts, 1995.

Both the UK and German experience of the use of participative processes is that the public is willing to participate, learn from the processes, and also bring added value to the process and decision. The challenge is to develop and adapt traditional tools—not least risk assessment—so that their application is embedded in deliberative processes, open to direct participant input, questioning and challenge.

It will require significant changes in planning procedures, particularly a need to break down the barriers of compartmentalised decision-making and more proactive planning of participation activities within processes. And as more resources will also be required, the question arises: who should pay? The non-statutory nature of the strategies drawn up by WDAs has provided them with a degree of freedom to experiment with new forms of participation. Waste Planning Authorities have been tied by the statutory consultation requirements and have therefore tended to 'do the usual', although some new approaches to participation are being tried. For example, Wiltshire County Council and Swindon Borough Council are (at the time of writing) experimenting with a waste forum to discuss the development of the waste local plan, including discussion of site selection criteria. It will be interesting to see the impact of the new guidance on Best Value in Waste Management (DETR, 2000f) on the integration of public consultation by WCAs, WDAs and Waste Planning Authorities.

What is most evident is that the link through to the siting process still needs consideration. Here local authorities may be able to instigate participation

BOX 8.7: Lancashire County Council Citizens' Jury 1999

Day	Content
1	• General introduction to issues before the Jury • Introduction to waste management problem in the County—County Council presentation • Waste management and risk assessment:—options for waste management, choice of appropriate option; concept of the Best Practicable Environmental Option—waste management academic presentation • Site visit—energy-from-waste incinerator
2	• Waste minimisation—local recycling group view • Recycling—national recycling campaign view • Composting—composting industry view • Site visits—recycling centre and also landfill and composting
3	• Anaerobic digestion—working group of the waste industry • Energy-from-waste incineration—industry view • County Council issues • District Councils perspective • Environment Agency—function and role
4	• Friends of the Earth—national views • Local interest groups' views • Industry view • Development Agency presentation on potential for community jobs and businesses
5	Whole day—Jury discussion and agreement on recommendations

when they are the decision authority, but still have to convince the private sector of the value. Contractual requirements may be necessary to force the issue. In Hampshire requirements for extended public participation were written into the waste management contract. The contractor (Hampshire Waste Services) has tried new forms of participation at the EIA preparation stage prior to submission of the planning applications for the three energy-from-waste incinerators. Contact groups have been formed related to each of the sites from people known to have particular interests and potential opinion formers in their local communities. The groups have met over a number of weeks to discuss the proposal and the EIA being undertaken. Comments and concerns have been integrated into the EIA work, including the scoping of the assessment and the design of the facilities. The group members have received background literature and also visited similar plant to those proposed. At the same time the company has run a more traditional participation exercise including exhibitions and public meetings.

CONCLUSIONS

Planning for sustainable waste management has suffered from national and local policy neglect, institutional fragmentation, unco-ordinated legislation and from guidance focused on what could be achieved rather than how to achieve it. The beginning of the twenty-first century sees new policy vigour and a clearer understanding that an integrated approach to waste planning is required which builds upon different responsibilities and expertise. Land-use planning still (i) addresses the broadest range of environmental impacts compared with other agencies and authorities, (ii) ensures preventative approaches to pollution control, and (iii) provides the primary means by which the public can be engaged in fundamental decisions which will directly affect the potential for waste to be reduced and recycled as well as for long-term mitigation of environmental impacts. This is a strength that needs to be capitalised upon through new deliberative decision processes. Some authorities have already recognised this potential. Great challenges still lay ahead in the further development of decision tools such as SEA, EIA and LCA which are responsive to the complexity of the process of deciding the BPEO for waste and siting the required facilities. Public engagement in the assessment process itself will be essential. Even greater challenges lie in developing a more holistic waste management planning which responds to the sustainability agenda, i.e. considering raw material use and product production upstream and linking with other key planning sectors.

9

Reconnecting Networks and Buildings: The Development Process and the Reshaping of Water, Energy and Transport Demands

SIMON MARVIN AND SIMON GUY

INTRODUCTION

THE PROVISION OF infrastructure—water and waste networks, electricity and gas services, and road infrastructure and public transport services—to new developments has always been a central issue in the relations between local planners, developers and infrastructure providers. The struggle over the extent of private-sector responsibility for extending infrastructure facilities to new sites or expanding the capacity of existing local networks has revealed and emphasised the strongly contrasting aims and interests of development actors. This has often led to animosity between public and private agencies highlighting divergent views about the 'costs' incurred and the 'impact' caused by development activity. This tension between public and private objectives has produced an image of provider–user interaction rooted in conflict. Debate about the dynamics of service provision has often appeared to revolve around the strength of developers to resist public authority demands to meet 'costs', and/or the power of the planners to extract benefits to mitigate the 'impact' of development on local communities.

This contest has been further complicated by radical changes to the social organisation of infrastructure provision prompted by processes of privatisation and liberalisation. An increasingly fragmented patchwork of infrastructure providers is delivering alternative packages of network services that are stimulating new debate about the 'costs' of network expansion. This is often reflected in struggles over the increased cost of service delivery borne by reluctant developers. However, negotiation over infrastructure provision is not always driven simply by capital cost considerations. Recent research suggests that the desire of infrastructure providers to reshape their networks in order to extract increasing value is leading to a new negotiation style based upon closer engagement with developers (Guy and Marvin, 1995a, 1996a). In these cases, infrastructure provision proceeds less on the basis of strategic discord and more on the identification of shared communities of interest in network management. The emergence of these new styles of collaborative infrastructure management is being mirrored by strong environmental, regulatory and economic signals highlighting the difficulties of simply continuing to expand and extend infrastructure networks.

The aim of the chapter is to 'rescue' a hitherto hidden set of institutional processes and introduce them to academic and policy-making debates around cities and sustainability. We argue that the current debate about developer contributions in relation to infrastructure networks is blinding us to those shifts and is obscuring significant changes in the relations between infrastructure providers and developers. We think that this is unfortunate as such shifts present new opportunities for the co-production of environmental value. Moreover, conventional planning discourse about infrastructure charges, standardised service fees, impact assessment and conflict between developers and infrastructure providers could actually hamper the emergence of this new logic. If the debate is not extended to take account of these new infrastructure practices then planners will miss a significant new opportunity for promoting new communities of interest, that encourage potentially more sustainable development activity that may provide wider community benefits.

The chapter is divided into five sections: First, we discuss the conventional view of infrastructure provision and the development process. Secondly, we examine the emergence of a new logic of infrastructure provision that questions the assumptions highlighted in the conventional view. Thirdly, we present three case studies, one each from the water, electricity and transport sectors, that each exemplify the new pattern of relations between different actors resulting from the new infrastructure logic and the ensuing co-production of environmental value. Fourthly, we will look back at the case studies and critically compare and contrast the styles of provision. Finally, we discuss the implications of the new development logic for planning.

CONVENTIONAL APPROACH TO INFRASTRUCTURE PROVISION

Conventional research has been rooted in the traditional style of infrastructure provision and characterised practice until the early 1990s (Guy and Marvin, 1996a). During the nationalised period of utility supply, networks were extended over the country, providing standardised levels of service at nationally agreed tariffs. A powerful supply orientation dominated the culture of network provision as publicly controlled utilities supplied excess capacity ahead of demand to support wider national and regional economic development objectives (Berrie, 1992; Peake, 1994). Infrastructure providers based network planning on the assumption that economic growth would continue to stimulate ever-increasing demand for transport, energy and water services. Rising demands were met by rolling out new networks, by enhancing the capacity of existing networks and by increasing economies of scale through large capital investment in network supply. New motorways, the roll-out of the electrical 'supergrid' and larger, up to two thousand four hundred megawatt, power stations were powerful emblems of modernity and became symbols of rising living standards. The extensions of networked services were the material sinews that quite literally connected and integrated modern society (Guy and Marvin, 1997).

Planners shared in this task by managing a rational and comprehensive system of land-use planning which provided substantial certainty for developers. But the planning system did not have a major role in the provision of infrastructure services and there was thus relatively little consideration of the role of infrastructure provision in developing processes (Healey, 1991, 1992). Local authorities had lost local control of utilities to large centralised publicly owned corporations, and infrastructure costs were largely met by major public programmes which set out to provide universal levels of service. However, from the early 1970s the state had serious difficulties underwriting the costs of infrastructure provision and increasingly looked towards developers to fund network extensions and connection to the mains (Healey et al., 1996; Loughlin, 1985; Simpson, 1983; Kirwan, 1990).

As infrastructure providers sought to recover the cost of extensions to their networks, the social organisation of infrastructure provision became increasingly formalised and routinised. Standardised practices followed three interlinked paths: the routine technical assessment of demand generated by new development; standardised costing of connection charges; and new institutional forms for co-ordinating infrastructure provision.

Accurately estimating demand for infrastructure services and the costs of connection to the mains networks has been very problematic. When dealing with the provision of networked services:

> the effects of an increase in demand from one site can be felt at several others where capacity may be reduced... The effects may have ramifications spreading over a considerable area [Simpson, 1983, p.66].

These uncertainties were further compounded by the additional problems of accurately measuring the condition and capacities of existing networks, estimating the level and timing of demand and the technical complexity involved in making a connection to the mains network. But as utilities sought to recover the cost of infrastructure provision they developed techniques to forecast more accurately the probable demand generated by new development based on information from developers on the size of development, its use, type of heating, etc. Alongside these technical assessments, infrastructure providers developed increasingly routinised negotiating practices and 'standard charges or contributions with respect to infrastructure hook ups' (Healey et al., 1996, 154).

Increasing routinisation often gave utilities powerful incentives to build demand into new development. When a utility received a request for a service it made an assessment of the cost of bringing a mains to the site and the probable revenue generated in sales. In the case of electricity:

> the greater the anticipated revenue, the less the cost to its developer, if electricity is to be the sole source of energy, the board will assume a bigger demand, and consequently a higher return on their investment; the cost to the developer will be reduced accordingly [Rowan-Robinson and Lloyd, 1989, 195].

New institutional arrangements were required to manage negotiations between infrastructure providers and developers in order to co-ordinate more effectively infrastructure servicing (NJUG, 1983). At a strategic level, the local planning authority role was based on the 'referral system' (Cantanese, 1988, 91). New development proposals were referred to infrastructure managers who reviewed the reasonableness and cost of the project, and these assessments were then passed back to the planners to be incorporated into the local planning and development control system.

Increasing standardisation of the infrastructure provision process brought the differing objectives to the participants into sharper focus (Loughlin, 1985; Rowan-Robinson and Lloyd, 1988, 1989). The local planning authority needed to be satisfied that there is sufficient infrastructure to support new development. Infrastructure providers required an assessment of the level of demand for services and a method of payment for providing the linkage to the mains network with an increasing emphasis on cost recovery through developer contributions. Finally, developers wanted to minimise the costs of infrastructure but make decisions about the level of infrastructure charges in the context of their appraisal of the feasibility of a specific development project. The conventional view has tended to characterise the social relations between these participants as highly conflictual and tension-ridden (Kirwan, 1990; Loughlin, 1985; Rowan-Robinson and Lloyd, 1988, 1989; Simpson, 1983; Wimouth, 1990). The participants are seen as having conflicting interests in their differing assessments of infrastructure network coverage, the location and level of spare capacity and the cost of providing connection. Debate has tended to focus on the difficulties in designing charging mechanisms and the tensions between infrastructure providers and developers (Hodge and Cameron, 1989; Kirwan, 1989).

A NEW LOGIC OF INFRASTRUCTURE PROVISION

1. The new visibility of infrastructure networks

The emergence of a new logic of infrastructure provision questions the central assumptions underpinning the conventional perspective. In particular the conventional supply logic has increasingly been challenged by a new public and political consensus about the environmental, social and economic limits to the 'capacities' of infrastructure networks. Key issues include the infrastructure demands of urban restructuring, the challenge of ageing and badly maintained networks, the need to create more environmentally sustainable infrastructure, the increased costs of investment and constraints on public expenditure. In the UK, the private sector has been given the key role in developing the policy response to these issues by the withdrawal of central government from infrastructure investment. Since the early 1980s, the utilities sector has been subject to the privatisation and liberalisation of telecommunications, energy and water networks, while the private sector has been increasingly involved in the provision (Guy and Marvin, 1997). These shifts have created considerable change in the process of infrastructure provision and contemporary relations between development processes and practices of infrastructure provision need to be placed in this broader economic, political and social context. With reductions in public expenditure and the pressure to increase returns, infrastructure providers have ceased simply to supply infrastructure ahead of development. Instead, increasing emphasis has been placed on short-term considerations in responding to local authority and developer requests for infrastructure provision. Providers now require greater certainty before making investments and often seek to increase contributions from developers to fund extra capacity, or to steer development towards areas of spare capacity. Also, large landowners with monopoly control of infrastructure can limit opportunities for other landowners and developers.

These changes have helped to reinforce the conventional view that the relations between the local authorities, infrastructure providers and developers are inherently conflict-ridden. In this context, it is no longer clear how local authorities can ensure that development has adequate infrastructure provision. The key issue here is how far a local planning authority is able to influence and co-ordinate the relations between new development and infrastructure provision. In response, the Department of the Environment is encouraging local authorities to use development plans to facilitate more effective co-ordination between development and infrastructure provision (DOE, 1995e). But it is not clear whether development plans are able to perform a central role on these relations in the context of privatised infrastructure provision. The privatised utilities now provide infrastructure services according to their own commercial criteria within the broad framework set by legislation and utility regulators (Guy and Marvin, 1995a). This has accelerated and reinforced the emphasis on cost recovery by seeking developer contributions to fund infrastructure provision. Equally significant from the developer's point of view is that the provision of infrastructure will involve negotiations with a range of providers, each with its own commercial interests and priorities. The key issues are the problems facing developers in co-ordinating and financing infrastructure provision for individual projects and how far these problems affect developers' strategies with respect to the location and form of development projects (Healey et al., 1996).

Despite these concerns, there has been very little research on the emerging relations between the development process and infrastructure process in this new context. While studies provide some insights into these changes, they were often undertaken prior to the privatisation of the complete package of infrastructure networks (Loughlin, 1985; Rowan-Robinson and Lloyd, 1988; Simpson, 1983). Yet much of the debate continues to be linked to the traditional questions of charges and distribution of costs, for example, the charges payable for connection to water and sewerage networks. While this is an important topic, we think this fails to acknowledge adequately the deeper significance of privatisation on infrastructure provision. The privatised model of infrastructure provision is now firmly established (Guy and Marvin, 1997). There is now potential to attempt an analysis of the implications of these changes on development processes. We will now briefly focus on the new strategies and relations of actors in the development process and link them to the wider forces, which shape their behaviour (Healey, 1992).

2. New logics of service provision

A new logic of infrastructure provision is emerging in contrast to the old certainties of the supply-oriented logic (Guy and Marvin, 1995a, 1996a). Infrastructure providers are no longer able simply to extend infrastructure networks in response to demands even if developers are willing to fund extensions. New limits are emerging which are creating a shift to a more demand-oriented logic of infrastructure provision. Awareness of the economic and environmental costs of supply-oriented investment has prompted widespread social resistance to new infrastructure plans. This new climate of social and political concern over infrastructure management strategies has mirrored a transformation in the regulatory and financial framework governing infrastructure decision-making. In the context of an increasingly competitive electricity market-place, less volume-related pricing, growing environmental concerns and a new focus on network efficiency, electricity utilities are having to reinvent themselves around a new network management logic. Similarly, profit-seeking water companies operating within tight environmental regulations are committed to maximising the efficiency of water supply (Guy and Marvin, 1996b). At the same time, social resistance to road schemes, cuts in the road-building programme and concern about the environmental implications of transport mean that transport policy is reconstructing itself around integration and management rather than the old logic of network expansion.

Operationally, this means that infrastructure providers are looking much more closely at the technical and economic performance of each part of their distribution networks and are planning improvements rather than simply expanding networks irrespective of cost. For example, 'hot' parts of electricity networks that have insufficient capacity to meet peak demands could be subjected to intense energy efficiency measures to reduce the level, or shift the timing, of peak consumption (Guy and Marvin, 1996c). Similarly, the water sector is more likely to adopt demand-side measures in areas suffering from water stress. Supply-led options are no longer the preferred mode of management as companies are forced to examine the efficiency of the network, reduce its leakiness and examine ways of customers saving water before considering expanding supply through new resource extraction (Guy and Marvin 1996b). The Department of the Environment has issued planning guidance commending local land use plans, which spatially harmonise domestic, leisure and working spaces in order to minimise car-based transport. The 'new' idea is overtly to shape transport demand through land use planning, encouraging individuals and organisations alike to think about their 'transport choices' in terms of where they live, work and shop. PPG 13 places a greater emphasis on the use of land use policies as a mechanism for reducing the need to travel, suggesting appropriate locations where travel demand can be minimised and supportive policy instrumented.

There are also new forms of differentiation between users on stressed networks. As infrastructure providers attempt to alleviate stress on congested networks, they are likely to engage with commercial and industrial users who create high levels of demand. These users are likely to benefit most from network-sponsored demand-side management (DSM) programmes. On 'hot' parts of the network, providers may seek to calm demand by sponsoring energy and water efficiency and conservation measures, or by finding alternatives to the private car. By contract, where the network is running 'cold' with spare capacity, initiatives may well be developed to stimulate demand and infrastructure providers may stimulate local economic activity by promoting inward investment.

While the conventional supply logic viewed new development as a largely passive form of demand whose growth was met with supply-oriented options, the demand logic seeks a closer form of engagement with users. Regional electricity companies are now marketing targeted energy services to industrial and commercial users rather than indiscriminately selling units of electricity. Privatised water companies are similarly keen to discriminate between customers based on their level of consumption and service needs. Infrastructure providers are seeking to develop new ways of engaging with large users in order to reshape patterns of demand to reduce stress on the networks. Electricity utilities are beginning to venture 'beyond the meter' to deepen relationships with electricity users by offering free energy audits and other energy services. Such initiatives signal a major refashioning of relationships between users and utilities within which energy savings activities can flourish. Large users of water services in the area of water stress are developing new ways of modifying water demands in partnership with the Environment Agency and water companies. In transport policy, the use of accessibility indices provides a more transparent model against which transport planners can attempt to reshape the form, design and location of new development to ensure that trip generation is balanced against the capacity of the local public transport system and the road network. Developers wanting to construct high-trip-generating developments in areas of low accessibility have to enter into discussion with the authority about how improvements to the public transport network can be made to improve access to the site.

In sum, the privatisation period appears to be characterised by the variety and range of approaches to the infrastructure provision process occurring across the country (Guy and Marvin, 1997). In some areas, providers are taking a more active role in the development process, promoting the development opportunity of services sites in their ownership (a return to their earlier role). Because networks can no longer be simply extended, new questions about the relationship between developers, infrastructure providers and planners are arising. In this new infrastructure era the bargaining process does not simply revolve around the question of 'costs' and 'conflict', but rather involves a more complex set of issues necessitating a reconfiguration of boundaries between the interests of developers, planning authorities and infrastructure providers. In this context, the actual network—its characteristics, levels of spare capacity and its environmental impact—no longer provides merely a background to negotiation but takes a central place in shaping the development process. The condition of the network—whether it is 'hot' or overstretched, or 'cold' or under-utilised—may play an active part in reshaping the location and form of individual developments. This process may also bring different actors into the bargaining process and can serve to emphasise environmental concerns. Here, the notion of costs and impacts fails to capture adequately the importance of the network itself as a shaper of environmental performance.

EMERGING LOGICS: CASE STUDIES

1. Understanding infrastructure provision

There has been relatively little research on the socio-technical processes fashioning infrastructure provision to new developments. The case studies (see Boxes 9.2–4) make visible the economic, social, regulatory and commercial factors shaping the development of different methods of infrastructure supply and their environmental implications, that is, the intensity of resource use and trip generation resulting from new-built developments. The analysis focused on practices of infrastructure provision to new-built development as a window through which changing methods of network management could be viewed. Specifically, we are concerned to understand how the reconfiguration of national, institutional structures driving infrastructure provision re-shaped local, infrastructure-related, development choices, and how these, in turn, shaped electricity, water and transportation supply and use. Interviews with occupiers, architects, developers and utilities negotiating the supply of electricity to a new industrial unit, water to a holiday village and transport infrastructure to new office developments allowed us to examine how DSM reshapes traditional forms of infrastructure provision through the creation of new coalitions of interest around more efficient resource use. The case studies provide both an overview of the new contexts of electricity, water and transport supply and use a detailed understanding of the micro-shifts in social organisation, commercial negotiation and technical specification brought about by a demand-oriented approach to infrastructure provision. These new coalitions of professional interest around DSM, the extent of any subsequent reordering of operational priorities by utilities, developers and local authorities, and any modification to development design and specification. Box 9.1 summarises the reshaping of the development process in each of the case studies.

2. Reshaping of water demand

Powerful regulatory shifts of an economic and environmental function have promoted the emergence of a demand-oriented logic within the water sector. OFWAT is measuring the economic efficiency of water companies against rigorous standards of performance, judged via the comparative regional 'cost' of water delivered by each company (OFWAT, 1992). Equally, the Environment Agency is tightly controlling new abstraction licences to encourage water companies to increase the efficiency of their networks, mainly through leakage reduction which can amount to twenty-five per cent of total water supplied (NRA, 1994). New technological innovations, such as smart metering systems and telematics-based leakage detection, are helping water companies to respond to this regulatory challenge (Guy and Marvin, 1995b). At the same time, the Council for the Protection of Rural England has pointed to the environmental impact of new reservoir schemes in terms of lost land, diminishing green belt area, natural sites and buildings of scientific interest (CPRE, 1993). Social resistance to proposed reservoir developments such as Broad Oak in Kent has also highlighted the difficulties of pursuing supply-oriented options. Those water companies in areas of severe water stress, particularly in drought areas such as the South-East are now starting to embrace demand-management strategies in response to these new pressures.

3. Building in energy efficiency

The emergence of demand management in the electricity sector is largely due to a powerful combination of regulatory, commercial and economic factors. OFFER has weakened the 'demand driver' that translated increasing sales into higher levels of profit in the pricing regime at the same time as granting

BOX 9.1: Comparative summary of case studies

	ELECTRICITY	WATER	TRANSPORT
Development Project	Wells kilo Toy Factory, Anglesey (Box 9.1)	Oasis Holiday Village, Kent (Box 9.2)	Office Developments, Hounslow (Box 9.3)
Network Stress	Growing energy demand requiring £1M investment for reinforcement of transformers and cable network.	Insufficient water resources to support capacity and major new development and environmental restrictions on waste and sewage disposal.	Insufficient road network car parking provision to cope with trips generated by new office developments.
DSM Logic	Energy-savings were identified by a free MANWEB energy audit. Measure included the use of low energy lighting, replacement of faulty power factor correction, improving efficiency of compressed air apparatus and installation of thermostats.	Water savings were identified by consultants. Measures included the installation of water efficient fixtures and fittings, the adoption of water conservation management procedures.	Local authority and consultants identify scope for improvement to public transport network. Developers contribute approximately £3m to create new public transport net-works and strengthen local traffic constraints.
Implications	An annual reduction of 40KW previous demand) leading to cost savings of £9,600 (17% or previous electricity costs). For example the May 1993 electricity bill of £5,273 was reduced to £3,770 in May 1994. This contributed to the avoidance of new investment in supply side infrastructure.	Water saving measures reduced potable demand from 1ML/day (million litres per day) to 0.8 ML/day. The recycling of treated grey waters further reduced potable demand by a further 25% to 0.6ML/day. These savings will allow the development to take place overcoming water and sewage constraints without major new supply infrastructure.	Creates new public transport networks including 25 Hoppa buses improving exist-ing services and establishing new routes. New 'on-street' parking controls deter commuters within 0.5 mile of developments. This initiative integrates the man-agement of the local transport network by balancing transport supply and demand.

electricity companies an additional revenue allowance of £1 per customer to fund energy-efficiency projects (OFFER, 1991). Critically, this has led to an internal industry debate about the economic costs of continuing to expand infrastructure networks. With suppliers concerned to avoid supply capacity that cannot be translated into profit, privatisation has focused utilities' interest on the efficiency and commercial effectiveness of their distribution networks. Demand-management activities have emerged as an important response to these concerns, a process further reinforced by the commercial benefits of utilities engaging with their most lucrative and profitable customers. These three shifts

BOX 9.2: Reducing water demand at a holiday village

A planning application by Rank Holidays and Hotel Development Ltd for the Oasis holiday village at West Wood in Kent provides a useful illustration of the potential of demand-management techniques in reshaping the development process in an area of acute water stress (Guy and Marvin, 1996b). Rank's consultants realised at an early stage that the water issues raised by the scheme could present a serious planning obstacle to the development. It was estimated that the scheme would normally require a supply of up to one million litres per day of potable water and around 0.5 ML/day^{-1} of non-potable water. There would be major difficulties in meeting these requirements at West Wood because the mains network was already committed—supplies were adequate only for the needs of existing rural communities and farms in the area. Unless an alternative could be found to the conventional supply-oriented option, it was considered highly unlikely that the scheme would be supported by the National Rivers Authority (now incorporated in the Environment Agency) or then obtain planning permission.

In response, the consultants radically reshaped the design and form of the development employing demand-management techniques. Demand for potable supplies was minimised by 'the elimination of unnecessary fixtures, the installation of water efficient fixtures and fittings and the adoption of water conservation management procedures' (Rank Holidays and Hotel Development Ltd., 1994, 87). These reduced potable demand to 0.8ML/day^{-1}. The recycling of treated grey waters would reduce potable demands by a further 25–30 per cent, to levels of 0.6ML/day^{-1}. Grey waters—from hand basins, showers and baths—would be collected, treated and then recycled via a dedicated grey water distribution network for topping up the water features and WC flushing. A separate network would collect black waters—from WCs—and treat them prior to discharge with surplus grey water to the aquifer for recharge. By utilising DSM techniques the developers and their consultants were able to deflect public opposition to the scheme and even to enhance their chances of gaining planning permission by embracing an innovative design stance. At the same time, the Folkstone and Dover water company has been able to attract a potentially lucrative customer, despite having little spare capacity on its system, while local planners have been able to capture significant inward investment while minimising its environmental impact on the water environment.

have also been mirrored by growing awareness of the environmental costs involved in a supply-led context, and pressure groups—such as the Association for the Conservation of Energy and Friends of the Earth—have highlighted the environmental benefits of DSM strategies in both carbon dioxide and sulphur dioxide abatement. Similarly, the fuel poverty lobby, including Neighbourhood Energy Action and National Consumers Council, has actively promoted energy efficiency. In this new context, electricity companies may no longer simply expand networks in response to new development proposals particularly where networks are at peak capacity requiring significant investment.

4. Creating new transport networks

The 'predict and provide' model of infrastructure planning has also come under threat within the transport sector where a similar range of social, economic, environmental, political and regulatory changes has been underway (Owens, 1995). There is now widespread recognition of the cost limits of continued road network expansion which seems merely to accelerate rates of car use and growing awareness of the environmental costs involved in continued road network expansion. Transport, in particular car travel, accounts for twenty per cent of the overall carbon dioxide emissions in the UK (see RCEP, 1994). Awareness of these economic/environmental costs of 'heroic engineering' initiatives symbolised by road-building has prompted widespread social resistance to new infrastructure plans. Demonstrations against road-building projects such as the M3 extension at Twyford Down have produced high-profile media coverage. A powerful grouping of the environmental lobby, including Friends of the Earth and Greenpeace, is widely credited with prompting the Conservative Government's U-turn on transport policy (Vidal, 1994, 3). Such demonstrations of public opposition mark a new chapter in public debate around infrastructure planning and send influential signals to the Departments of Environment and Transport on the acceptable form of future infrastructure investment. This new climate of social and political concern over infrastructure management strategies has stimulated a transformation in the regulatory/financial framework governing transport planning. In the transport sector, funding applications from local authority planners to the Department of Transport have been redrawn to cover integrated 'packages' of public and private provision, steering local transport planning policies away from narrowly engineering-inspired, road-building initiatives. In response to these regulatory shifts, and with demand for travel accelerating, transport planners at national and local levels are increasingly turning to demand-management strategies.

BOX 9.3: Reducing electricity demand in manufacturing

Wells Kilo is one of four big industrial plants on Holyhead, producing children's toys and play apparatus—slides, swings, prams, push-chairs. It had been occupying a relatively small, post-war factory which was both inefficient and gloomy. It was in the process of building a new factory, developed by the Welsh Development Agency, but little attention had been paid to energy efficiency in the design of new building. However, the local electricity company was attempting to reduce growth in electricity demand on the island in order to postpone or avoid the high capital cost of a new transformer to meet rising demand (Guy and Marvin, 1996c). Consequently, MANWEB approached Wells Kilo to examine the potential for reshaping electricity demand of the new factory.

Initial contact was limited to a free energy audit which provided a profile breakdown of demand. The factory was typically dark and dingy, the lighting and heating systems were old and inefficient and production was labour-intensive, with lots of energy used in manufacturing through energy-expensive machinery. Consumption was measured at around 300 kW, varying at different times of the year, at a cost of £57,000. Importantly, both costs and demand were expected to rise in the near future, a scenario that would not have worried a regionally electric company driven by the conventional supply-oriented logic. But, given MANWEB's demand-management logic, this was of great concern. MANWEB identified possible improvements to lighting and cooling systems and identified the more inefficient machinery—injection moulding machines and compressed air apparatus—and the potential for energy savings was clear. Adding these savings together would reduce electrical demand by some 40kW (13 per cent) and costs by £9,600 *per annum* (17 per cent). Notably, none of these potential savings necessitated advanced conservation technologies.

Each energy-saving measure had to be assessed against its payback period, or transferability to the new factory, and a decision made on implementation accordingly. Moreover, the long-term aims of the utility depended rather more on the energy profile of the new factory. MANWEB came in late on the design of the new factory—the physical body had already been erected—but there was still time to comment on the services specification. MANWEB offered their energy consultancy services free of charge. A series of recommendations was presented to the hired contractors including the latest high-frequency lighting, effective thermostatic heating regulators and magic-eye, energy-saving lighting controls. There was little debate and the specification was upgraded. The success of MANWEB's strategy was again apparent in the electricity bill. Comparing May 1993 with May 1994, we find a reduction from £5,273 to £3,770. This highlights the stark contrast between the conventional supply-oriented and demand-management approaches to infrastructure service provision. When the boundary of the building no longer acts as the frontier of utility activity, novel energy questions arise. Electricity ceases to be taken for granted and greater attention is directed to the factory as an energy system.

BOX 9.4: Reducing demands on private transport in West London

In December 1993, Hounslow Council published a strategy for the commercial area of the Great West Road (A4), the main arterial route from the west to central London which carries much of the traffic to and from Heathrow Airport (Hounslow, 1993). For many years, congestion along this trunk road has gradually worsened and the area has been in danger of becoming an impassable bottleneck. Hounslow Council and the Department of Transport were both keen that economic growth should continue—but only if extra traffic flows could be contained through the development of public transport options. With development pressures increasing in the Great West Road, Hounslow Council decided only to consider new office development in relation to improvements in public transport plus restraints on car use. They decided to use planning obligations to link planning permission to mutually agreeable conditions about public transport. The Council began by negotiating agreements with two major companies—Alfa Laval and Smith-Kline Beecham, which each wanted to develop new office space locally (Macrae, 1995). In return for tough parking controls and public transport improvements, the developers were offered higher plot ratios. This money would be put into the development of existing bus routes, plus the creation of new routes and the possible reopening of a disused train loop line and associated station refurbishment. This is only the start. Hounslow Council wants eventually to attract £3 million from developers to fund public transport improvements including 25 new 'Hoppa' buses and better train services, as well as paying for on-street parking controls to deter commuters within a half-mile radius of proposed developments. Environmental improvements and local skills training are also being negotiated. As David Bull, public transport officer with Hounslow Council, put it:

> The aim of this approach is to enter into partnerships with developers using section 106 obligations to increase the Pubic Transport Accessibility level (PTAL) at office sites so that over time the modal split is more favourable to public transport [Bull and Underwood, 1995, 1].

The Hounslow approach to development contributions suggests that a plan-led solution that emphasised the co-production of value could, potentially, allow more 'sustainable' development and create more employment opportunities and help with major improvements to the public transport network. There is ample scope for negotiations between the local authority and developers. As Bull and Underwood suggest, the local authority reduces potential car trips, improves the public transport and gains new development to help the local economy without adding to environmental problems. Developers can use areas that would normally be set aside for car parking as commercial floor space in office schemes to increase profits and help to pay for public transport improvements. In contrast to the old supply logic in which developers would be asked to contribute towards the cost of the highways improvements needed to deal with the additional trips generated by the new development, developers now contribute towards improving the quality and potential of the local public transport network.

RETHINKING THE DEVELOPMENT PROCESS

Comparing and contrasting the patterns of bargaining in the case studies with the conventional understanding of developer contributions raise critical questions about the conventional vocabulary of 'developer contributions' when applied to infrastructure provision. Here, the language of 'impacts', 'contributions' and 'bargaining' fails adequately to capture the creation of new forms of 'value' in these development contexts. Faced with these novel forms of service delivery, we must begin to ask what exactly a 'developer contribution' should represent and what we might mean by 'costs' and 'values'. Rather than see development exclusively in terms of 'impacts', we argue that in our case study examples new forms of 'value' have been created that would not have occurred in the absence of development activity. In this way, the new logic of infrastructure provision transcends the kinds of aims and objectives found in much literature on planning gain. Our case studies suggest that bargaining does not always have to be an adversarial affair. Rather, negotiation in particular development contexts can result in a mutual reshaping of development options in a process of close engagement between development actors.

Seen in this way, networks cannot be viewed as a neutral background or as simple technology. Instead, we need to view infrastructure networks as 'actors' in the development process. In this context, the demands placed on developers are not limited to questions about the economic costs of the networks, or the technical feasibility of supply. The new logic of network management means that developers are subject to new demands. The building is not viewed in isolation, but rather as a node on a network with the condition of that network having profound implications for how new nodes become linked. In areas where networks are seriously stressed, areas of water shortage, overburdened transformers or congested roads, a new development has to be configured in such a way that it lowers its demand on that network. Developers may be called upon to allow new actors and technologies into the design process, or they may be asked to provide services that will help existing users to reduce their demands on the network in order to allow the development to proceed.

In this context, 'cost' of service delivery is no longer the central issue. Instead, it is a question of how the developer and infrastructure provider configure the building and its demands on the networks in such a way that the development can happen at all! This requires a very different approach to the infrastructure problem. Planners and infrastructure providers need to develop new ways of mapping the diversity of network capacities. This includes: information on network conditions and how they vary; new types of knowledge about users and the relation between building specifications, technology and resource use; and the social construction of new relations and communities of interest to sustain the development of the new logic. The management of networks in this context is spatially contingent, leading to diverse management practices across 'hot' and 'cold' spots and infrastructure sectors even within a single plane area.

The new logic of infrastructure challenges many of the central assumptions of the conventional view of infrastructure provision, rendering problematic the calls for a return to standardised assessments of the environmental impact (see Chapter Seven above) of new development. Analysis or planning practice steeped in structural assumptions of conflict and development 'impact' must be questioned. Rather than developing standardised approaches, new forms of local assessment and contextual knowledge need to be established in order to relate new development to the particular capacities of existing infrastructure networks. Such assessments have to be negotiated between planners, infrastructure providers, developers and wide range of regulatory agencies.

This means acknowledging that processes of infrastructure provision and development are substantially more complex than previously accepted and that we have to rethink the concept of developer contributions. We need to move beyond the old debate which focuses on commercial contributions in a very narrow sense. Developers have to make a much more serious commitment to finding new ways of reshaping the demand of their development on the infrastructure network. This may involve considering new building practices, the inclusion of new technologies for water and energy savings or a different approach to the management of trip generation. Such contribution cannot be captured in simple cost formulae or standardised practices. Instead, developers have to work with infrastructure providers to shape their development to meet the capacities on stressed infrastructure networks. In this context, the bargaining process is not necessarily characterised by adversarial relations. Both the developer and infrastructure provider have a mutual interest in reshaping the form and design of a development to manage the level and timing of demand placed on the stressed network, to reduce the cost of infrastructure supply and to lower the long-run resource use and trip generation of the new development.

The new logic of infrastructure provision generates a much broader notion of the concept of value that goes beyond purely economic notions of costs and commercial contributions. By emphasising demand management, the logic can help to increase the efficiency of water and energy use in new development while also finding alternatives to car-based travel. The concept of value needs to be broadened to consider the wider environmental, social and economic benefits that the logic captures for the local community and the global environment. We argue that the conventional perspective has been unable to capture the importance of these shifts because of its focus on the importance of costs and an assumption that infrastructure provision is an inherently tension- and conflict-ridden process. While accepting that there are difficulties about costs, these have been largely transcended by the inability of developers simply to buy-in additional capacity on infrastructure networks. Instead, a new style and culture of infrastructure provision are emerging in which developers and infrastructure providers have a shared interest in reshaping the location, form and specifications of new developments to fit more sensitively onto increasingly stressed networks.

CONCLUSIONS

A powerful supply-oriented logic has traditionally shaped infrastructure management in Britain. While strong echoes of the supply logic still survive, we have highlighted the emergence of a new, more environmentally beneficial, demand-oriented logic of network management. This new logic is developing unevenly across infrastructure sectors, but our evidence suggests that a mix of public concern about the social and environmental impacts of new infrastructure, new regulatory signals and competitive commercial strategies is likely to stimulate the spreading of the new logic.

While conflicts and tensions between public and private goals clearly exist, there are presently significant opportunities for infrastructure providers, developers, regulators and policy-makers mutually to develop novel ways of minimising the environmental costs of infrastructure provision. Our research has illustrated how this new logic of network provision subtly, yet profoundly, changed the context within which the bargaining process unfolded. In light of this, we would argue that the debate about infrastructure provision needs to be expanded beyond the distribution of costs, assessment of individual impacts and the need for standardised procedures. In this way, rather than see infrastructure as mere background or context, we have argued for the need to examine the co-production of value from the standpoint of networks themselves. From this perspective, impact assessments of individual developments are extremely problematic as buildings tend to be located in groups and because the interests of developers, occupiers, utilities and the local community are clearly linked.

In sum, we argue that, as it becomes less feasible simply to expand infrastructure networks, the need to manage infrastructure services becomes more urgent. The new emphasis is upon the development of strategies through which the developer and infrastructure provider can configure buildings and their demands on technical networks in such a way that development can occur at all. Clearly what is required is a very different approach to the challenge of providing infrastructure for development. We urgently need a new vocabulary of the bargaining process which better captures the new logics of infrastructure provision and allows planners to deal with the different challenges of development in 'hot' and 'cold' spots and the different configurations of development actors involved at different times in different ways. Environmental planning and policy would then be strongly framed by changing social contexts of new forms of infrastructure provision more closely aligned to more sustainable urban futures.

10

The Environment and the Regions: A New Agenda for Regional Development

DAVID GIBBS

INTRODUCTION

PLANNING AND ECONOMIC development policy has increasingly come to adopt sustainable development as a central organising theme at various spatial scales. Following the 1992 Earth Summit in Rio de Janeiro, the United Nations Agenda 21 provided a framework for sustainable development to be placed at the heart of national, regional and local policy-making. In general terms the concept of sustainable development requires that human activities take place within the ecological limits of the planet. It is generally accepted that this requires consideration of inter- and intra-generational equity, greater democratic involvement in decision-making and, perhaps most importantly, the integration of environmental, economic and social decision-making. One of the most problematic elements of sustainable development is in implementing the integration of environmental and economic policy (Gibbs et al., 1996, 1998). It has been argued that this should involve a shift away from the environment being considered in the final stages of economic decision-making and toward the environment being considered at a strategic decision-making level. Attention should be directed to altering patterns of production and consumption based upon an efficient use of natural resources, a reduction in waste generation and the closure of resource loops (Friends of the Earth, 1997). Taken together these requirements represent a considerable challenge to the organisation of economic activity as it currently exists. In particular, it opposes the view that achieving economic goals is in some way a prerequisite for achieving environmental and social goals. However, progress in placing such aims at the centre of economic development policies has been limited. The most visible evidence of this process beginning to take place in the UK has been through the UK Sustainable Development Strategy (HMG, 1999) and the development of Local Agenda 21 initiatives. More recently there has been a growing debate over the potential for sustainable development to form a key component of the UK Government's revived interest in regional planning and policy.

In the UK, successive Conservative governments from 1979 onwards downgraded *regional* planning and policy in favour of a competitive regime for *urban* governance. In time this competitive regime was opened up to any area wishing to bid for funding. With the advent of a (New) Labour government in 1997, a regional dimension in both planning and policy returned to the UK political agenda. Legislation set up assemblies (but with markedly differing powers) in Northern Ireland, Scotland, Wales and Greater London. The establishment of Regional Development Agencies (RDAs) in eight of the nine English regions[1] from 1 April 1999, when they absorbed the existing bodies of the Rural Development Commission and English Partnerships, was the start of a key change in English regional governance. The Labour Party's revived commitment to regional devolution can be traced back (at least) to the work of the Regional Policy Commission (RPC), chaired by Bruce Millan (see Mawson, 1997, for the regional debate in historical context). The RPC considered the form of regional policy in the light of a manifesto commitment to greater regional government and produced its report in 1996 (Regional Policy Commission, 1996). Following the election of a Labour government in May 1997 a White Paper was subsequently published on 3 December 1997 (HMG, 1997) followed by the Regional Development Agencies Bill[2] on 10 December 1997.

A key theme in the regional policy literature from the Department of the Environment, Transport and the Regions (DETR) associated with the establishment of RDAs was the need to incorporate environmental issues into economic development strategies for local areas and the regions and to move towards the integration of economic, social and environmental issues through the concept of sustainable development (HMG, 1997; DETR, 1998k). The UK government's consultation on proposed changes to Regional Planning Guidance (RPG) also recognised the need for a broader approach to spatial planning, incorporating economic and environmental issues (DETR, 1998m). While this commitment to sustainable development was progressively watered down from the initial formulations of the RPC through to the White Paper and the passage of the 1997 Bill through Parliament, nevertheless the RDAs are still potentially key players in environmental policy formulation and delivery (Gibbs, 1998). The more contentious issue of how the RDAs and RPG should interact remains to be addressed—for example, while RPG involves elements of local democratic control through the central role of local authorities in the RPG preparation process, RDAs lack a direct democratic mandate (Benneworth, 2000; Murdoch and Tewdwr-Jones, 1999).

Thus, as with their other functions, the RDAs have not entered onto an empty stage—a number of key institutions and actors are already concerned with

[1] The ninth region, London, has its own RDA responsible to the Mayor of London, elected in May 2000. While the other regions have regional assemblies, London has its own Greater London Assembly.

[2] Subsequently the Regional Development Agencies Act 1998.

environmental policy, sustainable development and environmental governance. A number of questions arise from the formation of RDAs and the operation of RPG. First, although both the RDAs and RPG have sustainable development as one of their key responsibilities, will this be addressed seriously or will more conventional development initiatives take precedence? Secondly, what specific role will RDAs play, given that the environmental policy field in the UK already has a range of actors at the regional level? Finally, what is the justification for addressing issues of sustainable development through regional planning and economic strategies? In this chapter the development of recent policy initiatives and forms is outlined with a particular focus on regional planning, RDAs and sustainable development. These sections seek answers to the first two questions. Following this analysis, the chapter addresses issues of the appropriate scale of intervention for planning before concluding with some suggestions on potential policy initiatives that could be developed to contribute to sustainable development at the regional scale.

REGIONAL PLANNING AND SUSTAINABLE DEVELOPMENT

The lack of a strong regional dimension to planning has long been seen as a barrier to the implementation of sustainable development in the UK (Marshall, 1993). This is frequently contrasted with other parts of Europe where it has been argued that the regional scale is one which allows effective integration of economic, social and environmental policy areas (CEC, 1997a). The period from 1989 to 1991 saw the emergence of a new form of regional planning in England and Wales based on Regional Planning Guidance prepared for Government Office areas[3]. This provided strategic guidance for local authorities on the preparation of development plans and introduced some potential for introducing sustainability into regional planning. However, amongst other criticisms, it lacked a strong regional focus and paid insufficient attention to environmental concerns (DETR, 1998m). From this initial position under Conservative administrations, there has been a substantial revival of interest in regional planning following the election of a Labour government. The DETR proposed a substantially upgraded role for the regions in planning—regional planning bodies are responsible for preparing draft Regional Planning Guidance (RPG) in consultation with other regional stakeholders.[4] RPG now has a specific remit for implementing sustainable development, with a requirement for an environmental appraisal of RPG policies and proposals (DETR, 1998m). The response to this has been to see the emergence of sustainable development in most RPG

[3] Except in the South East where it covered the areas of the Government Offices for the South East, London and part of Eastern region.

[4] These new developments in RPG are also linked to developments in European policy, particularly the emerging European Spatial Development Perspective and the *de facto* production of regional and sub-regional plans in areas eligible for EU Structural Funds.

documents and moves towards integrating and co-ordinating land use planning and transport (Baker, 1998). Some regions have attempted to develop new integrative approaches for environmental issues, notably in South East England[5] (SERPLAN, 1998).

Consultation papers prepared by the DETR stress the need to strengthen regional governance and to improve the co-ordination of land use, transport and economic planning at the regional scale (DETR, 1998k, 1998m, 1999e). However, despite this shift in emphasis there is considerable regional variation in the extent of engagement within this broader sustainability agenda (Marshall, 1998). Reflecting the land use bias of planning policy, particular stress has been placed upon the implications of demand for housing and the perception of *restraint* as the key issue in a truly sustainable approach to the planning process in the UK (Rydin, 1999). In South-East England in particular, sustainable development discourses have been adopted at the sub-regional level to justify policies for restraint and to argue that some areas cannot accommodate allocations of new housing proposed within RPG. This fairly narrow focus points up one problem with the planning system with regard to sustainable development—the fact that the emphasis on land use planning makes it difficult to deal with broader economic and social issues (Breheny, 1997; Healey and Shaw, 1994; Murdoch and Tewdwr-Jones, 1999).

Of particular concern is the recognition that the revised planning policy could operate largely in isolation from the activities of Regional Development Agencies, albeit that RPG is intended to adopt a complementary approach to RDA economic strategies (DETR, 1999f). Revised Regional Policy Guidance for England and Wales has sought to ensure that RPG provides an overall framework that considers the environmental, economic and social consequences of a land use strategy and is subject to a rigorous environmental/sustainability appraisal. RPG is intended to provide a spatial framework, not just for development plans, but is also relevant to other strategies such as air quality, energy and waste, and for the investment and operational plans of relevant infrastructure and public service providers (Roberts, 1999). However, the formation of Regional Development Agencies (RDAs) in the English regions has introduced another element to operate alongside the planning process. To reduce the potential overlaps that may ensue, the UK Round Table on Sustainable Development, amongst others, has argued that RPG should be the wider spatial strategy within which RDAs act (UK Round Table on Sustainable Development, 1999). However, in the absence of a hierarchical approach to regional governance, overlapping responsibilities will continue to be present and tensions will inevitably arise between the different tiers of governance in future. The DETR (1998m, 4) proposed that the RDAs need to have 'due regard to' RPG, while 'proposals for the provision of housing, transport and other infrastructure have

[5] As with the RDAs, the new arrangements for planning guidance in London are likely to differ from those adopted for the English regions.

regard to and, where appropriate, support the RDAs' programmes of economic regeneration'. Recognition of the potential overlaps involved has led to the Government introducing regional sustainable development frameworks, intended to be 'high level documents that set out a vision for sustainable development in each region' (DETR, 2000g, 5). However, these are non-statutory and are only intended to act as a framework for other regional strategies.[6] As Harman (1998: 197) has pointed out, however, the number of regional bodies which need to 'have regard to' each other's work over the next few years is likely to 'end up giving the players a headache'.

REGIONAL DEVELOPMENT AGENCIES AND SUSTAINABLE DEVELOPMENT

Given the growing importance of the environment within policy-making, it is not surprising that the Regional Policy Commission (RPC), established by the Labour Party while in opposition to consider the form and structure of possible regional development bodies, contained an analysis of the benefits of integrating environmental and regional development policies. The RPC report recommended that regional level action was required, in conjunction with action at other spatial scales, to implement sustainable development and environmental improvement. The RPC proposed that a Labour government should provide a regional dimension to Local Agenda 21, working with newly created regional chambers and RDAs to establish partnerships for effective sub-national action. Under these proposals, regional economic strategies would have contained an environmental appraisal and an assessment of the environmental impact of regional economic development strategies. The RPC stressed that adopting sustainable development as the basis for development could create 'win-win' outcomes for both the economy and the environment. For example, the RPC drew upon research that suggested that there is substantial potential for job creation in environmental activities and industries (see for example OECD, 1997). Energy conservation and 'green engineering technologies' were highlighted as two examples where regional policy could help with creating jobs. This was also seen as an issue related to national economic competitiveness—in a growing world market for environmental technologies the UK was seen to be losing out to the dominant suppliers based in Japan, Germany and the USA.

While several of the environmental themes identified by the RPC were incorporated in the subsequent legislation, the importance attached to concepts like sustainable development has often been ambiguous. For example, the 1997 Bill itself called on Regional Development Agencies to take 'the environment and sustainable development' into account only 'where appropriate'. The White Paper stated that sustainable development would form one of the RDAs' five

[6] Substantial criticism by the Performance and Innovation Unit concerning the lack of co-ordination of regional initiatives led to the establishment of a Regional Co-ordination Unit to perform this function across all central government policies (*Planning*, 18 February 2000).

specific objectives (the other four being economic development and social and physical regeneration; business support, investment and competitiveness; enhancing skills; and promoting employment). Indeed, two key stated aims of the RDAs were said to be the promotion of 'sustainable economic development' (HMG, 1997, 9) and the integration of economic, social, democratic and environmental agendas. In a specific section of the White Paper devoted to 'Environment and Sustainable Development' it was further claimed that:

> RDAs will place the principle of sustainable development at the heart of their programmes. To ensure this, the Government will give them a specific statutory objective of furthering the achievement of sustainable development which we will monitor closely. They will integrate environmental, economic and social objectives [HMG, 1997, 39].

The RDAs were also seen as having a key role in a number of specific environmental aims—for example in relation to waste minimisation, energy efficiency, encouraging environmental technology developments and supporting Local Agenda 21 initiatives. It was envisaged that these objectives would be achieved through the development and implementation of regional economic strategies, which would integrate economic, environmental and social aims. Such strategies would also be the means to 'promote sustainable development and sustainable communities' (HMG, 1997, 22), although exactly how was not made clear, except that it would involve the RDAs working with local and regional partners for 'environmental improvements'. This lack of clarity was sidestepped at the time by reference to the future publication of a revised sustainable development strategy for the UK in 1999, which 'will seek to identify the main themes of sustainable development policy, and show how the various strands—such as regional policy—fit together' (HMG, 1997, 40). In the event, the revised strategy merely reiterated the role of RDAs in implementing sustainable development without providing detail of the Government's much vaunted 'joined-up thinking' to integrate policy areas (HMG, 1999).

The ambiguous nature of any commitment to sustainable development as a basis for regional strategies was clear from the more conventional views that prevailed elsewhere in the White Paper. In places sustainable development was narrowly equated with the physical built environment, such as through reusing redundant buildings, promoting quality in new developments and reclaiming derelict or contaminated land. Such ambiguity was highlighted by the fact that sustainable development did not feature in the list of twelve RDA *core functions* despite being one of the five *objectives* for RDAs. The former was a fairly conventional list of economic development policy areas where it was simply claimed that the environment and sustainable development are an area where 'RDAs will also contribute to policies and programmes' (HMG, 1997, 44).

Overall then, more conventional views of the role of the environment in regional development are likely to remain dominant. Thus, high quality natural environments are simply seen as a prerequisite for encouraging tourism and attracting inward investment and associated high value employment. This conventional view was given added weight in the White Paper through the argument that poor regional economic performance in the past has resulted in environmental degradation. This was said to be a consequence of a failure to invest in pollution reduction measures, the inability of firms with a poor economic performance to take environmental protection measures, and of business failure resulting in derelict or degraded land. The implicit message here then is that a growing regional economy is needed to create the necessary resources to tackle environmental problems—growth must come *before* environmental problems are addressed. The reliance is upon improved competitiveness (through conventional measures) which will then enable regions to turn to addressing environmental and social problems. However, seeing social and environmental goals as a function of achieving economic goals conflicts with the aim of sustainable development. It is perhaps worth observing here that this interpretation reflects a particular UK view of sustainable development. In other countries, by contrast, economic development, at least in policy statements, is demoted to a position below environmental and social concerns (O'Brien and Penna, 1997).

There is also little explicit linkage made within UK official documentation between the role of RDAs and the changing criteria for the use of European Union Structural Funds. While the RDAs will take a leading role in the disbursement of the Structural Funds, there is no explicit recognition of recent European Commission concerns about the failure to meet environmental requirements within the Structural Fund programme at the regional level (Keller, 1997), nor of recent proposals to 'green' the Structural Funds by developing a set of environmental indicators to assess the impact of projects and strategies (CEC, 1997b). A joint seminar held by the European Commission and the Environment Agency also sought to encourage the use of Structural Funds to encourage 'environmentally sustainable development' in the UK regions[7] (CEC, 1997c). This recommended developing environmental baselines against which to measure performance, integrating environmental profiles into Structural Fund programmes and encouraging adoption and diffusion of clean technologies and eco-industries. However, there is little indication that RDAs have taken this new EU agenda on board (Roberts and Jackson, 1999). This lack of clarity came through in proposals for the RDAs to track the state and development of the regions through Regional Competitiveness Indicators and measure performance. Initially these did not mention any environmental indicators to assess the impact of regional policy and in the subsequent guidance to RDAs on regional strategies, simply proposed the percentage of new houses built on previously developed land as a core indicator and net hectares of derelict land brought into use as an additional sustainable development indicator.

[7] Seminars were also held in France and Germany.

Despite this, subsequent strategy guidance given to the RDAs to develop their regional economic strategies indicated that, notwithstanding the White Paper's vagueness, sustainable development remained on the agenda for the RDAs:

> [The RDAs] most important task . . . will be to produce a regional strategy in relation to their purposes: economic development and regeneration; employment and the development of skills; and sustainable development [John Prescott quoted in DETR, 1998n].

In compiling their regional strategies, the RDAs were expected to appraise how these would promote sustainable communities, protect the environment and integrate economic, social and environmental objectives. However, the Regional Development Act requires the RDAs only 'to contribute to the achievement of sustainable development in the United Kingdom *where it is relevant to its area to do so*' (DETR, 1998n, emphasis added). This has left the implementation and interpretation of sustainable development open to individual RDAs.

In total then the UK policy literature does indicate that there has been a shift in thinking about the need to incorporate environmental issues into regional policy, both in relation to both planning policy and the RDAs. However, exactly what the incorporation of sustainable development into regional policy will mean in operational terms remains ambiguous (Friends of the Earth, 1997). As has been shown, the RDA White Paper was vague on the delivery of such environmental policy and in places equated this with a narrow view of the economic benefits to be gained and, even more narrowly, with infrastructural developments. Despite broadening the remit of planning within RPG to encompass environmental, social and economic issues, it remains very land use planning dominated. Issues central to the concept of sustainable development, such as greater democratic involvement, equity and community involvement, receive scant attention in either the RDA or RPG proposals. In relation to the initial question posed at the start of this chapter it appears that sustainable development may well be a secondary consideration after the development of more conventional economic and land use strategies for the regions and that most regional strategies will not place issues such as increased energy efficiency, clean technologies, waste reduction and closed-loop systems on their agendas. Indeed, the progressive watering-down of the sustainability message within UK regional policy serves to illustrate the failure of successive governments to seize the initiative and their continued reliance upon more conventional economic analyses, even where the past success of some of these (for example, inward investment policies) and the future success of others (for example, the knowledge-based economy) in lagging regions are dubious.

1. What role for Regional Development Agencies?

While the RDAs may have sustainable development and the environment as part of their agendas, there is a need to place this responsibility in the wider perspective of their capabilities. RDAs have relatively few powers, other than those of 'functional allocation' i.e. the responsibility to deliver policy initiatives, rather than powers of financial responsibility. The bulk of decision-making power for the latter remains with UK central government and, to a lesser extent, the European Union. Possessing these functional allocation powers could allow a reconsideration of the division of responsibilities and roles within the regions. However, there have been no proposals that the RDAs should replace existing governance institutions. For example, little transfer of responsibilities has been envisaged between DETR and the RDAs, and the Department of Trade and Industry (DTI) retains control over Regional Selective Assistance. Rather the RDAs will act as co-ordinators for partnership approaches by existing agencies and institutions (DETR, 1998n). As we have already seen, land use planning was specifically excluded from the RDA remit.

The potential for overlap and confusion of aims and initiatives is as substantial in the environmental field as it is in relation to other functions. At national level, neither MAFF, nor the Department of Culture, Media and Sport, is part of the existing Government Offices for the Regions (GORs). At the regional scale (albeit using different spatial definitions) the Environment Agency and English Nature continue to exercise statutory obligations in areas covered by the RDAs. The lack of congruence of these various boundaries gives rise to what has been described as England's 'disjointed meso' (Sharpe, 1993) and results from both the incremental nature of their development and the fact that the structures may reflect functional coherence for the single issue agencies concerned (UK CEED, 1997). In the case of the Environment Agency, for example, Local Environmental Action Plans (LEAPs) are based upon watershed areas. While there are obvious links between the work of the RDAs and these other agencies, they are not specifically mentioned as regional and local partners in RDA strategy guidance to be taken into account (DETR, 1998n). Similarly, there is little or no mention of the RDAs or of wider economic development strategies in the Environment Agency's LEAPs, despite the fact that they were developed in partnership with a wide range of local stakeholders including local authorities and business. At the sub-regional scale, local authorities, in partnership with other actors, continue to develop Local Agenda 21 and other environmental strategies, and it is not clear how the RDAs will contribute to co-ordinating these, if at all, at the regional scale, despite an explicit commitment to do so and the need for interaction between all the strategies encompassed in the regional sustainable development frameworks (DETR, 2000g).

As Marshall (1998) indicates, a shift towards the adoption of new ecological-economic policies by RDAs and regional assemblies in the English regions *could* occur. If this is the case, then regional governance may have some purchase on any shift towards sustainable development. While Marshall (1998, 438) argues that this would mean that 'regional political autonomy would have a relation to regional ecological autonomy', it is not clear how this would work out in practice. First, the boundaries of each remain mismatched. In the case of the environment, this is not just a matter of administrative and jurisdictional inconvenience, but may act as a key inhibitor of environmental planning. A reformation of boundaries along bioregional principles, or at least making the boundaries of existing regionalised structures coterminous, could go some way to resolve this, but seems unlikely in the short to medium term (see McGinnis (1999) for a discussion of the possibilities for this in a US context). Secondly, in the absence of a strong lead from central government such sustainable development strategies are likely to remain marginal to the perceived 'mainstream' of economic development (although see Jackson and Roberts, 1997). Thirdly, as with the entry of any new state form or structure, the formation of the RDAs and assemblies have implications for the access of different interests, political representation and policy determination (Patterson, 1999). Exactly how the interest groups involved represent their own interests and engage with those of other dominant groups through the new institutional forms remains to be seen. While regional assemblies have some element of legitimation, consisting as they do of indirectly elected councillors, RDA boards are non-elected. They are also intended to be business-led and, in the short to medium term at least, accountable solely to central government (Lynch, 1999). This may make them both easier to control from the centre and open to lobbying by coherent special interest groups organised at a regional level. Conversely, those interests not organised at a regional scale, such as environmental groups, may have little purchase on RDA activities[8] (Patterson, 1999). Moreover, conflict between the various regional strategies, such as between RPG and RDA strategies, may eventually be resolved only through reference to the Secretary of State, a process which negates some of the purpose of devolution.

Work by Marshall (1998) draws upon his research in Lower Saxony to devise a set of guidelines for what he terms 'environmentally intelligent regional governance' (see Box 10.1). By this measure, the situation in the English regions is not encouraging. What may be needed in the English regions is the development of strong elected regional assemblies which are able to set targets, develop policies and create partnerships with other actors such as utility companies and industry. Whether the existing assemblies will develop into directly-elected regional governments is still an open question. Developing regional environmental data sets, setting targets and developing performance indicators would all help to measure progress. Whether this occurs depends very much on individual RDAs. The relative weakness of current arrangements where there is weak democratic control or legitimation is noted by Haughton (1998), in relation to control over regional water companies in the UK, and is implicated in Marshall's point about the relative power of the private and public sectors.[9] The development of unelected RDA boards and the slow development of regional

[8] It is notable that where there is institutional capacity organised around an environmental agenda, such as in North West England, there was a much greater emphasis upon sustainable development issues in the Regional Economic Strategies.

[9] Bradbury and Mawson (1997) point out the high level of support for devolution amongst elites in Scotland and Wales, presumably to help advance their own agendas. Similar elite support is also evident in some of the English northern regions in particular.

BOX 10.1: Key Conditions for Environmentally Intelligent Regional Governance

- A strong regional jurisdiction
- Strong environmental sectoral planning
- Involvement of the economic arm of government
- Power balance between the private and public sectors
- Central government policy leaves space for regional initiatives
- Articulation between regional, sub-regional and local policies
- The presence of a strong sustainability discourse

Source: adapted from Marshall (1998).

assemblies (let alone directly elected ones) is likely to mean that the RDAs simply constitute one actor amongst many, at least in the early stages of their development.

The one encouraging sign to date is that there is evidence that some RDAs have incorporated sustainability and environmental issues into their regional economic development strategies (Benneworth, 2000; UK Round Table on Sustainable Development, 1999). This has been assisted by the fact that central government recognises that regional diversity means that a 'single prescriptive model' of RDAs is not applicable, even though in reality there has been strong central control over the form and content of such strategies. While this has some dangers, given that the absence of central requirements on environmental quality or sustainable development may allow regions to avoid the issue completely, it does create space for experimentation. While there has been some criticism that the original plans for the RDAs have been watered down substantially, some RDA chairs have seen opportunities for developing their own programmes based, for example, on European or joint public-private funding (Hetherington, 1998).

In future, then, it may be that the RDAs will develop more radical programmes around sustainable development, particularly in areas eligible for EU Structural Funds, where there has recently been specific encouragement to develop such a regional strategy:

> A full regional sustainable development strategy would necessarily address policy areas which lie outside the scope of Structural Fund intervention and may not always correspond to boundaries of the eligible programme area. Nevertheless, the Commission sees no reason why the European programme implementation apparatus in a region could not be used to contribute to the development of such a strategy [CEC, 1997c, Section 4].

However, the Commission proposes that the Environment Agency (and the Scottish Environmental Protection Agency) should be the main co-ordinating body to take such developments forward, as opposed to the RDAs. To conclude this section, as with much comment on the RDAs, the obvious message is that we shall have to 'wait and see' how they develop and what role they carve out for themselves given the nebulous state of current RDA development and formation.

2. Scale and sustainable development

Finally, there is the issue of the most appropriate scale on which to address issues of sustainable development. This concern with scale can also be related to a revival of interest in the importance of regional economies as key sites of development (see Storper, 1997 for example). In recent years it can also be argued that we have seen a process of the rescaling of environmental policy. Devolving sustainable development policy down to the regional and local level in the UK is part of a wider trend observable in several countries (see, for example, May et al., 1996, for a view on environmental governance in the USA, New Zealand and Australia). International agencies and national governments have increasingly delegated responsibility for action to sub-national and, in particular, local levels of the state. Recent UK environmental policy displays evidence of this rescaling process with some environmental responsibilities effectively being delegated upwards to the European level through the impact of successive European Environmental Action Programmes and through adopting European directives on, for example, integrated pollution prevention and control and urban waste water treatment (Lowe and Ward, 1998). Indeed, Hanf (1996) has argued that EU environmental policy has been a key factor in driving what he terms a 're-ordering of regulatory space' throughout the EU for delivering environmental initiatives. In the UK, however, much of the responsibility for implementing and policing these actions has been delegated downwards to local government and to specialist agencies of the state. In the latter case the Environment Agency has assumed a key role, implementing national environmental regulation at a sub-national level and producing Local Environmental Action Plans based on catchment areas, in conjunction with a range of local stakeholders. UK central government has additionally explicitly devolved environmental responsibilities downwards, for example by stressing local authorities as key sites for achieving internationally agreed environmental policy such as UN Agenda 21 (through the Local Agenda 21 process). This is not to over-emphasise the role of the central state—in the UK local authorities were glad to seize on to this new local agenda under previous Conservative governments because it represented an alternative to Conservative views on minimal local government and (re)legitimated local authority activities (Marvin and Guy, 1997).

The RDAs, RPG and regional sustainable development frameworks will continue this process of devolved responsibility. While the rationale for a regional approach to environmental issues is rarely stated, it is possible to put forward some arguments for this. First, there is an argument that a coherent management approach to 'natural' environmental ecosystems of necessity involves a larger spatial scale than individual local authority areas (UK CEED, 1997). Indeed, the need for this regional approach is explicitly recognised in the UK planning system through Regional Planning Guidance, for transport and solid waste management and, increasingly for water resource management. As we have seen, together with the development of Regional Air Quality Management Schemes in some parts of England, these have the potential for integration with RDA strategies. Secondly, it has also been argued that regions are potentially better vehicles for the expression of accountability and representation, operating at a meso-level between nation state and locality. They are thus closer to local areas than the nation state, but avoid the constraints of NIMBYism at that level (see UK CEED, 1997, for an outline of these arguments). In conclusion, then, there may be substantial justification for action on sustainability at the regional scale, but the effectiveness of such action in a UK context remains to be seen.

CONCLUSIONS

Given the recent establishment of Regional Development Agencies in the English regions, the changes to Regional Planning Guidance and the introduction of regional sustainable development frameworks, the tone of this chapter has necessarily been highly speculative. Establishing RDAs in the English regions will be a long-term process and, given that their first task of developing regional economic strategies was completed only in autumn 1999, we should perhaps not be too condemnatory in advance of the evidence.[10] Despite this, it is fair to say that the probability of any RDAs taking sustainability seriously as their key organising principle seems remote. Much more likely is an approach that sees sustainable development in fairly narrow environmental or infrastructural terms, or where it is marginal to other more mainstream economic policies. One certainty, however, is that the development of the RDAs has introduced new forms of institutional governance into the environmental and sustainable development policy arena. This has implications for how we understand the more pragmatic consequences of RDA establishment.

The devolution of some functions to the RDAs leaves other agencies and actors with their existing powers and responsibilities. In particular local authorities, through their Local Agenda 21 strategies and central involvement with RPG, and the Environment Agency, through Local Environmental Action Plans, remain key actors at the regional and sub-regional scales. Such governance structures may well remain confused unless there is a shift towards regional

[10] Final strategies were presented at the end of October 1999 and were approved by DETR in mid-January 2000 (Benneworth, 2000).

government. In revising RPG, the Government pointed to the need for democratic control over the planning process and, in arguing for this, rejected the possibility of RPG coming under the remit of the RDAs, given their dominance by business interests and their lack of democratic legitimation (DETR, 1998m). While there was speculation that revised planning legislation could come under the control of regional chambers, the more democratic option of subsuming both RPG and RDAs under the control of directly-elected regional assemblies does not appear to be an option at the time of writing. The compromise solution proposed is to continue with Regional Planning Conferences in some form, giving local authorities a major role working closely with Government Offices (DETR, 1998m). As has been outlined above, the development of regional assemblies to drive policy, set targets and monitor progress may be a key requirement in any shift towards a programme for sustainable development.

A starting point for the development of such a programme is that expressed in DETR guidance on sustainable development and regional strategies, which refers to 'a different model, where quality of life is enhanced by safeguarding the environment while still having economic growth and progress' (DETR, 1998n, para. 4.2.2). Much of the necessary change towards this new model remains the prerogative of national (and EU) government—carbon taxes, taxes on aggregates and reduced employment taxes for example. There remain though a number of areas that could be developed as part of a regional strategy. One of the key areas which needs to be developed is that around notions of capacity building, community enterprise, access to credit and capital and local trading. Such initiatives have particular links to debates around social inclusion and exclusion. While space does not allow these to be outlined here in detail, much invaluable work is already being done in this area (see Ekins and Newby, 1998 for example).

Such initiatives are only one part of the sustainability agenda for regional economic strategies. Invaluable though such developments are, they should form part of a coherent, holistic approach to sustainability which includes 'mainstreaming' sustainability through 'bending' more conventional programmes and ways of thinking. By way of conclusion, such approaches could include:

—Actions to encourage energy efficiency and renewable energy production, where a first step could be the construction of an audit of carbon emissions and flows on a regional basis and the development of strategies to reduce carbon emissions (McEvoy, Gibbs and Longhurst, 1998).

—The redirection of inward investment strategies on more 'environmentally friendly' lines, through demanding higher standards from inward investors or by targeting specific environmental sectors.

—The encouragement of closed loop waste systems and facilitating shared services at new and existing industrial sites. These ideas have been picked up in notions of eco-industrial parks that facilitate the interchange of waste products by firms and encourage collaborative effort (Brand and De Bruijn,

1998). For 'new-build' parks this may also be combined with layouts and buildings that encourage energy efficiency and utilise renewable energy sources. Such eco-industrial park developments are an increasing feature of economic development in the USA and in Europe, as well as more isolated examples from the UK at the Ecotech Innovation and Business Park at Swaffham in Norfolk sites and Dyfi Ecopark at Machynlleth in Wales.

—At the regional scale, an increasing emphasis has been placed upon the development of indigenous enterprise as opposed to inward investment strategies. Regional institutions could, in conjunction with the new Small Business Service, encourage Business Links and other groups within the region to provide advice to small firms on sustainable development. Given the difficulties of reaching such firms and, in some cases, of actually having an influence upon firm behaviour, this may need to be linked to other initiatives such as local public sector purchasing policies and supply chain networks.

—Encouraging the development of high technology sectors that can contribute to sustainability—the growing global market for environmental technologies and services provides an opportunity here for some regions. Many of the firms in these sectors are small and there may be opportunities for networking such firms to assist with global market access, as well as exchanging information and joint project bids. There is thus a role for regional institutions to act in a proactive manner to create the kinds of networking and 'institutional thickness' associated with cluster development. The argument here then is to rethink more conventional strategies, such as those envisaged in the Competitiveness White Paper (HMG, 1998), in a new, and more sustainable, fashion.

11

Postscript

CHRIS MILLER

During Mrs Thatcher's second administration, Healey (1985, 501) wrote:

> Despite political rhetoric, no government can dismantle the planning system without devising an alternative mechanism to manage the co-ordination of spatial externality effects and the mediation of conflicts over land use change and development.

Some fifteen years later, this observation has lost none of its validity. Moreover, public concern with that sub-category of 'spatial externality effects' which includes pollution, nuisance, noise and risk is similarly undiminished. The first four chapters of this book described the continued effectiveness of planning, strengthened with the environmental assessment regime, in anticipating and preventing these traditional concerns. But what of climate change and other externalities which are not confined to the immediate spatial and temporal scales? In Chapter One, we noted, among the recent additions to the list of Planning Policy Guidance Notes, one devoted to renewable energy and another concerned with the management of coastal areas (under threat from the raised sea levels which accompany global warming). The question arises: what role (if any) could planning play in preventing or reversing the conditions which now provoke increasingly urgent demands for more sustainable lifestyles?

According to Millichip (1993, 1118), planning control and policy can encompass the 'full range of temporal and spatial dimensions' which are inherent in the global remit as well as a concern for future generations which characterises sustainability. This transition can be made without difficulty since it represents a 'change of degree rather than kind'. This confidence in planning's adaptability is not shared by Jewell (1995), who points in particular to planning's ambivalent attitude to the question of 'need'. In its most frequently quoted definition, sustainable development is held to be 'development that meets the needs of the present without compromising the ability of future generations to meet their own needs' (WCED, 1987, 43). The notion of 'need' is therefore central. Need can be a material consideration provided it is 'related to the character of the use of the land'.[1] But this test is hardly onerous and, provided that its reasoning is not demonstrably erroneous, there is no reason why a planning authority may not justify refusing consent by arguing that a proposed development was

[1] *Westminster City Council* v. *Great Portland Estates plc* [1985] 1 AC 661 at 670.

superfluous to local requirements. However, the case law in this area has been more concerned with the separate question of alternative locations and, in regard to transport, consideration of 'need' is excluded[2] from discussion at the public inquiry which forms part of the procedures (under the Highways Act 1980) for approving a major road. But as Wood points out in Chapter Seven, the amended directive on environmental assessment obliges developers to provide, as part of the environmental statement, a description of the main alternatives to the project as well as the reasons for the particular choice. Whether this change (and, for the first time, an obligation on planners to justify planning *approval* as well as refusal) will result in 'need' becoming a more decisive consideration remains to be seen.

In Chapter Ten, Gibbs identifies '*restraint* as the key issue in a truly sustainable approach to the planning process'. It is not difficult to imagine planning guidance for a region like the South-East of England becoming increasingly couched in terms of a reluctance to allow market demand to determine the rate of development for residential use. But is it possible to imagine planning exercising restraint over other categories of non-sustainable development which are not so obviously linked to land use as housing? The case studies presented in Chapter Nine give some indication of what can be achieved—in terms of reduced water, energy and traffic demand—by negotiation between developers, planners and the utilities. 'Pollution prevention pays' (see Royston, 1979) was one of the clichés of the environmental movement of the 1970s, and enlightened self-interest will no doubt continue to play a role in the pursuit of sustainability. Implicit within sustainability is the notion that market forces are neither the sole nor the best indicators of 'need'. Certain activities entail so great an environmental risk and impose such demands upon natural resources that, irrespective of the economic demand which they may meet, they cannot be permitted. Anthropogenic threats to natural ecosystems are of such gravity, many environmentalists argue, that there must be a greater readiness to prohibit, and not merely to regulate, pollution. In other words: the state must become more prepared to say 'no' to activities which, although acceptable in traditional terms, are now recognised as offending against some aspect of sustainability.

There is no reason to believe that planning authorities must bear this regulatory burden alone. It is not difficult to imagine a body like the Environment Agency being given stronger powers to require manufacturers to employ processes which generate lower amounts of waste or which require a greater use of recycled material (see Chapter Eight). Product standards legislation is no less important: the EC regulation[3] banning the manufacture of the chlorofluorocarbons is a simple but effective contribution to halting the depletion of the ozone layer, and one which is independent of land use. The more sustainable development provides the motivation of various Community-wide programmes, the

[2] *Bushell* v. *Secretary of State for the Environment* [1981] AC 75, [1980] 2 All ER 608, [1980] JPL 458.

[3] Regulation 594/91/EEC [1991] OJ L67/67.

more we can imagine the Commission using its own enforcement powers against Member States whose failings are revealed by a growing array of ever more refined indicators of sustainability. It is significant that the first occasion[4] on which the Commission used its (post-Maastricht) power to impose a financial penalty was in respect of an environmental 'offence'—the unlawful disposal of toxic waste at a coastal site in Crete.

In the preservation of biodiversity—a central element of sustainability—the European Community (as well as the Member States) is a party to the CITES convention[5] which bans the trading of endangered species. But the preservation of threatened species also requires the protection of their habitats. Non-governmental organisations (NGOs) have probably been more effective than the European Commission in persuading Member States to incorporate this 'ecocentric' dimension in their land use policies.

With more than one million members, the Royal Society for the Protection of Birds is a very influential NGO and has the resources necessary to sustain long and costly public law actions. And although the successful outcome of the judicial review of the Lappel Bank decision[6] came too late to prevent the encroachment upon the mudflats of the Medway Estuary, it nevertheless served as a reminder (along with various cases in the European Court of Justice: see Chapter 5) that the designation of a 'special protection area' is not a trifling matter. The subsequent action[7] by Greenpeace, concerning the effects of oil exploration in the UK continental shelf, has demonstrated that the Habitats Directive may, with similarly purposive interpretation, be even more capable of restricting important economic activities in the interests, in this instance, of certain species of coral and marine mammals.

It is tempting to couple Greenpeace's successful action over Atlantic oil exploration with the House of Lords decision in *Berkeley*[8] as justification for concluding on an optimistic note—confident that these and similar third party actions, forcing the courts (albeit belatedly) to employ a purposive interpretation of environmental directives, may encourage legislation and policies aimed at accelerating the pursuit of sustainability. But despite its elevation to the constitutional level (Article 2) in the EC Treaty (following the Amsterdam summit of June 1997), it is unlikely that 'sustainable development' is sufficiently precisely defined to be justiciable and therefore capable of direct effect, in which case, public interest groups wishing to force the pace of the pursuit of sustainability will be able to

[4] Case C-387/97 *Commission* v. *Hellenic Republic* [2000] ECR -000 http://www.europa.eu.int/cj/en/act/0021en.htm

[5] *Convention on International Trade in Endangered Species of Wild Fauna and Flora* [1976] UKTS 101 (Cmd. 6647).

[6] Case C–44/95, *R.* v. *Swale BC ex parte RSPB* [1996] ECR I–3805; (1997) 9 JEL 139.

[7] *R.* v. *Secretary of State for the Trade and Industry and others ex parte Greenpeace Ltd.* (QBD, 5 November 1999).

[8] *Berkeley* v. *Secretary of State for the Environment* [2000] 3 All ER 897 in which their Lordships required the Secretary of State to insist upon the submission of an environmental statement even though it was recognised that this was unlikely to cause him to change his earlier appeal decision.

employ that remedy only in regard to specific Community directives whose objectives are phrased in precise and unconditional terms.

The preceding chapters describe several instances of HM Government being pressed, by various NGOs as well as the European Commission, to adopt stronger environmental policies than it would otherwise wish. But there are signs that future conflicts will be more complex and this book goes to press at a time (April 2001) when environmentalists have little cause for optimism. The International Conference on Climate Change at the Hague[9] ended without agreement on reducing carbon emissions. This failure came as governments across Europe were still pondering the events (in early September 2000) when the public demonstrated a very clear hostility to one particular policy—raising the price of fuel for road vehicles—with undeniable credentials in terms of sustainable development (*viz.* reduced consumption of fossil fuels). In various Member (and applicant) States, large sections of the population seem prepared, despite inconvenience to themselves, to voice their support for direct action (blockades of motorways and oil refineries) in protest against fuel prices. Increased excise duty on the fuel consumed by commercial vehicles can be recouped in higher prices on goods and services. The tax imposed on the landfilling of waste can be similarly passed on in higher prices to consumers of the goods which generated the wastes in questions. Some taxes, whether or not imposed for eminently green purposes, are more visible than others. The majority of road vehicles are owned by private individuals and any increase in the pump price of petrol (whether via taxation or in the market price of crude oil) has an immediate impact on the disposable incomes of a sizeable proportion of the electorate. And once the pursuit of sustainability is seen as being associated with such voter-unfriendly policies as higher taxes, politicians' commitment to the quality of the environment bequeathed to future generations will be sorely tested.

There is a limit to what can be achieved by fiscal policies alone, and political necessity will encourage the search for less painful incentives to reduced reliance on private motoring. Owens has argued that 'land use planning *in isolation* [her emphasis] is not an effective way of reducing travel demand' (1995, 47), but politicians can now be expected to pay it much greater attention. However, as the Royal Commission on Environmental Pollution has already warned, the annual rate of turnover of the built environment (RCEP, 1994, para 9.69) is far too low to permit the large-scale changes to existing settlements necessary for demonstrable changes in travel patterns. For the immediate future, planning's principal role will remain a regulatory one—withholding consent for dormitory suburbs, business parks and other out-of-town facilities for which travel by car is effectively compulsory.

In the longer term, two possible responses of the planning system to the sense of crisis which characterises 'strong' (to revive the terminology of Chapter One)

[9] Following the 1997 meeting in Kyoto, the Hague Conference was the fourth held under the auspices of the United Nations Framework Convention on Climate Change: see (1992) 31 *ILM* 849.

environmentalism present themselves. First, an extension of planning's 'techno-rational' approach in which environmental assessment is applied to wider categories of individual projects and to an increasing range of programmes and policies. Sheate (1997, 279) describes the 'tortuous history' of the early drafts of the proposed EC directive on strategic environmental assessment (SEA) and the UK government's reluctance—echoing the stance taken a decade earlier over project EA—to see formal legislation replacing voluntary appraisal. The European Community already requires applications for Structural Funds and the Trans -European Network (covering road, rail, air and water) to be accompanied by an SEA; and, as Wood points out in Chapter Seven, environmental appraisal of development plans is now commonplace.

Secondly, sustainability would come to permeate, to a degree not yet witnessed, national and regional planning policy guidance documents and it would be the central concern of development plans. Current doubts over the status of need as a material consideration would then become irrelevant, as would any residual sense of a presumption in favour of development. In effect, sustainability would become the guiding principle of the planning framework. Growing recognition of the gravity of our environmental threats may result in other agencies of the state undergoing a similar transformation. But since few of these threats are unlinked to land use, planning will continue to have a central role.

Bibliography

ADAMS, T. (1996), 'Gridlock in Waste Planning', *Waste Planning* 18: 3–5.

ALDER, J. (1993), 'Environmental Impact Assessment—The Inadequacies of English Law', *Journal of Environmental Law* 5(2), 203–19.

ANON. (1998), ' "Recalcitrant" Foundry Told to Abate Odours in Milestone Appeal', *ENDS Report* 277, 12.

ANON. (1999), 'Another West Midlands Foundry Prosecuted for Air Pollution', *ENDS Report* 296, 48.

ARUP ECONOMICS AND PLANNING (1994), *Assessment of the Effectiveness of Derelict Land Grant in Reclaiming Land for Development* (Report to DoE) (London: HMSO).

—— (1995), *Derelict Land Prevention and the Planning System: Final Report* (Report to DoE) (London: HMSO).

ASHFORD, N.A., and MILLER, C.S. (1998), 'Low-level Chemical Exposures: a Challenge for Science and Policy', *Environmental Science and Technology* 32, 502A–509A.

ASHWORTH, G. (1991), 'Ravenhead Renaissance—A Case Study' in Davies, M.R.C. (ed.), *Land Reclamation—An End to Dereliction?* (London: Elsevier Applied Science), 397–401.

BAKER, M. (1998), 'Planning for the English Regions: a Review of the Secretary of State's Regional Planning Guidance', *Planning Practice and Research* 13(2), 153–69.

BARKER, A., and WOOD, C.M. (1999), 'An Evaluation of EIA System Performance in Eight EU Countries', *Environmental Impact Assessment Review* 19(4), 387– 404.

BARLOW REPORT (1940), *Report of the Royal Commission on the Distribution of the Industrial Population* (Cmd 6153) (London: HMSO).

BARRETT, A., and LAWLOR, J. (1997), 'Questioning the Waste Hierarchy: the Case of a Region with a Low Population Density', *Journal of Environmental Planning and Management* 40(1), 19–36.

BEDFORDSHIRE COUNTY COUNCIL and ROYAL SOCIETY FOR THE PROTECTION OF BIRDS (1996), *Step-by-Step Guide to Environmental Appraisal* (Bedford: Bedfordshire CC).

BENNEWORTH, P. (2000), 'The Strategies were Just a Warm-up; We're Changing to Implementation', *Regions* 226, 16–32.

BERRIE, T. (1992), *Electricity Economics and Planning* (London: Institute of Electrical Engineers).

BIFFA (1997), *Great Britain Plc: The Environmental Balance Sheet* (High Wycombe: Biffa).

BOND, A. (1997), 'Environmental Assessment and Planning: a Chronology of Development in England and Wales', *Journal of Environmental Planning and Management* 40(2), 261–71.

BOURASSA, S. (1991), *The Aesthetics of Landscape* (London: Bellhaven).

BOX, J. (1998), 'Setting Objectives and Monitoring for Ecological Restoration and Habitat Creation' in Fox, H.R., Moore, H.M., and McIntosh, A.D. (eds.), *Land Reclamation: Achieving Sustainable Benefits* (Rotterdam: Balkema).

BRADBURY, J., and MAWSON, J. (1997), 'The Changing Politics and Governance of British Regionalism' in Bradbury, J., and Mawson, J. (eds.), *British Regionalism and*

Devolution: The Challenges of State Reform and European Integration (London, Jessica Kingsley/Regional Studies Association), 273–309.

BRAND, E., and DE BRUIJN, T. (1998), 'Industrial Ecology at the Regional Level: the Building of Sustainable Industrial Estates', paper presented at the Seventh International Conference of the Greening of Industry Network, Partnership and Leadership—Building Alliances for a Sustainable Future, Rome.

BREHENY, M. (1997), 'Urban Compaction: Feasible and Acceptable?', *Cities* 14(4), 209–17.

—— and HALL, P. (eds.) (1996), *The People: Where Will They Go? The Report of the Town and Country Planning Association Regional Inquiry into Housing Need and Provision in England* (London: TCPA).

BROUGH, C. (1993), 'Hazardous Substances Consent—UK Legislative Control from the Local Authority Viewpoint', paper presented at the 8th Annual European Summer School on Major Hazards, 13–17 September (Widnes: Halton Metropolitan Borough Council).

BULL, D., and UNDERWOOD, L. (1995), *Influencing the Choice of Work Trips to the Office: a Way Forward for Public Transport* (Hounslow: London Borough of Hounslow).

BURT, A., and BRADSHAW, A.D. (1986), *Transforming our Waste Land: The Way Forward* (London: HMSO).

CANTANESE, J. (1988), 'Planning Infrastructure for Urban Development' in Stein, J. (ed.), *Public infrastructure Planning and Management* (London: Sage), 81–93.

CARNWATH, R. (1992), 'Environmental Enforcement: the Need for a Specialist Court', *Journal of Planning and Environment Law* 799–808.

COMMISSION OF THE EUROPEAN COMMUNITIES (CEC) (1989), *EC Strategy on Waste Management* (Luxembourg: CEC).

—— (1996), *Environmental Impact Assessment—a Study on Costs and Benefits* (Luxembourg: CEC).

—— (1997a), *European Spatial Development Perspective: First Official Draft* (Luxembourg: CEC).

—— (1997b), *Call for Tenders by Open Procedure No. 97.00.57.001 Concerning the Thematic Evaluation on the Impact of Structural Funds on the Environment* (Brussels, Luxembourg: CEC).

—— (1997c), *Encouraging Environmentally Sustainable Development Through European Structural Fund Programmes in British Regions* Recommendations from European Commission Seminar, Manchester, 27–28 October.

—— (2000), *Managing Natura 2000 Sites* (Luxembourg: CEC).

CHEMICAL INDUSTRIES ASSOCIATION (1993), *Responsible Neighbours* (London: Chemical Industries Association).

—— (1995), *The Public Image of the Chemical Industry* (London: Chemical Industries Association).

CHERRY, G.E. (1974), *The Evolution of British Town Planning* (Leighton Buzzard: Leonard Hill).

CHRISTOU, M.D., and PORTER, S. (eds.) (1999), *Guidance on Land Use Planning as Required by Council Directive 96/82/EC (Seveso II)*, Report EUR 18695 EN (Luxembourg: Office for Official Publications of the European Communities).

CIVIC TRUST (1964), *Derelict Land—A Study of Industrial Dereliction and How it May be Redeemed* (London: Civic Trust).

COLUMBO, A.G., ARTOLA, A., GERVASI, C., HAQ, G., and MELAKI, I. (1996), *An Analysis of*

Environmental Impact Studies of Installations for the Treatment and Disposal of Toxic and Dangerous Waste in the EU (EUR 16389 EN) (Ispra: European Commission Joint Research Centre).

COUNTRYSIDE COUNCIL FOR WALES (1999), *Annual Report 1989–9 Part 2 (Digest of Statistics)* available at http://www.ccw.gov.uk/annualreport/english/digest.

COUNCIL FOR THE PRESERVATION OF RURAL ENGLAND (CPRE) (1993), *Water for Life: Strategies for Sustainable Water Resource Management* (London: Council for the Protection of Rural England).

CULLINGWORTH, J.B., and NADIN, V. (1997), *Town and Country Planning in the UK* (12th edn.), London: Spon).

CURRAN, J., and HART, I. (1998), 'Sustainable Development: Incorporation into Project Design' in Fox, H.R., Moore, H.M., and McIntosh, A.D. (eds.), *Land Reclamation: Achieving Sustainable Benefits* (Rotterdam: Balkema).

—— WOOD, C., and HILTON, M. (1998), 'Environmental Appraisal of UK Development Plans: Current Practice and Future Directions', *Environment and Planning B* 25(3), 411–33.

DAVOUDI, S. (1999), 'A Quantum Leap for Planners', *Town and Country Planning* 68(1), 20–4.

—— (2000), 'Planning for Waste Management: Changing Discourses and Institutional Relationships', *Progress in Planning* 53(3), 165–214.

DEPARTMENT OF THE ENVIRONMENT, TRANSPORT AND THE REGIONS (DETR) (1997a), *The United Kingdom National Air Quality Strategy: Guidance for Local Authorities* (Environment Circular 15/9) (London: Stationery Office).

—— (1997b), *LAPC/ IPC Appeals* (Guidance Note 1) (London: DETR).

—— (1997c), *Air Quality and Traffic Management* (LAQM. G3(97), London: DETR).

—— (1997d), *Determining the Need for Environmental Assessment (EC Directive 97/11/EC) on Environmental Assessment* (Consultation Paper) (London: DETR).

—— (1997e), *Implementation of EC Directive (97/11/EC) on Environmental Assessment* (Consultation Paper) (London: DETR).

—— (1997f), *Mitigation Measures in Environmental Statements* (London: DETR).

—— (1998a), *Digest of Environmental Statistics No. 20* (London: Stationery Office).

—— (1998b), *Sites of Special Scientific Interest: Better Protection and Management* (Consultation Paper) (London: DETR).

—— (1998c), *Prevention of Dereliction Through the Planning System* (Circular No. 02/98) (London: DETR).

—— (1998d), *Planning for the Communities of the Future* (London: DETR).

—— (1998e), *Sustainability Counts: Consultation Paper on a Set of Headline Indicators for Sustainable Development* (London: DETR).

—— (1998f), *Planning for Sustainable Development: Toward Better Practice* (London: DETR).

—— (1998g), *Policy Appraisal and the Environment: Policy Guidance* (London: DETR).

—— (1998h), *Review of Technical Guidance on Environmental Appraisal* (London: Stationery Office).

—— (1998i), *Guidance on Enhancing Public Participation in Local Government* (London: DETR).

—— (1998j), *Modern Local Government: In Touch with the People* (London: DETR).

—— (1998k), *Sustainable Development: Opportunities for Change—Consultation Paper on a Revised UK Strategy* (London: DETR).

Department of the Environment, Transport and the Regions (DETR) (1998m), *The Future of Regional Planning Guidance* (London: DETR).
—— (1998n), *Regional Development Agencies: Draft Guidance on RDAs' Strategies* (London: DETR).
—— (1999a), *Environmental Impact Assessment* (Circular 2/99) (London: Stationery Office).
—— (1999b), *Development Plans.* (Planning Policy Guidance Note 12) (London: Stationery Office).
—— (1999c), *Planning and Waste Management.* (Planning Policy Guidance Note 10) (London: Stationery Office).
—— (1999d), *Examination of the Operation and Effectiveness of the Structure Planning Process* (London: Stationery Office).
—— (1999e), *Planning Policy Guidance Note 11: Regional Planning Public* (Consultation Draft) (London, DETR).
—— (1999f), *Regional Planning* (Planning Policy Guidance Note 11) (London: Stationery Office).
—— (2000a), *Environmental Court Project: Final Report*, http://www.planning.detr.gov.uk/court/ index.htm.
—— (2000b), *Air Quality and Land Use Planning* (LAQM. G4(00)) (London: DETR).
—— (2000c), *Air Quality and Transport* (LAQM. G3(00)) (London: DETR).
—— (2000d), *The Contaminated Land (England) Regulations 2000* (Circular 02/00) (London: Stationery Office).
—— (2000e), *Waste Strategy 2000: England and Wales* (London: Stationery Office).
—— (2000f), *Waste Strategy Guidance: Best Value and Waste Management* (London: DETR).
—— (2000g), *Guidance on Preparing Regional Sustainable Development Frameworks* (London, DETR).
Department of the Environment (DOE) (1972), *Planning and Clean Air* (Draft Circular) (London: DOE).
—— (1973), *Planning and Noise* (Circular 10/73) (London: HMSO).
—— (1984), *Water and the Environment* (Circular 17/84) (London: HMSO).
—— (1985), *Development and Employment* (Circular 14/85) (London: HMSO).
—— (1989), *Environmental Assessment: a Guide to the Procedures* (London: HMSO).
—— (1990), *Tackling Vacant Land: An Evaluation of Policy Instruments for Tackling Urban Land Vacancy* (London: HMSO).
—— (1991a), *Water Industry Investment: Planning Considerations* (Circular 17/91) (London: HMSO).
—— (1991b), *Animal By-product Rendering* (Process Guidance 6/1(91)) (London: DOE).
—— (1991c), *Interpretation of Terms Used in Guidance Notes* (General Guidance 4(91)) (London: DOE).
—— (1991d), *Derelict Land Grant Advice: Derelict Land Grant Policy* (London: DOE).
—— (1991e), *Monitoring Environmental Assessment and Planning* (London: HMSO).
—— (1992a), *Planning and Pollution Control* (draft Planning Policy Guidance Note) (London: DOE).
—— (1992b), *Planning Control for Hazardous Substances* (Circular 11/92) (London: HMSO).
—— (1992c), *Proposals to Prevent Land Becoming Derelict* (Consultation Paper) (London: DOE).

—— (1992d), *The Strategic Approach to Derelict Land Reclamation* (London: HMSO).
—— (1992e), *A Review of Options* (Waste Management Paper No 1) (London: HMSO).
—— (1992f), *Development Plans and Regional Planning Guidance* (Planning Policy Guidance Note 12) (London: HMSO).
—— (1993a), *Town Centres and Retail Development* (Planning Policy Guidance Note 6) (London: HMSO).
—— (1993b), *The National Survey of Vacant Land in Urban Areas of England 1990*, (London: HMSO).
—— (1993c), *The Environmental Appraisal of Development Plans: a Good Practice Guide* (London: HMSO).
—— (1994a), *Review of Rural Water Supply and Sewerage* (London: DOE).
—— (1994b), *Planning and Pollution Control* (Planning Policy Guidance Note 23) (London: HMSO).
—— (1994c), *Planning and Noise* (Planning Policy Guidance Note 24) (London: HMSO).
—— (1994d), *Transport* (Planning Policy Guidance Note 13) (London: HMSO).
—— (1994e), *Nature Conservation* (Planning Policy Guidance Note 9) (London: HMSO).
—— (1994f), *Guidance to English Partnerships* (London: DOE).
—— (1994g), *Framework for Contaminated Land* (London: DOE).
—— (1994h), *Evaluation of Environmental Information for Planning Projects: A Good Practice Guide* (London: HMSO).
—— (1994i), *Good Practice on the Evaluation of Environmental Information for Planning Projects: Research Report* (London: HMSO).
—— (1995a), *Authorizations Conditions Relating to Odour* (AQ16(95)) (London: DOE).
—— (1995b), *Survey of Derelict Land in England, 1993* (London: HMSO).
—— (1995c), *Preparation of Environmental Statements for Planning Projects that Require Environmental Assessment: A Good Practice Guide* (London: HMSO).
—— (1995d), *Making Waste Work: The UK Strategy for Sustainable Waste Management* (London: HMSO).
—— (1995e), *PPG13: A Guide to Better Practice. Reducing the Need to Travel through Land Use and Transport Planning* (London: HMSO).
—— (1996a), *The Environment Agency and Sustainable Development* (London: DOE).
—— (1996b) *Decisions on Discharge Consent and Associated Appeals Transferred to Planning Inspectorate* (Press Release 579, 30 December 1996).
—— (1996c), *Local Authority Circular on Air Quality and Land Use Planning* (Consultation Paper) (London: DOE).
—— (1996d), *Survey of Land for Mineral Workings in England 1994* (London: HMSO).
—— (1996e), *The Reclamation of Mineral Workings* (Mineral Planning Guidance Note 7) (London: HMSO).
—— (1996f), *Changes in the Quality of Environmental Statements for Planning Projects* (London: HMSO).
—— (1997a), *Enforcing Planning Control: Legislative Provisions and Procedural Requirements* (Circular 10/97) (London: HMSO).
—— (1997b), *Enforcing Planning Control: Good Practice Guide for Local Planning Authorities* (London: HMSO).
—— (1997c), *General Policy and Principles* (Planning Policy Guidance Note 1) (London: HMSO).

EDULJEE, G. (1999a), 'EIA and Waste Management' in Petts, J. (ed.), *Handbook of Environmental Impact Assessment* (Oxford: Blackwell Science Ltd) ii, 300–30.

—— (1999b), 'Risk Assesment' in Petts, J. (ed.), *Handbook of Environmental Impact Assessment* (Oxford: Blackwell Science Ltd) i, 374–404.

EHRENFELD, J.R., CRAIG, E.P., and NASH, J. (1989), 'Waste Incineration: Confronting the Sources of Disagreement', *Environmental Impact Assessment Review* 35(3), 305–15.

EKINS, P., and NEWBY, L. (1998), 'Sustainable Wealth Creation at the Local Level in an Age of Globalization', *Regional Studies* 32(9), 863–71.

ENGLISH NATURE (2000), *Digest of Statistics*, available at http://www.english-nature.gov.uk/start/htm

ENNIS, F. (1996), 'Planning Obligations and Developers: Costs and Benefits', *Town Planning Review* 67(2), 145–60.

ENVIRONMENTAL ADVISORY UNIT (1988), *Heathland Restoration: A Handbook of Techniques* (Southampton: British Gas plc).

ENVIRONMENT AGENCY (1997), *Liaison with Local Planning Authorities* (Bristol: Environment Agency).

—— (1998a), *Corporate Plan 1999–2000 Our Forward Look to 2002* (Bristol: Environment Agency).

—— (1998b), *An Action Plan for Water Quality* (Bristol: Environment Agency).

—— (1998c), *Enforcement and Prosecution Policy* (Bristol: Environment Agency).

—— (1999), *Water Pollution Incidents in England and Wales 1998* (London: Stationery Office).

EPAQS (EXPERT PANEL ON AIR QUALITY STANDARDS) (1995), *Particles* (London: HMSO).

ESSEX COUNTY COUNCIL (2000), *The Essex Guide to Environmental Impact Assessment* (Essex Planning Officers' Association, Chelmsford: Essex County Council).

FORESTRY COMMISSION (1998), *England Forestry Strategy: a New Focus for England's Woodlands: Strategic Priorities and Programmes* (Edinburgh: Forestry Commission).

FORMAN, R.T.T. (1995), *Landscape Mosaics: The Ecology of Landscapes and Regions* (Cambridge: Cambridge University Press).

FRIENDS OF THE EARTH (1997), *Regional Development Agencies—an Opportunity Lost?* (Briefing Paper), (London: Friends of the Earth).

FROST, R. (1997), 'EIA Monitoring and Audit', in Weston, J. (ed.), *Planning and Environmental Impact Assessment in Practice* (Harlow: Longman).

GANDY, M. (1994), *Recycling and the Politics of Urban Waste.* (London: Earthscan).

GIBBS, D.C. (1998), 'Regional Development Agencies and Sustainable Development' *Regional Studies* 32(4), 365–8.

—— LONGHURST, J.W., and BRAITHWAITE, C. (1996), 'Moving Towards Sustainable Development? Integrating Economic Development and the Environment in Local Authorities', *Journal of Environmental Planning and Management* 39(3), 317–32.

—— —— and —— (1998), ' "Struggling with Sustainability": Weak and Strong Interpretations of Sustainable Development within Local Authority Policy', *Environment and Planning A* 30(8), 1351–65.

GILCHRIST, A. (1991), 'Logistics for Selecting the Fnal Solution' in Fleming, G. (ed.), *Recycling Derelict Land* (London: Thomas Telford).

GILES, N. (1992), *Wildlife After Gravel* (Fordingbridge, Hampshire: Game Conservancy Ltd).

GLASBERGEN, P. (ed.) (1998), *Co-operative Environmental Governance: Public Private Agreements as a Policy Strategy* (Dordrecht: Kluwer).

GLASSON, J., THÉRIVEL, R., and CHADWICK, A. (1999), *Introduction to Environmental Impact Assessment* (2nd edn.) (London: UCL Press).

GOLDSMITH, E., ALLEN, R., ALLABY, M., DAVOLL, J., and LAWRENCE, S. (1972), *The Ecologist* 2(1), 1–43.

GOSLING, M., and WALKER, A.J. (1992), 'Energy Efficiency within the Urban Design Process', *Cities* 9(2), 111–16.

GRANT, M. (1991), 'Development and the Protection of Birds: The Swale Decision'. *Journal of Environmental Law* 3(2), 135–52.

GRAY, P (1995), 'Waste Incineration: Controversy and Risk Communication', *European Review of Applied Psychology* 45, 29–34.

GREATER MANCHESTER WASTE REGULATION AUTHORITY (1996), *Greater Manchester Waste Management Plan* (Manchester: GMWRA).

GUNN, J., BAILEY, D., and HANDLEY, J. (1997), *The Reclamation of Limestone Quarries using Landform Replication* (Final Report) (London: DETR).

GUY, S., and MARVIN, S. (1995a), 'Reconfiguring Urban Networks: the Emergence of DSM in the UK', *Journal of Urban Technology* 3(2), 45–58.

—— and —— (1995b), *Planning for Water: Space, Time and the Social Organisation of Natural Resources,* Working Paper No. 55, Department of Town and Country Planning, University of Newcastle upon Tyne.

—— and —— (1996a), 'Transforming Urban Infrastructure Provision: the Emerging Logic of Demand-side Management', *Policy Studies* 17(2), 137–47.

—— and —— (1996b), 'Managing Water Stress: the Logic of Demand-side Infrastructure Planning', *Journal of Environmental Planning and Management* 39(1), 125–31.

—— and —— (1996c), 'Disconnected Policy, the Shaping of Local Energy Management', *Environment and Planning C: Government and Policy* 14(1), 145–58.

—— and —— (1997), 'Splintering Networks: Cities and Technical Networks in 1990's Britain', *Urban Studies* 34(2), 191–216.

HAIGH, N. (1987), *EEC Environmental Policy & Britain* (2nd edn., Harlow: Longman).

HANDLEY, J.F. (1996), *The Post Industrial Landscape: A Groundwork Status Report* (Birmingham: Groundwork Foundation).

——, GRIFFITHS, E.J., HILL, S.L., and HOWE, J.M (1998), 'Land Restoration using an Ecologically Informed and Participative Approach' in Fox, H.R., Moore, H.M., and A.D. McIntosh (eds.), *Land Reclamation: Achieving Sustainable Benefits* (Rotterdam: Balkema).

HANF, K. (1996), 'Implementing International Environmental Policies' in Blowers, A., and Glasbergen, P. (eds.), *Prospects for Environmental Change* (London: Arnold).

HARDIN, G. (1977), 'The Tragedy of the Commons', *Science* 162, 1243–8.

HARMAN, J. (1998), 'Regional Development Agencies: Not the Final Frontier', *Local Economy* 13(3), 194–7.

HAUGHTON, G. (1998), 'Private Profits—Public Drought: The Creation of a Crisis in Water Management for West Yorkshire', *Transactions of the Institute of British Geographers* NS 23, 419–33.

HCEC (HOUSE OF COMMONS ENVIRONMENT COMMITTEE) (1997), *3rd Report 1996–97 Session: The Environmental Impact of Cement Manufacture* (London: Stationery Office).

HCETRAC (House of Commons Environment, Transport and Regional Affairs Committee) (1999), *Town and Country Parks* (London: Stationery Office).

Healey, P. (1985), 'The Professionalization of Planning in Britain', *Town Planning Review* 56(4), 492–507.

—— (1991), 'Models of the Development Process: a Review', *Journal of Property Research* 8(3), 219–38.

—— (1992), 'An Institutional Model of the Land Development Process', *Journal of Property Research* 9(1), 33–4.

——, Macnamara, O., Elson, M., and Doak, A. (1988), *Land Use Planning and the Mediation of Urban Change* (Cambridge: Cambridge University Press).

——, Purdue, M., and Ennis, F. (1995), *Negotiating Development Rationales and Practice for Development Obligations and Planning Gain* (London: Spon).

—— —— and —— (1996), 'Negotiating Development: Planning Gain and Mitigating Impacts', *Journal of Property Research* 13(2), 143–60.

—— and Shaw, T. (1994), 'Changing Meanings of the "environment" in the British Planning System', *Transactions of the Institution of British Geographers* NS 19, 425–38.

Hetherington, P. (1998), 'Prescott Gets Half a Cake', *Guardian*, 20 November, 23.

Hirschhorn, J.S. (1991), 'Siting Hazardous Waste Facilities', *Hazardous Waste* 1(3), 423–9.

HLSCEC (House of Lords Select Committee on the European Communities) (1999), *11th Report 1998–99 Session: Incineration of Waste* (London: Stationery Office).

HMG (Her Majesty's Government) ('White Papers') (1985), *Lifting the Burden* (Cm 9571) (London: HMSO).

—— (1990), *This Common Inheritance: Britain's Environmental Strategy* (Cm 1200) (London: HMSO).

—— (1994), *Sustainable Development: the UK Strategy* (Cm 2426) (London: HMSO).

—— (1997), *Building Partnerships for Prosperity: Sustainable Growth, Competitiveness and Employment in the English Regions* (Cm 3814) (London: Stationery Office).

—— (1998), *Our Competitive Future: Building the Knowledge Driven Economy* (Cm 4176) (London: Stationery Office).

—— (1999), *A Better Quality of Life: A Strategy for Sustainable Development for the UK* (Cm 4345) (London: Stationery Office).

—— (2000a) *The Air Quality Strategy for England, Scotland Wales and Northern Ireland: Working Together for Clean Air* (Cm 4548) (London: Stationery Office).

—— (2000b) *Waste Strategy 2000 for England and Wales* (Cm 4693) (London: Stationery Office).

Hodge, I., and Cameron, G. (1989), 'Raising Infrastructure Charges on Land Development: Incidence and Adjustment', *Land Development Studies* 6(3), 171–82.

Hodge, S.J. (1995), *Creating and Managing Woodlands Around Town* (Forestry Commission Handbook 11) (London: HMSO).

Holder, J. (1996), 'A Dead End for Direct Effect?: Prospects for the Enforcement of European Community Environmental Law by Individuals', *Journal of Environmental Law* 8(2), 322–35.

Hounslow, London Borough of (1993), *The Great West Road-Strategy* (London Borough of Hounslow).

HSC (Health and Safety Commission) (1984), *Advisory Committee on Major Hazards: third report* (London: HMSO).

HSE (Health and Safety Executive) (1989), *Risk Criteria for Land Use Planning in the Vicinity of Major Industrial Hazards* (London: HMSO).

—— (1999), *Reducing Risks, Protecting People* (Sudbury: HSE Books).

Hunt Report (1969), *The Intermediate Areas* (London: HMSO).

Huxley Report (1947), *Conservation of Nature in England and Wales* (Cmnd.7122) (London: HMSO).

ILGRA (1998), *Risk Assessment and Risk Management: Improving Policy and Practice within Government Departments* (Second Report: Interdepartmental Liaison Group on Risk Assessment) (London: Health and Safety Executive).

Interdepartmental Committee for the Reclamation of Contaminated Land (1987), *Guidance on the Assessment and Redevelopment of Contaminated Land.* (Guidance Note 59/83, 2nd Edition) (London: DOE).

Jackson, T., and Roberts, P. (1997), 'Greening the Fife Economy: Ecological Modernization as a Pathway for Local Economic Development', *Journal of Environmental Planning and Management* 40(5), 617–33.

Jasanoff, S. (ed.) (1994), *Learning from Disaster: Risk Management after Bhopal* (Philadelphia, Penn.: University of Pennsylvania Press).

Jewell, T. (1995), 'Planning Regulation and Environmental Consciousness: Some Lessons from Minerals?', *Journal of Planning and Environment Law* 482–98.

Joint Nature Conservation Committee (1995), *The Habitats Directive: Selection of Special Areas of Conservation in the UK* (JNCC Report No. 270).

—— (1999), *The Birds Directive: Selection Guidelines for Special Protection Areas*, available at http://www.jncc.gov.uk/idt/body.htm

Jones, C.E., and Wood, C.M. (1995), 'The Impact of Environmental Assessment on Public Inquiry Decisions', *Journal of Planning and Environment Law* 890–904.

——, —— and Dipper, B. (1998), 'Environmental Assessment in the UK Planning Process', *Town Planning Review* 69(3), 315–39.

Keller, A. (1997), 'Strategic Environmental Assessment of the European Structural Fund Objective One Programme for the Highlands and Islands of Scotland', *European Environment* 7(2), 63–8.

Kirwan, R. (1989), 'Finance for Urban Public Infrastructure', *Urban Studies* 26(3), 285–300.

—— (1990), 'Infrastructure Finance, Aims, Attitudes and Approaches', *Urban Policy and Research* 8(4), 185–93.

Kivell, P.T. (1987), 'Derelict Land in England: Policy Responses to a Continuing Problem', *Regional Studies* 21(3), 265–73.

Krämer, L. (1997), *Focus on European Environmental Law* (2nd edn., London: Sweet and Maxwell).

Kreuser, P., and Hammersley, R. (1999), 'Assessing the Assessments: British Planning Authorities and the Review of Environmental Statements', *Journal of Environmental Assessment Policy and Management* 1(3), 369–88.

Land Capability Consultants (1989), *Cost Effective Management of Reclaimed Derelict Sites* (London: HMSO).

Land Use Consultants (1996), *Reclamation of Damaged Land for Nature Conservation* (London: HMSO).

—— and CAG Consultants (1997), *What Matters and Why: Environmental Capital a New Approach* (Cheltenham: Countryside Commission).

Last, K. (1999), 'Environmental Assessment and the Designation of Special Protection Areas : The Cairngorm Funicular Railway', *Environmental Law Review* 1(1), 133–40).

LEE, N., and BROWN, D. (1992), 'Quality Control in Environmental Assessment', *Project Appraisal* 7(1), 41–5.

LEU, W-S., WILLIAMS, W.P., and BARK, A.W. (1996), 'Quality Control Mechanisms and Environmental Impact Assessment Effectiveness with Special Reference to the UK' *Project Appraisal* 11(1), 2–12.

LEWIS, L.E., and HAYNS, M.R. (1989), 'Limitations on the Usefulness of Risk Assessment', *Risk Analysis* 9(4), 483–94.

LLEWELYN-DAVIES in association with ALAN BAXTER AND ASSOCIATES (2000), *Urban Design Compendium* (London: English Partnerships and The Housing Corporation).

LOUGHLIN, M. (1985), 'Apportioning the Infrastructure Costs of Urban Land Development', in Barrett, S., and Healey, P. (eds.), *Land Policy: Problems and Alternatives* (Aldershot: Gower), 229–48.

LOWE, P., and WARD, S. (1998), *British Environmental Policy and Europe* (London: Routledge).

LYNCH, P. (1999), 'New Labour and the English Regional Development Agencies: Devolution as Evolution', *Regional Studies* 33(1), 73–8.

MABEY, R. (1991), 'Derelict Land—Recent Developments and Current Issues' in Davies, M.R.C. (ed.), *Land Reclamation an End to Dereliction?* (London: Elsevier Applied Science), 3–39.

MACAUSLAN, P. (1980), *The Ideologies of Planning Law* (Oxford: Pergamon).

MCEVOY, D., GIBBS, D.C., and LONGHURST, J.W. (1998), 'Urban Sustainability: Problems Facing the "Local" Approach to Carbon Reduction Strategies', *Environment and Planning C: Government and Policy* 16(4), 423–32.

MCGINNIS, M.V. (1999), *Bioregionalism* (London: Routledge).

MACRAE, J. (1995), 'Council to Curb Office Parking', *Estates Times*, 27 January, 1.

MACRORY, R. (1992), 'Environmental Assessment and Community Law', *Journal of Environmental Law* 4(2), 273–304.

MARSHALL, T. (1993), 'Regional Environmental Planning: Progress and Possibilities in Western Europe', *European Planning Studies* 1(1), 69–90.

—— (1998), 'The Conditions for Environmentally Intelligence Regional Governance: Reflections from Lower Saxony', *Journal of Environmental Planning and Management* 41(4), 421–43.

MARVIN, S., and GUY, S. (1997), 'Creating Myths Rather than Sustainability: the Transition Fallacies of the New Localism', *Local Environment* 2(3), 311–18.

MAWSON, J. (1997), 'The English Regional Debate. Towards Regional Governance or Government?' in Bradbury, J., and Mawson, J. (eds.), *British Regionalism and Devolution: The Challenges of State Reform and European Integration* (London: Jessica Kingsley/Regional Studies Association), 180–211.

MAY, P., BURBY, R.J., ERICKSEN, N.J., HANDMER, J.W., DIXON, J.E., MICHAELS, S., and INGLE SMITH, I. (1996), *Environmental Management and Governance* (London: Routledge).

MILLER, C.E. (1988), 'Planning, Pollution and Hazard', *Urban Law and Policy* 9(2), 83–108.

—— (1993), 'Coke, Smoke and National Sovereignty: a Case Study of the Role of Planning in Controlling Pollution', *Journal of Environmental Planning and Management* 36(2), 149–66.

—— (1994), 'Planning, Pollution and Risk', *Town Planning Review* 65(2), 127–41.

—— (1999a), 'Environmental Law: the Weak Versus the Strong', *Environmental Law Review* 1(1), 23–36.

—— (1999b), *Planning and Pollution Revisited*, Report for the Royal Commission on Environmental Pollution. (Salford: University of Salford).

—— and Fricker, C. (1993), 'Planning and Hazard', *Progress in Planning* 40(3), 169–260.

—— and Wood, C.M. (1983), *Planning and Pollution* (Oxford: Oxford University Press).

Millichip, D. (1993), 'Sustainability: A Long-established Concern of Planning', *Journal of Planning and Environment Law* 1111–19.

MORI (1995), *Derelict Land in Britain—A Survey of Public Opinion*, Research Study conducted for Groundwork Foundation and Leedex (unpublished).

Morrish, B. (1997), *The Realisation of Ecological and Amenity Benefits Through Land Reclamation Programmes for Greater Manchester,* MSc Thesis, Faculty of Science, University of Manchester.

Murdoch, J., and Tewdwr-Jones, M. (1999), 'Planning and the English Regions: Conflict and Convergence amongst the Institutions of Regional Governance', *Environment and Planning C: Government and Policy* 17(6), 715–29.

MVA Consultancy (1996), *The London Congestion Charging Research Programme: Final Report* (London: HMSO).

National Audit Office (1994), *Protecting and Managing Sites of Special Scientific Interest* (London: HMSO).

National Joint Utilities Group (1983), *Model Guidelines for the Installation of Utilities Supplies to New Building Development* (Publication 5) (London: NJUG).

National Rivers Authority (1994), *Water—Nature's Precious Resource—National Water Resources Strategy* (Bristol: National Rivers Authority).

North West Development Agency (1999), *England's North West: A Strategy Towards 2020* (Warrington: NWDA).

O'Brien, M., and Penna, S. (1997), 'European Policy and the Politics of Environmental Governance', *Policy and Politics* 25(2), 185–200.

Office of Electricity Regulation (1991), *Energy Efficiency* (consultation paper) (London: OFFER).

Office of Water Services (1992), *The Cost of Water Delivered to Customers 1991–2: A Comparison of Unit Costs and Losses from Companies Distribution Services* (Birmingham: OFFWAT).

Orell, B., and Cryan, J. (1987), 'Getting Rid of the Hazard', *The Chemical Engineer* [August 1987] 14–15.

Organisation for Economic Co-operation and Development (1997), *Environmental Policies and Employment* (Paris: OECD).

Ortlano, L. (1984), *Environmental Planning and Decision-making* (New York: John Wiley).

Owen, G. (1994), *From Energy Supply to Energy Services* (London: Energy Savings Trust).

Owens, S. (1990), 'The Unified Pollution Inspectorate and Best Practicable Environmental Option in the UK' in Haigh, N., and Irwin, F. (eds.), *Integrated Pollution Control in Europe and North America*. (Baltimore, Mich.: The Conservation Foundation).

—— (1995), 'From "Predict and Provide" to "Predict and Prevent"?: Pricing and Planning in Transport Policy', *Transport Policy* 2(1), 43–51.

PA Consulting Group (1998), *Interim Evaluation of English Partnerships: Review of Structure, Strategy and Practices* (London: DETR).

PA Consulting Group (1999), *Interim Evaluation of English Partnerships: Final Report* (London: DETR).

Parkinson, R., Newman, A., and Nathanail, P. (2000), 'Contaminated Land: State of Local Authority Preparedness', *Land Contamination and Reclamation* 8(2), 133–43.

Patterson, A. (1999), 'Towards a Theory of Regional Governance', paper presented at the Annual Conference of the Royal Geographical Society (with the Institute of British Geographers), University of Leicester.

Peake, S. (1994), *Transport in Transition* (London: Earthscan).

Pearce, F., and Tombs, S. (1996), 'Hegemony, Risk and Governance: Social Regulation and the American Chemical Industry', *Economy and Society* 25(3), 428–54.

Perry, D., and Handley, J. (2000), *The Potential for Woodland on Urban and Industrial Wasteland in England and Wales—With a Review of the Dynamics of Urban and Industrial Wasteland* (Technical Paper 29) (Edinburgh: Forestry Commission).

Petts, J. (1988), 'Planning and Hazardous Installation Control', *Progress in Planning* 29(1), 1–75.

—— (1992), 'Incineration Risk Perceptions and Public Concern: Experience in the UK Improving Risk Communication', *Waste Management and Research* 10, 169–82.

—— (1994), 'Effective Waste Management: Understanding and Dealing with Public Concerns', *Waste Management and Research* 12, 207–22.

—— (1995), 'Waste Management Strategy Development: a Case Study of Community Involvement and Consensus-building in Hampshire', *Journal of Environmental Planning and Management* 38(4), 519–36.

—— (1996), 'Environmental Statement Quality: Experience from Independent Review', Paper presented at the Institute of Environmental Assessment and Environmental Auditors Registration Association Annual Conference, October 1996, Lincoln: Institute of Environmental Assessment.

—— (1997), 'The Public–Expert Interface in Local Waste Management Decisions: Expertise, Credibility and Process', *Public Understanding of Science* 6(4), 359–82.

—— (1998), 'Waste Treatment and Disposal' in Calow, P. (ed.), *Handbook of Environmental Risk Assessment and Management* (Oxford: Blackwell Science Ltd), 417–52.

—— (1999a), 'EIA versus other Decision Tools' in Petts, J. (ed.), *Handbook of Environmental Impact Assessment* (Oxford: Blackwell Science), i, 33–59.

—— (1999b), 'Public Participation and Environmental Impact Assessment' in Petts, J. (ed.), *Handbook of Environmental Impact Assessment,* (Oxford: Blackwell Science), i, 145–77.

—— (2000a), 'Municipal Waste Management: Inequities and the Role of Deliberation', *Risk Analysis*, 20(6) 821–832.

—— (2001), 'Evaluating the Effectiveness of Deliberative Processes; Waste Management Case Studies', *Journal of Environmental Planning and Management*, 44(2) 207–226.

—— and Eduljee, G. (1994), *Environmental Impact Assessment for Waste Treatment and Disposal Facilities* (Chichester: John Wiley & Sons).

——, Gerrard, S., Delbridge, P., Murrell, L., and Eduljee, G. (1996), *Perceptions and Communication Issues for Waste Management* (Research Report, CWM 151/96) (London: Environment Agency).

Portney, K.E. (1991), *Siting Hazardous Waste Treatment Facilities* (New York: Auburn House).

Powell, J.C. (1994), 'The Evaluation of Waste Management Options', *Waste Management and Research* 14, 512–26.

PRINDLE, W. (1991), 'Demand-side Management in the 1990s', *Energy Policy* 19(3), 205–7.

PURDUE, M. (1990), 'Defining Waste' *Journal of Environmental Law* 2(2), 250–61.

—— (1999), 'The Relationship between Development Control and Specialist Pollution Controls: Which is the Tail and Which the Dog?' *Journal of Planning and Environment Law* 585–94.

RANK HOLIDAYS AND HOTEL DEVELOPMENT LTD (1994), *Oasis Holiday Village-West Wood Environmental Statement* (London: Rank Holidays/HDL).

RCEP (ROYAL COMMISSION ON ENVIRONMENTAL POLLUTION) (1976), *Air Pollution Control: an Integrated Approach* (Fifth Report, Cmnd. 9149) (London: HMSO).

—— (1984), *Tackling Pollution—Experience and Prospects* (Tenth Report, Cmnd. 9149) (London: HMSO).

—— (1988), *Best Practicable Environmental Option* (Twelfth Report, Cm. 310) (London: HMSO).

—— (1991), *Emissions from Heavy Duty Diesel Vehicles* (Fifteenth Report, Cm. 1631) (London: HMSO).

—— (1994), *Transport and the Environment* (Eighteenth Report, Cm. 2674) (London: HMSO).

—— (1996), *Sustainable Use of Soil* (Nineteenth Report, Cm. 3165) (London: HMSO).

—— (1998), *Setting Environmental Standards* (Twenty-first Report, Cm. 4053) (London: Stationery Office).

READ, R. (1997), 'Planning Authority Review' in Weston, J. (ed.), *Planning and Environmental Impact Assessment in Practice* (Harlow: Longman).

REGIONAL POLICY COMMISSION (1996), *Renewing the Regions: Strategies for Regional Economic Development* (Sheffield: Sheffield Hallam University).

REISEN, F. (1998), *Strategic Environmental Assessment of Ground Contamination in the Redevelopment Process*, MA Dissertation in EIA and Management, University of Manchester.

ROBERTS, P. (1999), 'Guiding Regional Development Strategies', *Town and Country Planning* 68(1), 4.

—— and JACKSON, T. (1999), 'Incorporating the Environment into European Regional Programmes—Evolution, Progress and Prospects', *Town and Country Planning* 68(3), 85–8.

RODGERS, C. (1996), 'Conservation Law in Context' in Rodgers, C. (ed.), *Nature Conservation and Countryside Law*, (Cardiff: University of Wales Press).

—— and BISHOP, J. (1998), *Management Agreements for Promoting Nature Conservation* (London: Royal Institution of Chartered Surveyors).

ROGER TYM AND PARTNERS (1987), *Evaluation of Derelict Land Grant Schemes* (London: HMSO).

ROWAN-ROBINSON, J., and LLOYD, M. (1988), *Land Development and the Infrastructure Lottery*. (Edinburgh: T & T Clark).

—— and —— (1989), 'Distributing the Costs of Infrastructure: a Tale of Two Cities', in Grover, R. (ed.), *Land and Property: New Directions* (London: Spon), 187–96.

ROYSTON, M.G. (1979), *Pollution Prevention Pays* (Oxford: Pergamon).

RTPI (ROYAL TOWN PLANNING INSTITUTE) (1999a), *Good Practice Guide: Air Quality and Land Use Planning* (London: RTPI).

—— (1999b), *Planning for Biodiversity: A Good Practice Guide* (London: RTPI).

RYDIN, Y. (1998), *Urban and Environmental Planning in the UK* (London: Macmillan).

RYDIN, Y. (1999), 'For "Modernisation" Read "Business as Usual"?' *Town and Country Planning* 68(6), 177.

SADLER, B., and VERHEEM, R. (1996), *Strategic Environmental Assessment: Status, Challenges and Future Direction* (The Hague: Ministry of Housing, Spatial Planning and the Environment).

SANTEN, A. VAN (1993), 'Incineration' *Wastes Management Proceedings*, July, 18–21.

SCHNEIDER, E., OPPERMANN, B., and RENN, O. (1998), 'Experiences from Germany: Application of a Structured Model of Public Participation in Waste Management Planning', *International Journal of Public Participation* 4(1), 63–72.

SCOTT REPORT (1942), *Report of the Committee on Land Utilisation in Rural Areas* (Cmd 6378) (London: HMSO).

SELMAN, P. (1992), *Environmental Planning: The Conservation and Development of Biological Resources* (London: Paul Chapman Publishing).

SEPA (SCOTTISH ENVIRONMENT PROTECTION AGENCY) (2000), *National Waste Strategy: Scotland* (Stirling: SEPA).

SERPLAN (1992), *South East Regional Planning Guidelines* (London: SERPLAN).

—— (1998), *A Sustainable Development Strategy for the South East—A Sustainability Commentary* (SERP 402) (London: SERPLAN).

SGWP (STEERING GROUP AND WORKING PARTY APPOINTED BY THE MINISTER OF TRANSPORT) (1963), *Traffic in Towns: a Study of the Long Term Problems of Traffic in Urban Areas* ('the Buchanan Report') (London: HMSO).

SHARPE, L.J. (1993), *The Rise of Meso Government in Europe* (London: Sage).

SHAW, J.M. (1999), 'A National Spatial Framework', *Town Planning Review* 70(3), 1–4.

SHEATE, W.R. (1996), *Environmental Impact Assessment: Law and Policy: Making an Impact II* (London, Cameron May).

—— (1997), 'From Environmental Impact Assessment to Strategic Environmental Impact Assessment: Sustainability and Decision-making' in Holder, J. (ed.), *The Impact of EC Environmental Law in the United Kingdom* (Chichester: Wiley).

SIMMONS, P., and WALKER, G.P. (1999), 'Tolerating Risk: Policy Principles and Public Perceptions', *Risk Decision and Policy* 4(3), 179–90.

SIMPSON, B. (1983), *Site Costs in Housing and Development* (London: Construction Press).

SIMPSON, G.T. (1998), 'The Role of the Mineral Planning System in England in Achieving the Reclamation of Mineral Workings' in Fox, H.R., Moore, H.M., and McIntosh, A.D. (eds.), *Land Reclamation: Achieving Sustainable Benefits* (Rotterdam: Balkema).

SIOSHANSI, F. (1992), 'Demand-side Management and Environmental Externalities', *Utilities Policy* 2(3), 320–9.

SMITH, D. (1990), 'Corporate Power and the Politics of Uncertainty: Conflicts Surrounding Major Hazard Plants at Canvey Island', *Industrial Crisis Quarterly* 4(1), 1–26.

—— (1991), 'Beyond the Boundary Fence: Decision Making and Chemical Hazards' in Blunden, J., and Reddish, A. (eds.), *Energy, Resources and the Environment* (London: Hodder and Stoughton).

SNIFFER (SCOTLAND AND NORTHERN IRELAND FORUM FOR ENVIRONMENTAL RESEARCH) (1999), *Community Understanding of Contaminated Land Risks* (Stirling: SEPA).

SNOWBALL, D.J., and MACGILL, S.M. (1984), 'Coping with Risk: the Case of Gas Facilities in Scotland', *Environment and Planning* C 2(3), 343–60.

ST HELENS METROPOLITAN BOROUGH COUNCIL (1995), *Unitary Development Plan: Area Policies Sub-area 6* (Deposit Draft) (St Helens: St Helens MBC).

STALLWORTHY, M. (1998), 'Planning Law as a Tool of Environmental Protection: The UK's Slow Embrace of Environmental Assessment', *Journal of Environmental Law* 10(2), 363–97.

STANLEY, N. (1998), 'Public Concern: The Decision-makers' Dilemma', *Journal of Planning and Environment Law* 919–34.

STERN, P.C., and FINEBERG, H.V. (eds.) (1996), *Understanding Risk: Informing Decisions in a Democratic Society*. (Washington DC: National Academy Press).

STARKINGS, D. (1998), *Whose Landscape is it Anyway*? MTPl Dissertation, University of Manchester.

STEVENS COMMITTEE (1976), *Planning Control over Mineral Working* (London: HMSO).

STORPER, M. (1997), *The Regional World: Territorial Development in a Global Economy* (New York: Guilford).

STREET, E. (2000), 'Powers over Pollution' *Planning*, 3 March 2000, 13.

STRUTHERS, W.A.K. (1997), 'From Manchester Docks to Salford Quays: Ten years of environmental improvements in the Mersey Basin Campaign', 11 *Journal of the Chartered Institution of Water and Environmental Management* 1–7.

THÉRIVEL, R. (1998), 'Strategic Environmental Assessment of Development Plans in Great Britain', *Environmental Impact Assessment Review* 18(1), 39–57.

—— and BROWN, L. (1999), 'Methods of Strategic Environmental Assessment' in Petts, J. (ed.), *Handbook of Environmental Impact Assessment* (Oxford: Blackwell Science), i, 441–62.

TOMBS, S. (1993), 'The Chemical Industry and Environmental Issues' in Smith, D. (ed.), *Business and the Environment: Implications of the New Environmentalism* (London: Paul Chapman).

UK (BIODIVERSITY) STEERING GROUP) (1995), *Volume 1: Meeting the Rio Challenge* (London: HMSO).

UK CEED (CENTRE FOR ECONOMIC AND ENVIRONMENTAL DEVELOPMENT) (1993), *Response to the Government Consultation Paper—Regional Development Agencies: Issues for Discussion* (Cambridge: UK CEED).

UK ROUND TABLE ON SUSTAINABLE DEVELOPMENT) (1999), *Sustainable Development—Devolved and Regional Dimensions* (London: UK Round Table on Sustainable Development).

UNIVERSITY OF ULSTER (1998), *Accessing Private Finance: The Availability and Effectiveness of Private Finance in Urban Regeneration* (London: RICS).

URBAN TASK FORCE (1999), *Towards an Urban Renaissance* (London: E & FN Spon).

US ENVIRONMENTAL PROTECTION AGENCY (1991), *Code of Federal Regulations* (Title 40 CFR Part 258) (Washington DC: USEPA).

—— (1994), *Health Assessment Document for 2,3,7,8 Tetrachloro dibenzo-p-dioxin (TCDD) and Related Compounds* (review draft) (Washington DC: USEPA).

UTHWATT REPORT (1942), *Expert Committee on Compensation and Betterment: Final Report* (Cmd 6386) (London: HMSO).

VICTORIA ENVIRONMENTAL PROTECTION AGENCY (1990), *Recommended Buffer Distances for Industrial Residual Air Emissions* (Publication No. AQ 2/86) (Melbourne: Victoria Environmental Protection Agency).

VICTORIA GOVERNMENT (1991), 'State Environmental Protection Policy: Siting and Management of Landfills Receiving Municipal Wastes', *Victoria Gazette S40* (Melbourne: Victoria Government).

VIDAL, J. (1994), 'Road Building "Only Makes Traffic Worse" ', *The Guardian*, 20 December, 3.

VILE, M.J.C. (1967), *Constitutionalism and the Separation of Powers* (Oxford: Clarendon) (discussing Montesquieu, *De l'Esprit des Lois* [1748] Book XI ch.6).

WALKER, G.P. (1991), 'Land Use Planning and Industrial Hazards: a Role for the European Community', *Land Use Policy* 8(3), 227–40.

—— (1994), *Hazardous Substances Consents: a Review of the Operation of Statutory Planning Controls over Hazardous Substances* (London: Department of the Environment).

—— (2000), 'Urban Planning, Hazardous Installations and Blight: an Evaluation of Responses to Hazard-development Conflict', *Environment and Planning* C 18(2), 127–43.

—— and BAYLISS, D. (1997), 'Development Plans and Hazardous Installations', *Planning Practice and Research* 13(1), 23–4.

—— and BICKERSTAFF, K. (2000), *Polluting the Poor: an Emerging Environmental Justice Agenda for the UK?* (Critical Urban Studies: Occasional Paper) (London: Centre for Urban and Community Research, Goldsmiths College).

—— and DRAYCOTT, P. (1996), 'Mapping Technological Hazards: Spatial Patterns of Major Accident Hazards in England', Occasional Paper New Series A 7, Stoke on Trent: Division of Geography, Staffordshire University.

—— and MACGILL, S.M. (1985), 'Planning Control of Industrial Hazard in a Major Metropolitan Planning Authority', *Environment and Planning B* 12(4), 463–78.

——, MOONEY, J., and PRATTS, D. (2000), 'The People and the Hazard: the Spatial Context of Major Hazard Management in Britain', *Applied Geography* 20, 119–35.

WALKER, G.P., SIMMONS, P., IRWIN, A., and WYNNE, B. (1998), *Public Perception of Risks Associated with Major Accident Hazards* (Research Report 194/1998) (Sudbury: Health and Safety Executive Books).

—— —— —— and —— (1999), 'Risk Communication, Public Participation and the Seveso II Directive', *Journal of Hazardous Materials* 65, 170–90.

WCED (WORLD COMMISSION ON ENVIRONMENT AND DEVELOPMENT) (1987), *Our Common Future* (the 'Brundtland Report') (Oxford: Oxford University Press).

WEBLER, T., KASTENHOLZ, H., and RENN, O. (1995), 'Public Participation in Impact Assessment: A Social Learning Perspective', *Environmental Impact Assessment Review* 15(5), 443–63.

WESTON, J. (1997), 'EIA and Public Inquiries' in Weston, J. (ed.), *Planning and Environmental Impact Assessment in Practice* (Harlow: Longman).

—— (2000), 'EIA, Decision-making Theory and Screening and Scoping in UK Practice', *Journal of Environmental Planning and Management* 43(2), 185–203.

WHITE, P.R., FRANKE, M., and HINDLE, P. (1995), *Integrated Solid Waste Management: A Lifecycle Inventory* (London: Chapman & Hall).

WIGLEY, K.E. (2000), *Testing an Attribute Based Approach to Contaminated Land Assessment*, MA Dissertation in EIA and Management, University of Manchester.

WIMOUTH, D. (1990), 'Urban Infrastructure Issues in Australia: a Review in the Context of International Experience', *Urban Policy and Research* 8(4), 159–68.

WIRTSHAFTER, R.M., and HILDEBRANDT, E.W. (1992), 'Energy Performance Connection Fees', *Energy Policy* 20(12), 1161–73.

WITHRINGTON, D., and JONES, W. (1992), 'Enforcement of Conservation Legislation' in Howarth, W., and Rodgers, C. (eds.), *Agriculture, Conservation and Land Use* (Cardiff: University of Wales Press).

WOLSINK, M. (1994), 'Entanglement of Interests and Motives: Assumptions Behind the NIMBY-theory on Facility Siting', *Urban Studies* 31(6), 851–66.

WOOD, C.M. (1976), *Town Planning and Pollution Control* (Manchester: Manchester University Press).

—— M. (1995), *Environmental Impact Assessment: a Comparative Review* (Harlow: Longman).

—— DIPPER, B., and JONES, C.E. (2000), 'Auditing the Assessment of the Environmental Impacts of Planning Projects: Results', *Journal of Environmental Planning and Management* 43(1), 23–47.

—— and JONES, C.E. (1997), 'The Effect of Environmental Assessment on UK Local Planning Authority Decisions', *Urban Studies* 34(8), 1237–57.

WOOD, G., and BELLANGER, C. (1998), *Directory of Environmental Impact Statements: July 1988–April 1998* (Working Paper 179) (Oxford: Oxford Brookes University).

WOOLF, H. (1991), 'Are the Judiciary Environmentally Myopic?', *Journal of Environmental Law* 4(1), 1–14.

—— (1996), *Access to Justice: Final Report* (London: HMSO), http://www.open.gov.uk/ lcd/civil/finalfr.htm.

Index